Masculinity in
Breaking Bad

Masculinity in *Breaking Bad*

Critical Perspectives

Edited by
BRIDGET ROUSSELL COWLISHAW

Foreword by Robert G. Weiner

McFarland & Company, Inc., Publishers
Jefferson, North Carolina

LIBRARY OF CONGRESS CATALOGUING-IN-PUBLICATION DATA

Masculinity in Breaking bad : critical perspectives / edited by
Bridget Roussell Cowlishaw ; foreword by Robert G. Weiner.
    p.   cm.
Includes bibliographical references and index.

ISBN 978-0-7864-9721-8 (softcover : acid free paper) ∞
ISBN 978-1-4766-1991-0 (ebook)

1. Breaking bad (Television program : 2008–2013) 2. Masculinity
on television.   I. Cowlishaw, Bridget Roussell, editor.

PN1992.77.B74M38 2015
791.45'72—dc23   2015003654

BRITISH LIBRARY CATALOGUING DATA ARE AVAILABLE

Cover image © iStock/Thinkstock

Printed in the United States of America

McFarland & Company, Inc., Publishers
  Box 611, Jefferson, North Carolina 28640
  www.mcfarlandpub.com

Table of Contents

Foreword

ROBERT G. WEINER

Ok, I admit it; I am a newbie to *Breaking Bad*. I didn't watch the program when it first aired on AMC. I hate commercials so I rarely watch any regular television at all, preferring either DVD sets or streaming for viewing. I'll also disgracefully admit that I was shamed into watching the show. My friend and librarian colleague at Texas Tech, Ryan Cassidy, basically embarrassed me in front of one of my Honors classes in which he was guest lecturing. My best friends, Joe Ferrer and Tom Gonzales, also kept at me to watch the show. Practically every time we would hang out they would ask me if I had seen it yet. Both Mr. Cassidy and Mr. Ferrer were "getting on my case" for being someone who was "Mr. Popular Culture" but had never seen *Breaking Bad*. Both were constantly telling me what a great show it was. The premise just didn't grab me: a teacher who "breaks bad" and makes meth. Somehow, that just didn't sound interesting (I was wrong).

I am not the type of individual who necessarily follows trends in my television or movie watching or even in my study of popular culture. I don't care what the critics or *Rotten Tomatoes* say. I like to find out for myself and watch films or shows before I read any critical comments if I read them at all. I figured, however, if everyone is talking about this show there might be something to it. So over Christmas break I watched *Breaking Bad* and continued to watch it. I had never actually binge-watched anything before. I didn't watch anything else for more than a month and watched every episode available at the time, even spending nearly 24 hours without sleep watching the episodes by myself. I was "hooked" from the first episode. I would often see or call my friends and tell them what I predicted might happen in future episodes even though they had already seen them. They were amused at my enthusiasm.

1

Here was a show that had compelling characters, a great setting (Albuquerque, New Mexico), and a plot that was not only good from the first episode on, but continued to be good throughout its five seasons. Let's not forget the acting! In addition to the great scriptwriting and premise, the acting is stellar. There is a good reason the show won or was nominated for so many Emmy awards. Anna Gunn, Dean Norris, Jonathan Banks, Bob Odenkirk, Giancarlo Esposito, Betsy Brandt, and all the rest of the cast and guest stars did an amazing job. But Bryan Cranston, I could hardly believe it. Here was the guy from *Malcolm in the Middle* playing this kind of heavy? I am convinced that Cranston is one of the finest actors of the 21st century. Sometimes things really are that good and no amount of pretending that something is overrated makes it overrated (for example, the Beatles, Led Zeppelin, *Casablanca*, *The Godfather*, *Seinfeld* and *M*A*S*H* are not overrated. There is a reason why these artists and films are consistently brought up as examples of excellence). *Breaking Bad* falls into this category, with Vince Gilligan's writing and directing and Cranston's acting helping make the show one of the finest programs of the 21st century. Walter White is truly the anti-hero/villain for our times, as this collection attests.

The 1950s and 1960s have often been thought of as the "Golden Age of Television." Certainly television was beginning to find its way into the houses of millions of people across the world and become a force that could not be ignored. It is true that in terms of programming there were some excellent shows like *Alfred Hitchcock Presents*, *Naked City*, *77 Sunset Strip*, *The Twilight Zone*, *Playhouse 90*, *Andy Griffith* and *The Prisoner*. Even today, these programs hold up with timeless storytelling, compelling characters, and good acting and scriptwriting. However, today we really are in a "GOLDEN AGE" (as my friend Mr. Ferrer likes to tell me) of television watching. With streaming services, DVDs, Blu-Rays, it's theoretically possible to watch nearly anything at any time of the day or night, making binge-watching a current pastime. The paradigm of television has changed with many streaming services offering original content and posting whole seasons all at once, so, again, viewers no longer have to wait weeks for the next episodes nor be bothered with annoying commercials. I can't imagine what the original viewers of *Breaking Bad* had to endure waiting for the next episode or season. The quality has gone up, too, with shows like *House of Cards*, *True Detective*, *American Horror Story*, *Walking Dead*, *Orange Is the New Black,* and, of course, *Breaking Bad.*

This begs the question of the popularity of a character like Walter White (not to mention Frank Underwood, Marty Hart, Rick Grimes). Is White a hero? A villain? A modern cowboy? An anti-hero? A criminal mastermind? A family man? A teacher? A drug kingpin? It is these questions and more that this carefully curated collection attempts to answer. The answer is a little more complex. White is all of the above and yet he can't be pigeonholed into any one of them. This is what makes his character and the show so compelling. It took Cranston and Gilligan to bring White alive and viewers all over the world continue to discuss and debate the nuances of show and the characters. As I watched *Breaking Bad*, I found myself rooting for Walter White on various occasions. At times I wondered if I was a moral degenerate. Let's face it—White is not exactly the sort of person you would want to hang out with and be best friends with. White is not the type of person most of us would want in our daily lives. Yes, he can on occasion do something honorable and selfless, but he can also be brilliantly manipulative and just plain evil. However, we can't help but admire, root for, and even love Walter White. As played by Cranston, he has a certain charm and is frankly a "badass." In many movies, televisions series, novels, serials and the like, endings are often unsatisfactory. It is hard to come up with a good ending, but *Breaking Bad* had one of the most satis-fying endings I've ever seen. I wanted White to conquer and "get back" at those who had "wronged" him despite all the despicable things he had done previ-ously. (Again, I sometimes wonder about the morality of rooting for White.)

Breaking Bad has now become a mini-cottage industry. You can take tours around Albuquerque and see the places where the show was filmed, including the famed Heisenberg/White house. You can eat at the restaurant featured as "Los Pollos Hermanos." You can buy t-shirts, stickers, jewelry, mugs, and even blue meth-colored candy (which to my mind is going a little too far). The Pontiac Aztek had a spike in sales because White drove it. This demonstrates just how deeply *Breaking Bad* has ingrained itself into our popular conscious-ness and become part of the American myth (but I know Europeans, South Americans, Africans, Asians all the love the show, too, so it is a world phe-nomenon). It makes me wonder because everywhere I go when I wear my Heisen-berg shirt, I get positive comments—even in a community of 1,000 people like Challis, Idaho—showing just how universal *Breaking Bad* has become. The story is not even completely over because we have a new series based on characters featured in *Breaking Bad* with *Better Call Saul* starting up.

Bridget Roussell Cowlishaw has put together a finely tuned collection of essays on the crucial show of the early 21st century. Her hard work and tenacity in seeking out high-quality, well-written essays shows us how the scholarly dis-course related to modern television programs can affect popular culture in areas related to questions of gender and masculinity, business, philosophy and ethics, politics, family studies and even library studies. Not only is this volume useful for academics, but for all *Breaking Bad* devotees. Cowlishaw is to be commended for being a pioneer in helping us understand why *Breaking Bad* has captivated so many. Walter White has become one of the pivotal icons of the 21st century; this collection helps us understand why.

Preface

This book had its genesis at the 2014 Southwest Popular/American Culture Conference in Albuquerque, New Mexico. I had made a habit of initiating my graduate students into the rites and rituals of the academic conference at the SWPCA for many years, but when I gave up my tenured teaching position in order to do my own writing, I thought I had made my last pilgrimage to Albuquerque (even as my husband Brian went on to become a co-chair in the conference's rapidly growing Science Fiction and Fantasy area). The memory of loitering on Central Avenue with some of my students as one of them explained that this city was the setting for *Breaking Bad* (the subject of her presentation) had long faded from my memory along with all the other urgings by students that I "really should watch *Breaking Bad*." I would love it, they told me. It's about ethics and morality, they said. From high atop my Ph.D. in Rhetoric, I smiled down. I didn't think a show about a high school teacher cooking meth with a former student had any compelling questions of ethics with which to challenge me. Three years later, though, I found myself again on Central, rushing from showing some of my fellow conference attendees a rooftop location (where Walter White watched Gus Fringe *not* get into his car in the parking garage) to arrive on time for a panel on *Breaking Bad* I was chairing at the Hyatt.

It was at the 2014 conference that I first met Susan Johnston who was at the time editing a collection to which my husband was a contributor. She introduced me to Ian Dawe and they both attended most of the *Breaking Bad* panels I chaired (thanks to the kind permission of Nick Gerlich). The very best presentation I heard at the conference was Jeff Pettis' and as my husband and I drove Jeff and his friend out to To'hajiilee one afternoon, I found myself talking to him like a star grad student: he should add a note about this and he should send the essay in for publication there. On another afternoon, Susan and I cornered Marc Valdez to insist he publish his elaborate research on locations used in *Breaking Bad*. (That book came quickly to fruition but is not among those in my Annotated Bibliography because it deals with locations, not the show itself. It is required reading for a visit to Albuquerque, however.) After I had answered the question of what research has been done about *Breaking Bad* for the umpteenth time (with "I don't know. Someone needs to write up an annotated bibliography"), Susan and I decided I should pull together this collection. In a fit of good judgment, I invited Stephanie Gross (who I knew from my days at the University of Oklahoma) to join us as she was watching the series for the first time and feeling compelled to write about it in relation to her scholarship on Machiavelli.

The intention from the start was that this collection would be focused on the issue of masculinity—not because gender studies is the primary field of any of the contributors but because—according to our reading of it—it is the primary theme of the series. Brian, Stephanie, and Susan bring literary analytical perspectives. Ian brings his background in film studies and his special interest in sequential art. Jeff is deft at employing Michel Foucault who is arguably the most fruitful theorist through whom to read *Breaking Bad*. Nick and Lori are the business and fandom scholars such an anthology must include. I specifically wanted each of these topics addressed—this is not a collection of essays culled from casting a broad H-net Call for Papers. These are focused analyses by some of the smartest scholars I know.

There was only one issue I knew must be addressed but which did not seem appropriate to an essay of its own: the Skyler question. My solution was to create the three Round Table discussions in which we explore how Skyler has been received and what that might mean. More than anything, these Round Table discussions point to where we hope our humanities and social science colleagues who do specialize in gender studies will create new scholarship.

As I kept telling people in the halls of the Albuquerque Hyatt as I pitched the idea of this book: *Breaking Bad*'s popularity has only begun to peak. Netflix has provided the platform for a new kind of popular culture surge, one where a show finds its largest audience a year after its on-air run has ended. I know my Annotated Bibliography will very quickly be out of date as new scholarship is hitting the press while this book is going to print. Still, it is a start and I am pleased to include in it not just peer-reviewed scholarship but also the substantive analyses that have appeared in various online venues. Though the artistry of the craftspeople who created it make *Breaking Bad* the worthy recipient of many awards, we believe the series is popular because it has touched the zeitgeist. It has started conversations about contemporary American concepts of being a man (which are, of course, always constructs) while not eliding the moral and ethical questions involved. These questions are not mere academic exercises. We need to ask ourselves what kind of man we have been constructing and what kind of man we want to be responsible for constructing.

Introduction

This collection of *Breaking Bad* analyses is predicated upon an assumption well summarized in Peter Rollins' motto "If it isn't popular, it isn't culture." To their contemporaries, Shakespeare, Mozart, and Dickens were popular entertainment. Today, we see their works as something more—as landmarks in western culture. If we, the authors of this book, are not exactly arguing that Vince Gilligan and his fellow artists are modern-day Shakespeares (though this editor would be happy to make such a statement on her own), we are at least asserting that the popularity of this particular television series merits serious attention from scholars who would understand the early twenty-first-century zeitgeist. Far from banishing it from scholarly consideration because of its popularity (a move that still exists among academic snobs), we are drawn to *Breaking Bad* precisely because it has struck a chord with viewers. One might argue that, by such criterion, every cuddly kittens video that goes viral in social media merits study. We counter such suggestions with our analyses of how this series does more than simply capture viewers' attention. It plays with its medium's conventions, invokes previous visual artistry, and violates the expectations of its audience to great effect. We consider it an exploration in light and sound of contemporary western understandings of masculinity. As such, it tells us about ourselves. But *Breaking Bad* goes one step further: it offers us a story with multiple layers of meaning open to various interpretations *within the framework of a critique*. This book takes the view that the universe of *Breaking Bad* is not a postmodern one of relative values—though it has been read as such. Rather, it is a world where every evil action has a consequence that obliges the serious viewer to evaluate Walter White not merely as another anti-hero, but as the protagonist in a tragedy—a tragedy that might have been conceived by Shakespeare or Dickens and to which Mozart could have provided the score.

This book begins with Susan Johnston's analysis of the representation of fatherhood in *Breaking Bad*. This is an inevitable examination if a viewer considers the series within the context of prime-time television in which a paterfamilias is the protagonist. It is interesting to note that Bryan Cranston as lead actor in itself evokes memories of the comedic paterfamilias of *Malcolm in the Middle*—the fin de siècle trend of father as unruly child. The role of the father as "the man who protects this family" receives an ironic critique in *Breaking Bad* as Walter's claims to be doing it all for his family is gradually revealed to be the central lie in his substantial arsenal of untruths.

Susan's consideration of fatherhood is immediately followed by Ian Dawe's reading of *Breaking Bad* as a traditional Western. It is from this tradition that Walter White's understanding of what "being a man" is drawn: staking a claim, shooting it out with rivals, and choosing between being the outlaw and being the family man. This analysis, it seems to us, is necessary in any consideration of *Breaking Bad*. In its cinematography, its setting, and its music, this series presents itself to the viewer as self-consciously Western—right down to a tough guy traveling the desert in a black hat. Bringing his background in film studies, Ian considers the various genres of Westerns and where *Breaking Bad* fits within them.

As I explained in the preface, there are questions of the series' reception that touch upon its theme of masculinity—questions that did not lend themselves readily to a distinct essay of their own. Instead, I have elected to put the contributors to this collection into conversation with one another about what these issues might have to say about the series and its viewership. The first of these is the question of what Emily Nussbaum, writing for *The New Yorker*, called "Bad Fans." It is a discussion of all possible explanations for what we see as the willful misreading of the text that is *Breaking Bad*. We hope that this will spark further discussion among scholars and researchers.

Brian Cowlishaw's examination of the relationship between intellectual ability and credible masculinity is the necessary consideration of Walter White's unique quality (whether one chooses to see him within the context of prime-time paterfamilias, gunslingers of the wild west, or cable television anti-heroes): his knowledge of science. In choosing to focus its examination of masculinity on an intellectual, *Breaking Bad* makes an unexpected move and reveals how uncomfortably our culture combines "being a man" with "being a brainiac."

This volume then steps outside of the humanities and into the realm of business and marketing for its necessary examination of those masculine proving grounds so important in *Breaking Bad*. R. Nicholas Gerlich and Lori Smith Westermann explore the series' capitalist concept of manhood in which masculinity is always bound to the acquisition of capital, profits, and strategy. It is often overlooked that Walter White makes the move from the realm of science and education to the battlefield of business in his journey to becoming Heisenberg. To "provide" is, after all, "what a man does" in the world of *Breaking Bad*.

Stephanie Stringer Gross then goes on to consider exactly what kinds of strategy are needed on the capitalist battleground. Employing Machiavelli as Walter White's uncredited mentor, she considers how winning with such strategy requires besting the inherently feminine force of Fate. Indeed, there are places in the text where *Breaking Bad* can be read as pinning Walter's cunning directly against the forces of chance and luck.

This essay is followed by the second round table discussion, which focuses on the issue of fan hatred for the character of Skyler White. This ultimately became an exploration of whether or not the text supports reading her as an unsympathetic character.

In an analysis related to both Walter White as paterfamilias and as a strategizing businessman, Ian Dawe examines the series' preoccupation with the rugged individualist man's need to leave a legacy behind him. It is not only the series' protagonist who is motivated by legacy. All the men of *Breaking Bad*—with the interesting exception of Jesse Pinkman—are caught up in concern for what they will leave after them, how they will be remembered when they are gone.

The final essay, by Jeffrey Reid Pettis, deals with perhaps the most obvious concern of hegemonic masculinity: power. With its reputation for the formal preference for quirky camera angles and the thematic preference for characters observing or watching or surveilling each other, *Breaking Bad* lends itself to a Foucaldian analysis of power. In this series, who is watching whom has everything to do with which man wins.

The last round table discussion turns from masculinity to femininity, asking if *Breaking Bad* can be read as a feminist text.

Finally, this book offers the reader an annotated bibliography of *Breaking Bad* analysis because there is nothing in the world so helpful to a scholar as a comprehensive annotated bibliography. We hope that even the casual reader will find a use for this feature as a guide for further reading and discussing.

• Family Man •

Walter White and the Failure of Fatherhood

SUSAN JOHNSTON

"That's right, Daddy did that. Daddy did that for you" (212, "Phoenix"), says Walter White (Bryan Cranston) to baby Holly, pointing to the ill-gotten gains that are spreading like mold through the walls of their home. This model of fatherhood as service, a sacrificial offering, is echoed by a different father, Donald Margolis (John de Lancie), in the very same episode, in a way that implicates both men in the far-reaching tragedy of Don's daughter Jane's (Krysten Ritter) death. Although both Walt and Donald articulate a fundamentally custodial idea of paternal masculinity, of the father as provider and protector, /FILM reviewer Hunter Stephenson points out that already in the previous episode, "Mandala" (211), Walt has "[chosen] a new life over the nurturing of his current one as a father, a husband," by choosing the deal with Gus Fring (Giancarlo Esposito) over the birth of his baby. Stephenson calls this "the dark side," remarking that "as Walt's tunnel vision for the thrill of the drug world and its unknown power narrows, the fates of other characters in his life fade like weakness.... Blood and loyalty: Walt seems on the verge of tossing them out of the window at 80 mph like a cold cup of coffee. He is not only breaking bad, he is breaking all respect for life" ("TV Buzz"). But "Phoenix" goes still further, matching its powerful image of Walt-as-father, tenderly placing baby Holly on her side, to the carelessness with which he accidentally shifts someone else's daughter onto her back and then to his murderous neglect of the unconscious Jane as she subsequently chokes to death on her own vomit.

Gus Fring, who is the occasion but not the cause of Walter White's turn

13

to the dark side, himself echoes the violent contradiction at the heart of "Phoenix" the following season when he tells Walt "a man, a man provides. And he does it even when he's not appreciated or respected or even loved" (305, "Màs"). Fastidious, murderous, potent and fearless enough to challenge even the drug cartels in the fortress of their own power, Gus nonetheless invokes the formidable and enduring grip of custodial masculinity on Walt's imagination, and on ours. And when Walt is later invited into Gustavo Fring's suburban home for a meal (311, "Abiquiu"), Gus invokes food as memory of family. Yet despite the toys and Gus's own references to "the kids," his kitchen, traditionally in American television the heart of the home and the family, is darkly shadowed, empty of all but Walt and Gus: for whom, then, does Gus provide? Against this darkening backdrop we see that the custodial masculinity Gus preaches to Walt is itself, like the home he occupies, merely a façade, one that both points to and masks the ways the dangerous and powerful have justified their any and every action. As Margaret Lyons has observed, "*Breaking Bad* doesn't have a dad."

This essay begins by reading Walt himself in terms of the commitment to fatherhood he claims, and then turns to examine other father figures in the show, documenting the ways in which the idea of the father emerges in *Breaking Bad* in terms of its concrete articulation in custodial relationships, particularly Hank and Walt Jr.; Walt and Walt Jr.; and Walt and Jesse. Situating these relationships in the context of contemporary work on fathers and fatherlessness, the chapter concludes by arguing that Walt's self-justifying defense of his actions, predicated on this idea of fatherhood, compromises the audience by drawing them into sympathy with and support for the villain of the piece.

Critic Brian Faucette reads producer Vince Gilligan's assertion that the series wanted to take "a man who transforms himself from Mr. Chips into Scarface" (MacInnes) as a response to a modern crisis of masculinity, one in which male loss of authority and control can only be addressed by "embrac[ing] older models of masculinity based on violence, intimidation, and control" (74). For Faucette,

> the importance of being seen as a provider and a protector is one of the key themes the series addresses as it presents an image of an America where it is no longer possible for most men to be the "bread winner" without having more than one job. Despite the fact that Walt is a man with advanced degrees in science and a teacher, he is forced to work after school at a car wash to help keep the family afloat. Walt's wife Skyler (Anna Gunn) who is eight months pregnant reminds him to not let the owner screw him on his work hours

again. Her statement shows her concern for the family but also indicates that in effect Skyler is the person who is in charge in the home, which is a situation that as the series moves forward it seeks to destabilize in an attempt to make Walt feel masculine and in control [76–77].

In the end, Faucette contends that Walt's rise and fall warns against the dangers of restoring the hegemony of a masculinity that centers on "father, husband, and provider" (84), seeing Walt's transformation as a caution against the ways these ideas of masculinity have been used to reassert control over marriage, home, and nation (84–85). Yet compelling as this view is, it relies on Faucette's presumption, first, that Walt's custodialism is genuine, and, second, that such masculinity is in itself at best outmoded or bankrupt and at worst the corrupt longing that breeds violence and oppression inside the family and out. As such, it conflates custodialism with hegemonic masculinity-as-power-over, and thus with all that power finally entails; but as I will suggest, the show points not to the bankruptcy of custodial masculinity, but to its hollowing out.

Revisiting the term "hegemonic masculinity" in 2005, more than twenty years after its early development in the context of field work in Australian high schools and the labor movement, Connell and Messerschmidt sought to clarify the scope of the concept. Hegemonic masculinity, they noted, is not "normal," but "normative": while "only a minority of men might enact it…. It embodied the currently most honored way of being a man, it required all other men to position themselves in relation to it, and it ideologically legitimated the global subordination of women to men" (832). Blending insights from local empirical research, feminist theory, social psychology, psychoanalysis, Gramscian Marxism, and gay activism (830–2), the term asserted the historicity of hegemonic masculinities as part of the gender hierarchy and therefore changeable: "Hegemonic masculinities therefore came into existence in specific circumstances and were open to historical change. More precisely, there could be a struggle for hegemony, and older forms of masculinity might be displaced by new ones" (832–3). In other words, masculinities are multiple, cultural, and historical; they are performed and enacted by practices and behaviors; and what is normative among them changes from place to place and time to time, but amongst these multiple masculinities social and ideological mechanisms will work to shore up and inculcate a normative model. Faucette, for example, reads the birthday party scene in the *Breaking Bad* pilot (101), dominated by Walt's brother-in-law Hank (Dean Norris) in a boisterous, gun-loving display of masculinity and authority, as highlighting both the failure of Walter's milquetoast masculinity and the social practices through which hegemonic masculinity is reified and normalized. Faucette says, "For men like Hank the gun is an extension of their masculinity and their authority. Walt shows the first signs of dissatisfaction with his status as a man when his brother-in-law, son, and the other men laugh at him. In that moment he comes to realize that his family sees him as effeminate because he does not measure up to a man like Hank" (76).

Nor is it surprising, given the history of the term "hegemonic masculinity" in masculinity and men's studies, that, as Connell and Messerschmidt report, the concept has "reduce[d], in practice, to a reification of power or toxicity" (839), as it has done for Brian Faucette. "Because the concept of hegemonic masculinity is based on practice that permits men's collective dominance over women to continue ... in some contexts, hegemonic masculinity actually does refer to men's engaging in toxic practices—including physical violence—that stabilize gender dominance in a particular setting" (Connell and Messerschmidt 840). And here Demetriou's distinction between external hegemony, "connected to the institutionalization of men's dominance over women," and internal hegemony, "a social ascendancy of one group of men over others" (341), has proven valuable.[1] As the complicated responses of both Skyler and her sister, Marie Schrader (Betsy Brandt), to the transformations of their respective husbands from one mode of masculinity to another suggest, the unifying idea of a global dominance over women fails to account fully for "women's relations with dominant masculinities" (Connell and Messerschmidt 847). As the early exposition of these relationships make clear, the competition between Hank and Walt, already visible at Walt's 50th birthday party when Hank insists that Walt handle his gun, is mirrored in the competition between Skyler and Marie (101, Pilot). As Skyler packs up her garage-sale finds for her Ebay customers, Marie nitpicks: these online auctions only earn petty cash, a novel would be more lucrative than a short story collection, how's the sex with Walter now that he's fifty? As a sequel to the perfunctory "birthday sex" scene in the same episode, Marie's question trumpets her own success through Hank's dominant masculinity over her sister and Walter. Indeed it is difficult to read Skyler's shift from the bored, sexually controlling figure who offers Walt perfunctory sexual stimulation early in the pilot to the thrilled, and sexually dominated, lover of the episode's close as anything but an indictment of women's ongoing complicity in this external hegemony.[2] Walt's sexual assault on Skyler in the first episode of Season Two ("Seven-Thirty-Seven"), which she resists, does seem to indicate that there are limits to Skyler's complicity in this coercive dominance. At the same time, this assault, like the unresisted one that concludes "Madrigal" (502), foregrounds the distinction between the custodialism Walt mouths and the dominance he performs. Guffey and Koontz, who quite rightly find Walt's assault on Skyler in their own kitchen "truly disturbing," note this contradiction: "The fact that Skyler is pregnant adds another layer of horror to Walt's attack. The White house is becoming less and less of a refuge as Walt brings more and more of the violence of his other life home with him, harming those he loves and slowly destroying their home life. What Walt is supposedly doing for the good of his family is destroying it" (62). The menace of this scene is arrested only by the return of Walt Jr., but as we see in the chilling final scene of "Madrigal," with its echo of the Season One pilot's erotic closer, the "forgotten rape" (Wilder) of "Seven-Thirty-Seven" is a harbinger of things to come, for this time Walt's kisses and his hand sliding to cup Skyler's breast are something twisted and evil, with no love behind any of it, only power, and a willing joy on Walt's part in how he now so completely dominates his wife. It is a truly chilling rape scene, and Anna Gunn somehow projects Skyler's skin actually crawling at Walt's touch, expressing perfectly the trapped horror she feels. Walt has brought the darkness all the way home at last (Guffey and Koontz 320).

In drawing forward these instances of sexual assault, that is, of violence in and of the home, I am not reiterating the condemnation of hegemonic and masculinized violence so ably demonstrated elsewhere. Rather, I am highlighting the deceit of Walt's claim to nurture and provide. For over five seasons, *Breaking Bad* demonstrates repeatedly that the nurturing and providing, the family care, that Walt's vaunting rationalizations trumpet, has little to do with custodialism or with care. Jamie Paris defines "custodial masculinity" as "relationships where men take on the responsibility for ensuring the human flourishing of another person"; typically or even archetypically as they enter "a new community" (3). For Paris, custodial masculinity is antithetical to Connell's hegemonic masculinity (5), and entails not what he calls the "morally flat" sense of the term (7), of merely keeping someone alive and safeguarding them, but the richer and indeed sacrificial sense in which men act as fathers, placing the flourishing of another above the self (6–7). Now, Paris is not rejecting the critical analysis of power in masculinity studies out of hand, but noting, in contrast to such influential figures as Raewynn Connell and Michael S. Kimmel, and in line with David Popenoe, that such analyses have neglected to consider men in forming relationships with others, as they have neglected to consider those relationships in any dimension except that which maps the valences of power. "Custodial masculinity," then, is for Paris a term of art which seeks to redress "one of the real crises of modern masculinity" (9). He says, "As men become more and more disconnected from their communities and their families, and as we increasingly raise generations of men without men as primary caregivers, I fear that men are seeing their lives as not being meaningfully connected to others, and are living as what [Charles] Taylor calls atomists, who believe that 'all goods are in the last analysis the goods of individuals'" (Taylor 128; qtd. Paris 10).

The distinction Paris draws may be clearer in the context of Season Two's "Over" (210) and Walter's confrontation with his brother-in-law, Hank. The family is celebrating Walt's remission from cancer with a party celebrating the return to that normalcy he has left behind for his secret life as "Heisenberg," and as in Walt's birthday party (101, Pilot), Hank is spinning tales about his macho world as a police officer. And as at that earlier party, Walter Jr. is hanging on his uncle's every word, his hero-worship palpable.[3] This time, however, Walt strikes back at Hank's bravado, reasserting his role as the man of the family over and against Hank's familiar surrogacy in that role (see, for example, "...And the Bag's in the River" [1.03] and "Seven-Thirty-Seven" [2.01]) by insisting on serving Walt Jr. (R.J. Mitte) repeated tequila shots:

HANK: What you doing there?
WALTER: What does it look like I'm doing?
HANK: The kid's 16. You going for Father of the Year?
WALT: [to Walt Jr.] What are you looking at him for? We're celebrating.
...
HANK: I'd take a pass on that one if I were you, okay? Think we've been bogarting this puppy long enough.
WALT: Hey, bring. The bottle. Back.
HANK: Sorry, buddy. No can do.
WALT: My son! My bottle! My house! ["Over"].

In this scene, Walt asserts a masculinity hegemonic rather than custodial; his filling and refilling of his son's glass, while it imitates the nurturing care for another that is the hallmark of custodial masculinity, is instead destructive and debilitating, as Walt Jr.'s drunken vomiting into the pool points up. What is more, the destructiveness of Walt's "booze-fueled pissing contest with Hank," which as Guffey and Koontz note takes "Walter Jr. as the playing field" (117), is quite clearly a response both jealous and envious of the care that the childless Hank shows for his nephew, one motivated by the possessiveness Walt snarls at his brother-in-law: "'My son! My bottle! My house!" We may say, in other words, that it is the apparently "masculinized jerk" (Guffey and

Koontz 28) Hank who exemplifies the ethics of care Paris wants to articulate as a proper sphere for men and the masculine, and the diffident, gentle intellectual whose prideful and atomistic longing for the dominance of hegemonic masculinity can grasp custodialism only as custodianship, that is, as a species of control. Despite the machismo Hank performs, especially for that audience of other police officers and drug enforcement agents, his care for his wife, Marie, for his sister-in-law, Skyler, and for his nephew reveal precisely the importance of the distinction between Walt's narcissistic and atomistic masculinity, in which his vaunted care for his family is primarily about his own pride, and the custodialism Jamie Paris feels that contemporary theorizing of masculinity has left behind at its peril. Moreover, to dismiss, as Faucette seems to do, the idea of a masculinity that provides and nurtures as simply part of an inevitably toxic stew of hegemonic masculinity is to hasten its loss.

The term "ethics of care," here, may well recall the controversies over gendered moral development in feminist theory of the 1970s and 1980s, when Carol Gilligan recast the work of developmental theorist Lawrence Kohlberg to insist that "moral maturity" for women specifically is characterized by a view of the human self as enmeshed in a complex web of relationships, relationships that give rise to "the contextuality, narrativity and specificity of women's moral judgment" (Benhabib 78). Care ethics in this early stage tended to emphasize, as Gilligan did, the attachment between mother and baby as a paradigm for an ethics defined by relational and contextual thinking in contrast to what Hamington terms "formulaic and analytic approaches to morality that treat ethics as abstract manipulations of principles or consequences" (1130). In the 1980s, Seyla Benhabib summarized the debate between traditional and care ethics as between the notion of the generalized and the concrete other. Traditional—that is, classical liberal ethics—calls on us to "abstract from the individuality and concrete identity of the other. We assume that the other, like ourselves, is a being who has concrete needs, desires and affects, but that what constitutes his or her moral dignity is not what differentiates us from each other, but rather what we, as speaking and acting rational agents, have in common. Our relation to the other is governed by the norms of formal equality and reciprocity" (87; emphases in original). By contrast, an ethics of care calls on us to occupy "the standpoint of the concrete other": "We seek to comprehend the needs of the other, his or her motivations, what s/he searches for, and what s/he desires. Our relation to the other is governed by norms of equity and complementary reciprocity: each is entitled to expect and to assume from the other forms of behavior through which the other feels recognized and confirmed as a concrete, individual being with specific needs, talents and capacities" (87; emphases in original).

More modern accounts of care ethics eschew the incompatibility Benhabib identified between ethics of rights and ethics of care, noting that care ethics is not an alternative to other approaches to justice and morality, substituting attachment and relationships for rights, but a supplement to those traditional moral domains, one that acknowledges that individuals are not, in fact, autonomous and atomistic, but caught up in social relationships that cannot be simply elided as we estimate the consequences of our actions (Hamington 1131). It is, as Nel Noddings insists, "a relational ethic," in which the "motive energy" of the carer "is directed (temporarily) away from her own projects and towards those of the cared-for" (53): in such a view, the cared-for is both a bearer or rights, a human person with his or her own ends and desires, and a beloved other, a "bright particular star" (Shakespeare 1.1.98) whose moral claim consists precisely in being beloved. The relationship between carer and cared-for, moreover, is both role-based and reciprocal, because it is one of mutual recognition and response (Noddings 53) from the cared-for to the carer's expression of attention and respect, so that "when, for whatever reason ... the cared-for is unable to respond in a way that completes the relation," the burden lies on the carer, though "reciprocity is then almost entirely defined by the cared-for's response of recognition" (54).

In this vein it is worth contrasting Walt and Hank's response to Walt Jr.'s disability. Walt Jr. has cerebral palsy,[4] a neurological impairment that expresses itself physically, in his slurred speech and reduced mobility. Jami L. Anderson notes that Walt Jr.'s cerebral palsy is just one of a whole series of impairments, including Marie Schrader's kleptomania, Hank's post-traumatic stress disorder, and Jesse's addictions (104). Anderson is primarily concerned with Walter Sr., and what she perceives, fairly importantly, as his unhealthy obsession with his own able-bodiedness (112–13): he does not fear death, but the failure—of bodily control and of fatherhood—it betokens (104–5). Her reading is both confirmed and complicated in the pilot episode, when Skyler and Walt take Walt Jr. to buy a new pair of jeans. First, the very name of the store, Family 1st Clothing, points to a kind of grimly economical householding, so that the scene is marked by the same tension over money we have seen elsewhere in the episode, writ large in Walt's humiliating second job at the car wash and small in the erratic water heater and Skyler's querying of a $15.88 credit card charge. Second, we see a rare moment of connection and care between Walt and his son, as he helps him on with his pants in the fitting room, a gesture whose performance may be read as providing the occasion for an embrace or, rather more darkly, parodying one. But most significant is Walt's response, seconds later, to the other teenagers in the store who are mocking Walt Jr. Their behavior echoes moments earlier in the episode when Walt himself is mocked, first by the high school student in his chemistry class and, later, by the same student as he scrubs tires at the car wash. Both those earlier scenes highlight Walt's powerlessness, particularly in the toxic hegemony of masculinities; it is no accident that in each case it is not the queen bees with which every high school is richly endowed who denigrate Walter, but the jocks. At the same time it matters that Skyler looks repeatedly but wordlessly at Walt, pleading with him to do something about the boys mocking their son, especially in terms of that complicity with hegemonic masculinity I have indicated. Here, though, for the first time, we see Walt's propensity for violence manifest itself, as he trips the biggest of the laughing jocks in the store and threatens him with further violence. The scene is oddly satisfying, but it is so precisely because it appeals to our own lurking sense of the fitness of Walt's response, a sense dependent, I want to say, on our complicity with Skyler's sense that it is the role of the father to protect his family.

As Laura Hudson notes, this seems to be "the exact model of manhood that Walt embraces," the one Gus Fring expresses too, but at bottom this identity is not about Walt's altruism or his care for his family, but "an affirmation of his own power and identity" ("Die Like a Man"). Hudson goes on:

> Masculinity in *Breaking Bad* is a brittle thing, one so terrified of weakness that any display of vulnerability must be punished, and any slight against another man's power answered with violence—or else perceived as a weakness....
>
> This model of manhood also requires control not only over your own life, but over the lives of others. Think about all the most iconic moments in the show, the badass lines that made us want to pump our fists: "Say my name." "I am the danger." "I am the one who knocks." "I won." Every single time, it's about dominance—not just about having power, but about taking power away from someone else.

In this sense we may read Walt's response to the jocks at Family 1st Clothing as of a piece with his outraged tearing off of the disability parking pass in his car, grabbing his crotch in response to his boss at the car wash, and indeed that later party scene with Walt and Hank. Even when he enacts the roles of father or husband, Walt is not oriented toward those others as persons but toward himself; his response, to use the language of care ethics, seeks to affirm merit in himself as a carer, rather than the wellbeing of the cared-for, beloved other. Yet his claim that he is thinking about his family is part of the deception Walt practices on us.

Hudson sees the contest between Walter and "alpha-male" Hank as not only about "who has more power. It's about which brand of power is superior: brains or brawn" ("Die Like a Man"). But this view fails to notice the relationship between Hank and Walt Jr., which in the end is predicated on genuine care for and of the other, rather than on mere "hero-worship," as the first episode suggests. We see this care at work in "And the Bag's in the River" (103), when, misled by Skyler's clumsy lie to Marie about researching drugs for a short story, Hank tries to "scare [Walt Jr.] straight" (Guffey and Koontz 24) by taking him to the "Crystal Palace" motel to view the human wreckage dwelling there. It is worth contrasting this care to the utter disdain for others—not just these broken beings, but those yet to come—evidenced in Walter White's willingness to cook crystal methamphetamine in the first place. Hank seems to share Walt Sr.'s marked preference for the "normal," and normalized, body, his lie to Wendy the Meth Whore (Julia Minesci) that Walt Jr. broke his leg in an appropriately masculine pursuit, football, thus resembling Walt Sr.'s rejection of Junior's disability through tearing off the parking permit. But as Guffey and Koontz contend, Hank's lie seems designed to save Walt Jr.'s pride rather than Hank's own: "There's a tremendous amount of compassion under Hank's testosterone-fueled dickishness" (24). It is this compassion, rather than hero-worship, that leads Walt Jr. to call on surrogate-father Hank rather than his own father, Walt, when he is caught trying to buy beer underage (105, "Gray Matter"); in a surprisingly display of sensitivity, Hank rebukes Walt Jr. for preferring a surrogate to his Walt himself, asking his nephew how Walt would feel.[5] Such scenes may seem at odds with the bluster and bravado of the character Laura Hudson calls "prototypically macho" and "uber-masculine," and indeed as Hudson remarks, Hank's own investment in his performance of masculinity is highlighted when he works to hide his post-traumatic stress disorder (208, "Better Call Saul") from his brother-in-law and colleagues at the Drug Enforcement Agency ("Die Like a Man"). But while Hank in this sense is clearly implicated in a masculinity "deeply pernicious, a cultural dogma that damages, warps and limits men, isolating them from their emotions and from others" ("Die Like a Man"), it is not clear that this "toxic masculinity" does indeed isolate from others. Rather, Hank himself seems aware that his masculinity, part of a deeply-rooted sense of identity, takes in an ethics of care. Thus does he see his own beating of Jesse Pinkman (Aaron Paul) as a betrayal of his own ideals and identity. He tells Marie:

"I'm supposed to be better than that.... I've been—unraveling, y'know? I don't sleep at night anymore. I freeze, I freeze up. My chest gets all tight, I can't breathe. Just—I panic.... What I did to Pinkman—that's not who I'm supposed to be. All this, everything that's happened, I swear to God, Marie, I think the universe is trying to tell me something and I'm finally ready to listen. I'm just not the man I thought I was. I think I'm done as a cop" [307, "One Minute"].

As an aside, this same episode introduces "The Cousins," Leonel and Marco Salamanca, who in the episode's teaser learn the brutal lesson that "La familia es todo" (The family is all) from Hector Salamanca. Yet as we see this motto played out in the lives of the characters, the series draws a harsh line between the ethics of care such a view may produce, as in Hank's offer to look after Walt's family (104, "Cancer Man"), and the virulent revenge fantasy that leaves Vince Gilligan's fictive Albuquerque awash in blood (e.g., 413 "Face Off" and 516 "Felina").

This is a distinction worth making, not least because without it we risk mistaking one for the other. For Jamie Paris, custodial masculinity in its true form turns on the bond that forms between men and the boys they care for, a "symbiotic bond … where they come to care about something by caring about the boys as ends in themselves" (11). Here Paris is following the work of Harry Frankfurt, who in The Reasons of Love remarks that "Caring about something may be, in the end, nothing more than a certain complex mode of wanting it. However, simply attributing desire to a person does not in itself convey that the person cares about the object he desires. In fact, it does not convey that the object means anything much to him at all" (11). This is to say that love is a mode of caring, but not the only mode; it is not mere preference, for example, or the desire for possession, since both these modes are kinds of "wanting it," and take the other, not as a beloved person with his own ends and desires, but as an object, a means to be deployed to ends that are my own. Frankfurt says, "Loving someone or something essentially means or consists in, among other things, taking its interests as reasons for acting to serve those interests. Love is itself, for the lover, a source of reasons. It creates the reasons by which his acts of loving concern and devotion are inspired" (37; emphases in original). Here it is worth contrasting Walt's failure to respond to Holly's birth, preferring instead to make his deal with Gus Fring, discussed briefly above, with Hank's immediate abandonment of his pursuit of Jesse Pinkman when he hears Marie has been in an accident and is being rushed to the hospital (306, "Sunset"). Though the pursuit of "Heisenberg" and the breaking of his blue meth empire are powerful enough motivators for Hank to give up a promotion and risk his career, they are insufficient in the face of the over-riding imperative of his love for Marie. And this is so, I suggest, despite her flaws; she is the orienting value of his life because he loves her, which is to say, as Harry Frankfurt suggests, that love takes the beloved as intrinsically and infinitely valuable, independent of her worth or her deserving.

The same cannot be said of Walter White and his so-called beloved ones. Although when we first meet Walter, he is making a video in which he declares, "Skyler, you're the love of my life, I hope you know that" (101, Pilot), he consistently chooses his alternate life and the power and domination it provides him over care for her and their family, even though that life puts them at risk. What is more, the Gray Matter back-story, told only partially and through flashbacks, points to another, older love, the gorgeous brunette of the chemistry classroom flashback in "And the Bag's in the River" (103), now Gretchen Schwartz (Jessica Hecht). We might think this affair is long in the past, but it's worth noting that the emerald-clad woman Walter spots at the car wash right before he faints ("Pilot") bears a remarkable resemblance to that younger Gretchen. Clearly this scene, though momentary, asserts in the language of emotional realism[6] that governs the show's "first-person" shots from Walter's point of view, at least a counterweight to his declared commitment to Skyler at the start of the episode; it is elaborated by the accusations Walt levels at Gretchen in Season Two's "Peekaboo" (206), where he accuses her and husband Elliot of "cutting [him] out." Ultimately for Walt even love is finally about possession, as we see when he escapes with Holly (514, "Ozymandias") when the game is finally up. Eric San Juan has noticed this as well, remarking that "when we see Walt do things for his son it's often to prove a point or to get one over on Skyler" (23). It is, in this sense, individualistic and self-centered rather than other-directed: not love, but, as Frankfurt would say, merely a kind of wanting.

In marked contrast, Walt Jr. shows himself to be, in truth, the "big man" his father calls him, so patronizingly, in the first episode's cold open ("Pilot"). His cerebral palsy functions connotatively throughout the series to point up the adolescent struggle for independence, more conventionally represented through the driving lessons he takes from his friends (note that in "Down" [204] his lesson from his father stops short when Walt refuses to let Walt Jr. compensate for his disability by using both feet on the pedals). As Jami L. Anderson remarks, Walt Jr.'s stammer "perfectly expresses the slurred rage of a character who wants to, but cannot, fully understand or take control of the situation he is in" (104). Unlike Walt, Sr., though, Walt Jr. sees such control not as power or domination over others, and in fact he rejects that model of manhood even as he rejects his father's "fugue state," through his retaliatory renaming of himself as "Flynn" and not "Walter Jr." (204, "Down"). It is striking, too, that after his parents' separation, "Flynn" reverts to "Walt Jr." (302, "Caballo Sin Nombre"), which again suggests that whatever (self) control or independent identity the boy seeks to carve out, it is in the context of family and community and not apart from or, indeed, above them.

Critical to this reading of Walt Jr. is his response to his father's failure to honor his sixteenth birthday (410, "Salud"). Badly beaten by Jesse, Walt has slept through Walt Jr.'s celebration, but despite his disappointment Walt Jr. drives to his father's apartment and cares for what Guffey and Koontz aptly call "his battered, drug-addled, whining, weeping, tighty-whitey-wearing father" (282–3). This tender scene between father and son is undercut by Walt's miscalling his own son "Jesse" as he drifts off to sleep. When he wakes, Walt recalls his own father's final illness and death from Huntingdon's disease, revealing his own contempt for weakness and disability even as we see again Walt Jr.'s love for his father, rooted in his "realness" rather than in perceived or performed strength and perfection. It is this acceptance of imperfection, of his own and others' all-too-human embodiment, that leads Anna Mae Duane to call Walter Jr. the "real hero" of *Breaking Bad*. She says,

> For Walter White, manhood means not just being a redeemer and benefactor (after all, he's doing it for his family, right?) but a conqueror of the chaos and darkness that comes with being embodied, with being human. Walter's sense of entitlement, which undeniably finds its purchase in having a white male body, also resides in the belief that only an able body is worth having. He, unlike those trapped within the realm of "minors and invalids," will accept only a body that doesn't require thinking about at all.

Indeed, for Duane, Walter's transformation into Heisenberg is provoked by his cancer, by the failure of the able body. To be Heisenberg is to cease to be "in danger" and to become "the danger" (406, "Cornered") and to exercise control, to refute "the weakness he associates with illness": Duane says, "Walt's decisions stem from a fundamental desire to be the one doing the breaking, rather than the one who has to live with the uncertainty of being perceived as broken." Walt Sr. might seem then to parallel Hank, whose self-loathing in response to his spiritual and physical crippling echoes Walt's desire for perfection, but is ultimately redressed by his acceptance of help from others. Hank learns, in other words, from "Gomie," from his wife Marie's single-minded love for him, and from the nephew he loves, to accept at least partially his own brokenness, as Walt Jr. himself has done.

Duane identifies Walt Jr.'s willingness to call for help, telling the 911 operator that his father is threatening his mother ("Ozymandias"), as the heroic move that "dismantles Heisenberg's plan to beat both death and the law," and it is worth noting that the same scene gives us Walt Jr./Flynn fighting to protect his mother from his raging and violent father. He has, in other words, chosen in extremity—as his uncle Hank has done, laying down his life in the service of the law—to risk his life for his family, to reject the radical self-centeredness that is the hallmark of Walter's toxic masculinity and to choose instead care and the community.

In this Walt Jr. is both like and unlike the feckless Jesse Pinkman, Walt's surrogate son. Laura Hudson calls Jesse "more creampuff than criminal," saying that "despite his flaws and his posturing, he's always been a good guy: compassionate, caring and even sensitive … unable to take part in the sociopathy of the people around him and deeply traumatized when forced to commit violence" ("Die Like a Man"). The viciously gendered language so typical of his character, in his usage of "bitch" and "pussy," in this sense, is both, as Hudson remarks, a marker of power deployed against another, and a sign of the "very narrow cultural script for being a man" that Jesse can act out but not fully become. She says, "What these words tell us is that men aren't just defined by what they are; they're defined by what they're not supposed to be" ("Die Like a Man"). Yet as Hudson also remarks, it is striking that Jesse Pinkman almost never uses these denigrating, toxically gendered terms to women, although he is seeks to claim power over others by using them to render other men feminine and thus exploited, weak, submissive. When we first meet Jesse, too, he is escaping out his lover's window as Hank and his DEA agents raid the meth lab he has set up as "Cap'n Cook" ("Pilot"), an introduction which points to a penchant for exploitative relations rather than to the kind of care and custodialism I am contending for here. Yet, as we learn in "Down," Jesse cared for his aunt, who died of cancer, while she was undergoing chemotherapy, and part of the estrangement between Jesse and his parents indeed seems to be predicated on what he sees as their failure of care towards Mrs. Pinkman's dying sister ("Down"). And while his romantic relationship with Jane Margolis, a recovering addict, seems marred by carelessness, particularly with regard to the drugs he uses nearly constantly, the failures and fecklessness Jesse exhibits here bear no resemblance to the toxic and atomistic masculinity we have already seen, for example, in Walt's relationship with Skyler. What is more, the grief and self-loathing Jesse reveals after

Jane's death (213, "ABQ") aligns him not with the self-absorbed Walt, whose deliberate refusal of care is directly responsible for Jane's death, but with her heartbroken father, Donald Margolis, whose struggles to care for his flailing adult daughter he shared so poignantly with Walt himself ("Phoenix"). This is to say that Jesse, blaming himself for Jane's death, understands it as a failure of care, and it is in this understanding, however tragic, that we begin at last to see the fullness of the distinction between him and his surrogate father, Walt.

In this vein, Jesse's later romance with another recovering addict, Andrea Cantillo (Emily Rios), and her young son Brock (Ian Posada) is also telling. While Jesse's care for Andrea and Brock is initiated by his romantic interest in her, the paternal role he plays during Brock's illness (which Jesse assumes is accidental and due to ricin poisoning, but which in fact seems to be another of Walt's deliberate strikes against those Jesse cares for) makes it clear that he is seeking not only a romantic relationship, but a familial one (412, "End Times"). Indeed Jesse's relationship with Brock, including the money Jesse gives Andrea to move to a better neighborhood (402, "Thirty-Eight-Snub"), one where Brock will be less likely to meet the fate of her murdered eleven-year-old brother, Tòmas, is anticipated by his care for the strange, silent little boy of "Peekaboo" (206). The Young Boy (Dylan and Brandon Carr) himself is, of course, foreshadowed by the beetle Jesse refuses to kill but who is nonetheless crushed by Skinny Pete (Charles Baker) in the episode's teaser. Walt has sent an unwilling Jesse to threaten the two meth addicts, Spooge (David Ury) and his "woman" (Dale Dickey) after they robbed Skinny Pete at knifepoint of the meth he was dealing (205, "Breakage"), and it is against the filthy and hellish landscape of Spooge and his girlfriend's meth house that we first meet the Young Boy. The child is, as Guffey and Koontz observe, "the heart-ripping part of the episode ... an innocent in hell" (92), and it is worth noting that the hell the child dwells in, "this cycle of addiction, desperation, criminality, and violence" is the hell that "Jesse and Walt are actually producing in the RV, and what the viewer is complicit in as the audience roots for the two protagonists" (Guffey and Koontz 93). For Walt this hell remains fundamentally unreal, even as he fully understands the effects of meth and is himself implicated in a widening gyre of criminality and violence. For Jesse, however, who is both "the conscience of the show, or at least a barometer of the damage Walt inflicts" (Hudson, "Don't Cry"), the drive to save the young boy is both a marker of his care for those he sees as innocent and an indictment of his own role in manufacturing that hell—the guilt he seeks to expiate but that will later nearly destroy him (509, "Blood Money").

I should, however, make it clear that although in my reading of Breaking Bad Jesse sees Walt as a substitute father, Walt does not reciprocate. Adam Pinkman (Michael Bofshever) appears only rarely in the series, but our first encounter with him, in "Cancer Man" (104), points to his fraught relationships with Jesse and his younger brother, Jake (Ben Petry). We first meet Jesse's parents and young Jake as they are seated around a small dinner table in a well-appointed home, though in that scene much of the rest of the home is deeply shadowed. The three are discussing Jake's music lessons, his soccer practice, his teachers: the stilted conversation makes it clear that for the Pinkmans, Jake is a talented prince whose special gifts must be fostered at all costs:

> MR. PINKMAN: I don't understand why they're forcing you to choose between the piccolo and the oboe. You show so much promise with both.
> JAKE: They can't have any switching between woodwinds because no matter how divided up, someone would be left out.
> MRS. PINKMAN: Well, rules are rules, I guess.
> MR. PINKMAN: Sure, rules are rules. I'm all for that. But I'm telling you, you really shine on that oboe. You have real talent, and I'm not just saying that.
> JAKE: Thanks.
> MRS. PINKMAN: What about Mr. Pemberton? Is he giving you enough individual attention?
> JAKE: I'd have to say so. He tries to talk to each one of us at least once during every practice.
> MRS. PINKMAN: That's good. Feedback's important.
> MR. PINKMAN: It's key, I think—Hey, so how was soccer practice? ["Cancer Man"].

Guffey and Koontz read this episode not in terms of the parents' coldness, but as "a realistic and convincingly brutal depiction of a family dealing with addiction" (30); without blaming the parents, though, I want to say that their coldness, Adam Pinkman's especially, to his sons does highlight the distinction I was trying to make earlier between kinds of custodialism. The Pinkmans provide for their sons, and do so well, it is clear; at the same time, it is also clear that both their sons remain radically uncertain of their parents' love for them, as the poignant exchange between Jesse and his younger brother later in the episode makes clear:

> JESSE: Like, "Oh, we can't let that scumbag warp the mind of our favorite son."
> JAKE: I'm the favorite? Yeah, right. [You're] practically all they ever talk about.

I want to call the Pinkmans' relationship with their sons care of them, rather than care for them, in the custodial sense I have been treating care here; care ethicist Nel Noddings would suggest that the boys' response points to the failure of mutuality and reciprocity in the caring relationship here. Care ethics calls for the carer to be attentive to the particularity of the cared-for, to acknowledge and be receptive to their "expressed needs." She points out that "when things go wrong, when the cared-for does not recognize the effort of the carer, there is no caring relation.... In contrast, a virtue carer may simply point to her own virtuous acts and urge the cared-for to shape up" (53). Indeed we might also say, with Harry Frankfurt, that Adam Pinkman's valuing of Jake's talents—for piccolo, for oboe, for soccer—is itself a version of love that responds in the first instance to merit, which is to say that Mr. Pinkman's love must be earned because it is at least partly concerned with the way the beloved object reflects his own sense of worth. Frankfurt says, "I don't deny that some sense might be given to the notion of something being unworthy of my love if loving it were somehow demeaning. But ... the fact that it is demeaning would be a function of my loving certain other things" (Voorhoeve 230).

With this relationship as background, then, Jesse's attachment to Walter White as a kind of surrogate father makes a certain amount of sense, because Walt's attachment appears to Jesse to remain despite his fecklessness, his recklessness, his criminality. Indeed it might even be said that Jesse's worth to Walt lies precisely in those things that for his parents make it necessary to set him aside. San Juan suggests, as well, that "the few instances of true selflessness we see from Walt—or as close to true selflessness as Walter White can muster—generally center around Jesse" (24), although San Juan also recognizes that, estranged from his own parents, Jesse still needs to be controlled by someone. Their relationship is abusive, but nonetheless Jesse sees Walt as pushing him to improve, to be the best that he can be (San Juan 25–26). At the same time I think San Juan errs when he says that "Jesse ... opens up something inside Walt that allows some genuine goodness to seep through" (26). I contend that Walt's apparent care for Jesse is merely a reflection of Walt's attachment to other things, particularly the power, money, and influence that come from the criminal empire Jesse has helped him build. Even in the risk and expense Walt goes to rescuing Jesse from his downward spiral and sending him to rehab after Jane's death ("ABQ"), seems in large part to be motivated by his need for a minion. In this Walt's capacity for care is far from the sacrificial love offered up by Hank, *Breaking Bad*'s other surrogate dad. In fact, at the death ground of To'hajiilee, Hank lays down his life in the service of a more abstract kind of custodialism, opposing the ramifying evil of Walt's meth empire and Jack's gang, ASAC Schrader to the very end (514, "Ozymandias"). And though Walt has pleaded for Hank's life, offering up even his entire criminal fortune as ransom, it is worth noting that Walt also insists Hank swear he will not pursue his investigation any more. In order to save his own life, in fact, Walt asks that Hank give up the things he holds most dear. In the end, in other words, Walt insists, as he has throughout, that others lay down their lives for him. The defining moments of their relationship, then, are not those moments of so-called tenderness that enable Walt to manipulate Jesse, but his spiteful betrayal of his surrogate son to the neo–Nazis ("Ozymandias") and thus to appalling slavery.

Critics of masculinity in *Breaking Bad* have tended to read the show in terms of the "toxic masculinity" it expresses, whether, like Hudson, they read it in the end as "more like wish fulfillment than condemnation (Hudson, "Die Like a Man"), or, like Brian Faucette, they see it "illustrat[ing] the dangers of the 'self-made man' and 'hegemonic masculinity' in the formation of American masculinity at a time of great upheaval" (85). Yet these readings are made possible, I contend, in large part because they do not adequately address other models of masculinity, or work to see in flawed creatures like the blustering and racist Hank Schrader, the posturing, unreliable, weak Jesse Pinkman, and the despised son, no longer Walt Jr. but Flynn, that other models of the masculine might be on offer, might, indeed, be worth dying for. In the midst of the terrible darkness that Walter White has wrought, however, a darkness that, like a 737 down over ABQ, ramifies cancerously throughout New Mexico, it is telling that these three men, whose spiritual and physical brokenness, in various ways, Walt contemns, find the resources to stand against him at the last. Hank dies rather than fail in his duty by covering up the gang's crimes; Flynn places his mortal body between his mother and the father he now recognizes as a killer and a criminal ("Ozymandias"); Jesse—even Jesse, in the end, murderer and meth-dealer though he be, refuses to kill Walter White and in so doing not only takes back control over his own life, but his identity as the man who cared for others rather than himself ("Felina"). The cost such custodialism exacts from each of them—recall here that Jesse has returned to slavery and torture rather than risk the life of young Brock, his girlfriend's son, at the hands of the captors who have already murdered Andrea (515, "Granite State")—is, I propose, adequate proof that these men evince what Paris calls custodial masculinity at its finest, as a sacrificial love that lays itself down for another, and not the pallid and self-serving façade of it that Walter wears.

That despite our growing suspicion of masculinity, particularly in its hegemonic variants, we continue to value that mode of the masculine that lays down its life for another, that spends itself in care, is shown, I think, by those viewers and reviewers who see Walt's admission in the final episode, that he was doing it for himself and not for his family ("Felina"), as itself a kind of redemption for Walt, a final provision for the ones he loves.[7] Matt Seitz, quoting a number of commenters and correspondents defending Walt, says,

> Some viewers desperately, desperately, desperately need for Walt to be somehow a "good guy." As in, good at heart. Good, deep down. Flawed but worthy of redemption. And also an incredible badass, a man with a plan. Heisenberg! A guy who really is doing it all for his family, though he's made some mistakes along the way, Lord knows—but give the dude a break, look at the pressure he's under!
>
> To defend Walter White, however feebly, is, I suggest, to concede the value of that mode of masculinity Walt pretends to, that idea that "a man provides" that Gus Fring, in his dark and empty house, likewise pretends to, but which at the last proves a mask that must be blown off. In none of us is it pure or unmarred, but, as Jesse and Walt Jr./Flynn show in their every move, it is what we honor and long for: a father who thinks we are worth dying for.

Notes

1. See, for example, Connell and Messerschmidt's thoughtful response to Demetriou and their reformulation of the concept of hegemonic masculinity (844–47).

2. Faucette addresses some of these scenes as well, but focuses on Walt's adoption of hegemonic masculinity as a mode of seizing sexual control rather than on Skyler's cession of that control (77–8).

3. The directions for the birthday party in the Season One official scripts read "Walt can't help but notice his son's hero-worship. Hank seems to be everything Walt isn't: bold, brash, confident" (Gilligan et al., Loc. 21).

4. Actor R.J. Mitte, who plays Walter Jr., also has cerebral palsy, though because Mitte's case is quite mild, he had to learn to walk with crutches and to emphasize the slurring characteristic of Walt Jr.'s speech in order to play the role (Strauss).

5. Guffey and Koontz likewise remark that Hank here "shows sensitivity towards the emotional currents of the family, including Walt's pride" (37).

6. I am indebted to Guffey and Koontz (1) for drawing my attention to Ien Ang's term "emotional realism," which depends on connotation rather than denotation to convey recognizable feelings, so that the specific experiences depicted are taken "as symbolic representations of more general living experiences" (Ang 44): television audiences, then, ascribe emotional meanings to the events and characters depicted on-screen, and these emotions "form the point of impact for a recognition of a certain type of structure of feeling" (45).

7. See, for example, Hudson; Paskin; Seitz.

Works Cited

Anderson, Jami L. "A Life Not Worth Living." *Breaking Bad: Critical Essays on the Contexts, Politics, Style, and Reception of the Television Series*, ed. David P. Pierson. Lanham, MD: Lexington, 2014. 103–118. Print.

Ang, Ien. *Watching Dallas: Soap Opera and the Melodramatic Imagination*. London: Routledge, 2013. Ebook.

Benhabib, Seyla. "The Generalized and the Concrete Other: The Kohlberg-Gilligan Controversy and Feminist Theory." *Feminism as Critique: On the Politics of Gender*, ed. Seyla Benhabib and Drucilla Cornell. Feminist Perspectives Ser. Minneapolis: University of Minnesota Press, 1987. 77–95. Print.

Connell, R.W. (Raewyn), and James W. Messerschmidt. "Hegemonic Masculinity: Rethinking the Concept." *Gender & Society* 19.6 (2005): 829–859. JStor. Web. 3 June 2014.

Demetriou, Demetrakis Z. "Connell's Concept of Hegemonic Masculinity: A Critique." *Theory and Society* 30 (2001): 337–61. SpringerLink. Web. 3 June 2014.

Duane, Anna Mae. "Why Flynn Is the Real Hero of *Breaking Bad*." Salon.com. 29 Sept. 2013. Web. 13 June 2014.

Faucette, Brian. "Taking Control: Male Angst and the Re-Emergence of Hegemonic Masculinity in *Breaking Bad*." *Breaking Bad: Critical Essays on the Contexts, Politics, Style, and Reception of the Television Series*, ed. David P. Pierson. Lanham: Lexington, 2014. 73–86. Print.

Frankfurt, Harry G. *The Reasons of Love*. Princeton: Princeton University Press, 2004. Print.

Gilligan, Vince, prod. *Breaking Bad*. AMC Network, 2008–2013.

Gilligan, Vince, Patty Lin, George Mastras and Peter Gould. *Breaking Bad: Season 1 Scripts*. Albuquerque: Topanga Productions (Sony Pictures). Kindle.

Guffey, Ensley F., and K. Dale Koontz. *Wanna Cook? The Complete, Unofficial Companion to Breaking Bad*. Toronto: ECW Press, 2014.

Hamington, Maurice. "Feminist Care Ethics and Business Ethics." *Handbook of the Philosophical Foundations of Business Ethics*, ed. Christoph Luetge. Dordrecht: Springer, 2013. SpringerLink. Web. 1129–1143. 10 June 2014.

Hudson, Laura. "*Breaking Bad* Recap: Don't Cry for Walter White: He's Already Dead." Wired.com. 12 Aug. 2013. Web. 17 June 2014.

_____. "Die Like a Man: The Toxic Masculinity of *Breaking Bad*." Wired.com. 10 May 2013. Web. 8 June 2014.

Kimmell, Michael. "Masculinity as Homophobia: Fear, Shame and Silence in the Construction of Gender Identity." *Theorizing Masculinities*, ed. Harry Brod and Michael Kaufman. Research on Men and Masculinities Ser. 5. Thousand Oaks: Sage, 1994. 119–41. Print.

Kleinman, Howard. "Jesse Pinkman and Male Self-Hatred." Life in an Electric Box. 3 Aug. 2012. Blog. 17 June 2014.

Kovvali, Silpa. "*Breaking Bad*'s Big Critique of the Macho (and Its Problem with Women)." *The Atlantic*. 1 Oct. 2013. Web. 11 June 2014.

Lyons, Margaret. "*Breaking Bad*'s Walter White Is the Ultimate Absent Father." Vulture.com. 7 July 2012. Web. 29 April 2014.

MacInnes, Paul. "*Breaking Bad* Creator Vince Gilligan: The Man Who Turned Walter White from Mr Chips into Scarface." *The Guardian*. 19 May 2012. Web. 3 June 2014.

Noddings, Nel. "The Language of Care Ethics." *Knowledge Quest* 40.4 (2012): 53–6. ProQuest. Web. 10 June 2014.

Paris, Jamie. "On Custodial Masculinity in Kipling's Writing for Children." M.A. Thesis. University of Regina. Regina, Saskatchewan, 2008.

Paskin, Willa. "Did 'Team Walt' Win?" [blog]. Slate.com. 30 Sept. 2013. Web. 20 June 2014.

Popenoe, David. "Parental Androgyny." *Society* 30.6 (1993): 5–11. SpringerLink. Web. 17 June 2014.

San Juan, Eric. *Breaking Down Breaking Bad: Unpeeling the Layers of Television's Greatest Drama*. North Charleston, SC: CreateSpace, 2013. Print.

Seitz, Matt Zoller. "Seitz on *Breaking Bad*, and Why Viewers Need to Whitewash Walter White." Vulture.com. 18 Sept. 2013. Web. 20 June 2014.

Shakespeare, William. *All's Well That Ends Well. In The Riverside Shakespeare*, ed. G. Blakemore Evans. Boston: Houghton Mifflin, 1974. 499–544. Print.

Stephenson, Hunter. "TV Buzz: AMC's *Breaking Bad* Finally Crosses the Dark Side." /FILM. 18 May 2009. Slashfilm.com. Web. 1 June 2014.

Strauss, Gary. "For Teen Star of *Breaking Bad*, Real-Life Disability is No Obstacle." *USA Today*. 2 Feb. 2008. Usatoday.com. Web. 9 June 2014.

Taylor, Charles. *Philosophical Arguments*. Cambridge: Harvard University Press, 1995.

Voorhoeve, Alex. "Harry Frankfurt: The Necessity of Love" [interview]. *Conversations on Ethics*. Oxford: Oxford University Press, 2009. 215–31. Print.

Wilder, Alice. "The Forgotten Rape of Skyler White." HuffPost College. 13 Sept. 2013. Web. 5 June 2014.

• Western Men •

Breaking Bad's Outlaws
and Family Men

IAN DAWE

The Western is traditionally a genre associated with a specific kind of masculinity. Key genre tropes such as the man on a horse, squinting into the setting sun, or standing, legs apart, still, reaching for a hip-mounted iron shaft as another man does the same, draw the attention, consciously and subconsciously, to a consideration of the masculine. The camera angles, poses, preoccupation with firearms, drinking and rugged looks are all part of the visual textual vocabulary of westerns, and all are to be found in the world of *Breaking Bad*. Exploring the visual and moral universe of the Western is much like exploring the inner universe of the American male, a collection of imperatives, duties, obligations and attitudes that underwent dramatic changes during the 20th century, evolving on-screen in the American Western and being reflected back, stark and brutally incisively, through the so-called "Spaghetti" Westerns. One way of reading that moral landscape is to posit two primary sorts of male characters: the Outlaw and the Family Man. Whether these are different characters, conflicting characters, cooperating characters or the same character at different points in their evolution, the tension between those two states is played out in *Breaking Bad* through its major male characters with just as much force and dramatic power as any of the classic westerns. Reading the show in those terms can help us to understand its genre connections and appreciate what it has to tell the audience about the choices and duties facing the American man.

In terms of film genre, a risk when considering the Western it, as Schatz

33

puts is, "The western ... seem[s] to represent [a genre] in which the evolutionary 'cycle' seems more or less complete." The genre has long since passed, even in its American incarnations, from its historically embedded and culturally coded beginnings. It has embraced the specific generic elements that give it mass appeal, branched out to reconsider its archetypes (particularly with regards to the hero), and finally reached into knowing self-parody and satire. In other words, we all seem to intuitively "know" what a Western is, even if we have never seen one. The genre was so deeply embedded in popular culture, so soon after the invention of the cinema, that there have been many eras in which the western was almost equivalent to cinema itself.

In *Breaking Bad*, a number of the Western themes come into play, partially due to the visual patina of Albuquerque and surroundings and partially due to some important thematic motifs. *Breaking Bad* falls squarely within the tradition of the Western film, and the western cultural narrative, a tradition with a history that extends back over a century. But the Western is a very flexible genre, capable of adapting other forms to it. For example, *The Magnificent Seven* (dir. John Sturgess, 1960) is a remake of Akira Kurosawa's *Seven Samurai* (1954). The Western also influences other forms in visual or thematic ways, as when the poses struck by the participants in *Star Wars* (dir. George Lucas, 1977) during lightsaber duels deliberately recall Samurai postures prior to a deadly duel—but just as deliberately mimic the low-angle, menacing poses struck by Western gunfighters. Consider Porter's *The Great Train Robbery* (1903), one of the canonical early American films. Although it contains many of the archetypes that had already become staples of the genre, it was in fact shot in New Jersey by the Edison Company while similar, real events were still taking place. This is history and myth reinforcing each other, almost in "real-time." Clearly based on earlier stage traditions, it is remarkable to see how "complete" the western was even at this very early point in its development. The film's best-known shot, a flat, full-frame close-up of a mustachioed man shooting his six-shooter gun into the camera lens, was in fact an earlier stage tradition. Westerns would soon be telling stories of moral choices and hard-won landscape, but *The Great Train Robbery* shows us the essence of the genre—in some ways the arguable essence of American genre cinema: action, violence, masculinity, dangerous stunts, dynamic camera work, flashy special effects and bold marketing. This description might just as appropriately be applied to *Breaking Bad*, right down to its innovative, moody, web-based[1] marketing campaign.

As the Western became codified and popular through the silent era and deepened its popularity through the age of the "serial," certain character and narrative codes became an essential component of the genre. "For example, the Western hero, regardless of his social or legal standing, is necessarily an agent of civilization in the savage frontier. He represents both the social order and the threatening savagery that typify the Western milieu" (Schatz, 457). Therefore the white settlers had their share of family men: people who were attempting through settlement and peaceful building to create a new world out of a so-called "wild" landscape. Consider a film such as John Ford's *Stagecoach* (1939), where good, Christian European settlers must be escorted through territory occupied by Native Americans led by Geronimo. The U.S. Calvary also comes to their aid in the final, legendary battle sequence. Without ever consciously commenting on it, the film implicitly casts the whites as "innocents" attempting to survive against a hostile country, filled with "Indians" whose only desire is to kill them for no good reason. The Indians are "wild" and portrayed as such: cunning and ruthless, planning a sneak attack. Whereas the Europeans are made up in brilliant white, are led by a man with narrow eyes and a grim disposition, stoically facing the challenge of this unwelcoming environment with strength and resolution. The metaphors for the American experience are rich and deep, bringing a mythic quality to an ultimately tragic story of genocide and murder.

Breaking Bad is filled with those resonant western themes, with wild forces beyond the imagination of settled, white, suburbanites (the Mexican cartel and its accompanying violence, with Tuco Salamanca nicely filling the role of western villain and later, the twins Leonel and Marco Salamanca, with their lack of dialogue and deep understanding of a slightly mystical culture, evoking the murderous "Indian"), extensive vistas that frame the American southwest in mythic terms (such as the iconic image of Walter White rolling a barrel full of money through the desert in "Ozymandias" [514]) and the male preoccupations with power and self-determination that resonate throughout the cultural history of the region to the present day.

Homestead

The White family themselves can be read as prototypical American "homesteaders" in the wild west. They have a house, literally a "ranch" house, and right from the pilot episode, we see that Walter is a family man, a person committed to providing for his home and family without asking for help, even if that means working two jobs, neither of which appears to bring him much professional satisfaction. His cancer diagnosis threatens to remove him from his life situation, and threatens even the modest middle-class respectability he has managed to accumulate. Here we have a western narrative: the family is threatened from an outside force that has a wild nature. He protects the family against the threat, ergo he is a family man, protecting the homestead. But *Breaking Bad*'s wonderful twist on the familiar story is that Walter, by producing dangerous drugs, has become an outlaw. Significantly, in order to create this new identity, his first act is to create a second "homestead": The Crystal Ship.

The RV that forms the first mobile "cook lab," dubbed "The Crystal Ship" by Jesse Pinkman, is Walter White's wagon train, his homestead and his freedom. The choice of a "cook site" is a perennial issue throughout the run of *Breaking Bad*, starting with the RV and moving through a professional lab facility, suburban homes being fumigated and back to the RV again. The argument for the use of the RV is that it is portable and provides privacy. In the episode "Sunset" (306), Walter even uses the RV's questionable legal status (residence or vehicle?) to avoid detection. The RV is purchased with $7,000, all the money that Walter has in the world as the series opens. Just as his ancestors may have spent all of their resources on a wagon train west, so Walter commits all of his hitherto accumulated wealth and uses it to start a new life (a theme found in many westerns, including Jim Jarmusch's classic *Dead Man*, 1995) and start it on Indian land, no less, thus furthering the American sense of manifest destiny. The RV occupies unsettled territory and turns it into a factory, a mechanism of industrial production for a product valuable to western society. In *Dead Man*, the main character leaves his fortune in the east to come west to a town called literally "Machine," distilling this western motif to its essence, and further demonstrating how *Breaking Bad* uses these subtle textual notes to trigger unconscious connections to the Western genre.

The Crystal Ship represents freedom to Walter White just as American pioneers may have seen their wagons representing the same concept, and this applies on several levels. It is a mobile mechanism that he can use to "conquer" the forces that would conspire to change his life for the worse. It generates money, and it allows Walter to express himself through his own peculiar brand of chemistry. It allows him to be the sort of chemistry teacher he had always tried to be, working side-by-side with his former student, Jesse. Like the pioneers who opened the American west, the technology in which they invested (in their case horse-drawn wagons and carriages) sometimes failed to function correctly, losing axles on the plains and sometimes the wagons had to be converted into temporary settled homes. Walter and Jesse, too, must deal with the technical challenges of their vessel of freedom, as in the episode "4 Days

Out" (209), where the RV breaks down and they are obliged to spend the weekend in it before Walter improvises a battery to get it running again. Surviving by their wits in a wilderness, surrounded by less than reliable technology and constantly faced with the threat of dehydration, Walter and Jesse play the role of fierce American pioneers with their chosen home.

Walter and Jesse eventually abandon and destroy their RV, but this is no different from the attitude their ancestors may have had in the "old west" about their chosen method of conveyance. The wagons were always meant to be taken apart at the end of the journey, but it's interesting to note how much Walter and Jesse are willing to fight for their chosen home, their pioneer instrument, in contrast to their actual residences. The White house, though it does contain Walter's family and is very much in line with the settled, rancher mentality of American settlers, is also casually sacrificed at the end of the show to the "wild" forces of judgment and allowed to go "fallow," filled with graffiti and other destruction. Walter will fight for the RV, but not for the house that he seems to view as an admission of defeat to even have purchased in the first place. (Recall that, in a flashback sequence in "Full Measure" [313], Walter sniffs at the house when he and Skyler tour it as prospective buyers, saying only that it will "do.") Jesse's homes are also tools to be used to make a point (buying his parents' house) or temporary dwellings that he rents in order to get some personal space. When he turns his home into a junkie flop-house/ party pad in early season five, he is acting in a way that is contrary to the civilizing impulses of the western hero, inviting the swirling forces of natural and societal chaos to come in and stay for the duration. He does this partially out of a growing sense that his actions don't have consequences (a disturbing thing to him) and partially out of a desire to tempt fate and destroy all that he has earned for himself in defiance of his mentor, Walter. By specifically not protecting the homestead, Jesse in this period is rather like a character who lets his once well-trimmed garden go fallow, and "gives up" on the imposition of society on the wilderness. This is a specific form of rebellion against everything Walter White is working towards, and it is the moment where Jesse tries to own an identity in opposition to Walter's Family Man persona: an Outlaw.

Outlaw vs. Family Man

There is an important difference between the Crystal Ship and a covered wagon, one that highlights our main point of discussion here. The covered wagon was fundamentally a vehicle for the transport of a person and their family from one place to another. It was a tool designed to expand the influence and reach of the family, under the guidance of a strong 19th-century man, a "family man," no less. Whereas the RV, despite all of Walter's public justifications for what he does, is in his hands the instrument of a person engaged in crime. It is the vehicle of the outlaw, and represents his form of rebellion against the homestead. It is equally telling that *Breaking Bad* uses the RV to demonstrate a rebellion against family values and an aggressive imposition of industrial criminality on the west, since the RV was marketed as a vehicle for family vacations and is culturally associated with family-related activity. Walter has taken a mechanism representing family values and turned it to rampant, dangerous criminal behavior, all supposedly in the service of protecting his family. In other words, Walter believes he is becoming an outlaw in order to be a better family man.

The Western idiom offers these two types of strong male characters, outlaws and family men, and often places them in conflict with each other. John Ford's classic 1938 film *Stagecoach* features John Wayne as the outlaw Ringo, pressed into defending a mixed group of civilians through "Indian country" on a relatively defenseless stagecoach. Ringo is not a family man, as his ties to home and family are never explicitly mentioned, although his humanity is illustrated in his compassionate attitude towards the "fallen woman" in the coach. He attempts to become a family man: he yearns for the day when he can settle down, but his role in the film is to provide flashy masculine adventurous exploits, putting his own stated motivation in conflict with his character's actions, something echoed in Walter White. Tim Holt's character "Lieutenant Blanchard" is the true family man of the *Stagecoach*, a square-jawed, stiff and humorless hero, fighting out of grim duty and necessity. Here is a classic example of one of the important differences between outlaws and family men: the outlaw might say that he wishes for something more, but he can enjoy the violence that comes along with his station. Family men can't express any enjoyment, otherwise they run the danger of being considered morally suspect. Outlaws yearn to be family men, but family men seem to be constantly on guard against becoming outlaws.

Even when an outlaw "goes straight," American westerns cannot allow him to completely escape the past. There might be forgetting, but there is no forgiving. Consider one of Ford's later films, *The Man Who Shot Liberty Valance* (1962). Here, the plot hinges on a middle-aged senator, played by James Stewart, and the revelation that he was involved in the murder of a man many years before. Stewart's character is torn by guilt over this long-ago act even though he has married and entered respectable society. There is, in fact, quite a bit of cachet that comes along with having killed a man in the culture of the "wild west," and Stewart is offered accolades as "the man who shot Liberty Valance." But it is only when a contemporary of his, played by John Wayne, admits that it was actually he who fired the killing shot all of those years ago that Stewart can fully embrace the role of "family man" and U.S. senator of unimpeachable character. One act of violence, in the morally absolute world of 19th century, White, Protestant America, appears to be enough to tip a man's character from one of the two available extremes to another.

Sometimes Western films do occupy themselves almost completely with outlaws, particularly later "revisionist" westerns such as *The Wild Bunch* (1969, Sam Peckinpah) or *Unforgiven* (1992, Clint Eastwood). But even early westerns like *The Great Train Robbery* tell the story from the perspective of the villain. Outlaws, particularly as portrayed in the Peckinpah films, seem to be having a lot more fun than their family man counterparts such as those seen on TV shows like *Bonanza*, where a stern father figure protects those on the ranch, or even in films such as *The Great Train Robbery*, where the ordinary citizens are portrayed as little more than simple stooges on the sidelines as the real battle rages between the "good guys" and the "bad guys." The outlaws in westerns have a knowing sense of humor, a seemingly deeper understanding of the rituals and artifice of 19th-century American society, than their straight-laced counterparts. Consider a sequence early in *The Wild Bunch* in which a group of outlaws rides into town with the express purpose of robbing a bank, but dressed as soldiers. On the way in, they accidentally bump into an elderly lady crossing the street, and rather than act as ruffians, they pick up the lady's parcels and help her on her way as she links arms with the group's leader, Pike (played by William Holden). By deliberately emphasizing the rituals of polite society, they both parody them and use them to hide in plain sight. This extra level of self-awareness is one of the more attractive features of the "outlaw" type. Family men, in films such as *The Wild Bunch*, are seen marching with the temperance league in a humorless and joyless procession at the beginning of the film. They demonstrate no sense of irony or self-awareness, believing that making stern proclamations and marching with signs and other such forms of social and civil discourse will affect change in the world, leading them closer to the sort of society they came west to build. Outlaws, on the other hand, are cynics, or at least realists, in these stories, demonstrating little interest in building anything and rather accumulating as much wealth as possible and subsequently escaping to somewhere where they can spend it with impunity.

In later quasi–Westerns such as *From Dusk Till Dawn* (dir. Robert Rodriguez, 1996), the outlaw characters such as Seth Gecko (George Clooney) express this sentiment explicitly, professing no ambition other than to "pound liquor."

Revisionist westerns such as Eastwood's *Unforgiven* address the outlaw-family man dichotomy more directly. Though released in 1992, the film's script dates from the late 1970s, inspired by, in part, the film *The Shootist* (1976, Don Siegel) about a gunfighter dying of cancer who wishes to end his life in a gunfight. Starring an aging but effective John Wayne, *The Shootist* neverthe-less plays out Western male heroic archetypes from an earlier age. Wayne's char-acter is allowed to be sympathetic only when acting in a mentoring/fatherly capacity for the man played by Ron Howard. For his misdeeds, there is no for-giveness, and he remains an outlaw to his final scene. Eastwood's film addresses this more directly, telling the story of William Munny, a vicious and notorious outlaw who has since "gone straight" and become a family man—the other acceptable western male choice. When hard financial times strike him and his young family, Munny reluctantly turns back to killing, this time in the employ of several local prostitutes who seek revenge on a cowboy who mutilated and attacked one of their colleagues. Eastwood plays Munny as haunted and regret-ful, seeking forgiveness and peace above all and retrospectively carefully hiding the record of his past deeds from his young children. In that sense, he is much like Jesse, with his preoccupation with redemption and building something noble out of an ignoble past. But whatever spiritual fate or moral reckoning may await William Munny, he is determined to be remembered a certain way when he passes from the earth, just as he is determined to leave enough money for his children to get a good start in life. In this sense he reflects Walter's per-spective, although Munny lacks Walter's egotism and stubbornness. Indeed, Eastwood allows Munny to be buffoonish and sweet throughout the film, making his eventual transformation back into his old, cold, calculating outlaw self that much more arresting in the final sequence, when he goes on an alcohol-soaked killing spree that wins him the money and the influence nec-essary to make a brand new start, but loses his ability to claim any moral high ground or to hide his violent disposition from his children. Munny is an outlaw, despite his claim to be a family man and his efforts to fly that flag.

Hank and Steve

A potential third type of male character sometimes found in the land-scape of American Westerns could be called the "lawman," but unless the Western is truly revisionist, such as *Unforgiven*, the law figures in these films are usually men with families, or at least men who desire families, and they conform to the legal order of the surrounding society. In other words, a "lawman" in a traditional American Western is still a conservative figure for the most part—and if he isn't, then he is a remarkable exception. *Unforgiven*, for example, features the sadistic and twisted character of "Little" Bill, played by Gene Hackman, who is the state-appointed authority figure but who abuses his power and lives alone. Most of the time, the lawman is the central source of authority and the representative of the civilizing power of the state, such as Marshal Wilcox from *Stagecoach*, played by George Bancroft. They adopt a paternalistic attitude towards all the people under their authority in the setting presented, and generally these characters are played with that grim, determined, square-jawed pose of the American male hero.

Breaking Bad's numerous similarities and kinships with any or all of these archetypes offer us an intriguing reading of the show and its characters. Here, the "lawman" is Hank Schrader, and while he may not be exactly the buttoned-down and square jaw type normally associated with a traditional portrayal of American heroism, he is truly devoted to family and to his country in a very uncomplicated way, and in his locker-room, shoulder-punching masculinity he does conform to very much an "all-American" type. Hank is even provided with his own version of "Tonto" or other such loyal sidekick in the character of Estaban "Steve" Gomez. In keeping with revisionist western tradition, Gomez is more often right than wrong in his work. This is a trope that dates back to Sancho Panza, the sidekick of Don Quixote, who sees true reality (noting that what Quixote sees are not giants, but windmills) and keeps his Knight on a relatively straight and narrow path. He is more cautious, more realistic and in the extreme parodic form, wiser. Consider the satirical film *Big Trouble in Little China* (dir. John Carpenter, 1986), in which the sidekick of Kurt Russell's hero is consistently correct about every major plot decision, just as Russell is consistently incorrect. This level of parody illustrates a deep truth to that dynamic. But it should be noted that neither Hank nor Steve ever expresses any doubts or ambiguity about their work or its moral contours. Their only complaints seem to be those perennial police/military gripes about not being given the resources they feel are necessary to effectively complete their work.

Hank and Steve, in fact, would have been right at home in the police station of any number of American westerns, with their feet up on the desk, having the same sorts of conversations, right down to their arch–American character names. Hank and Steve are always on the side of "justice" as they see it, and even though Hank sometimes pushes at the explicit command authority under which he operates, he does so in the service of the larger mission. In western genre terms, they represent the long arm of the federal government, tasked to stand on the barricades of the south against drugs and all of the violent crime that business brings with it. Their goal is to make Albuquerque and indeed all of New Mexico into a safe community for families and children to have barbecues in their backyard and live free from any threat of violence or disturbance. *Breaking Bad* specifically pitches the threat in these terms, implying that the DEA at the very least believes that if they stopped all of their activity, the city would be overrun by crime. However correct or incorrect this perception may be, it is a direct expression of the role of the Western hero, to hold back the forces of chaos that threaten to consume the civilized culture of the region.

Gus

Gustavo Fring, on the other hand, is clearly in the "outlaw" category, as are his close associates Mike Ehrmentraut and Saul Goodman ("A *criminal* lawyer," as Jesse Pinkman describes him in "Better Call Saul" [208]). He operates in the style of an upper class Mexican or South American crime lord, that is, with all the trappings of civilization, decorum and dignity. In purely genre terms, Gus and his behavior have lots of resonance, particularly in the first generation of revisionist American westerns of the 1960s, such as *The Wild Bunch*. In that film, the major American characters are mercenaries but they place themselves in the service of a Mexican warlord, hijacking a train full of U.S. Government munitions, to assist him in his rise to power in early 20th century Mexico. Consider, in *Breaking Bad* terms, how Walter and Jesse are helping this Latin American criminal organization flourish in the Unites States (and later, Europe), bringing financial benefit for themselves but potentially great harm to their community an their country. Though at first they don't see themselves as in Gus' service as much as his new business partner, Gus doesn't appear to have any confusion about his status. The Americans are mercenaries who produce a useful product that will bring him more power. And, as in keeping with the warlord character in *The Wild Bunch*, Gus is acting in clear defiance of the law, international and domestic, but is still acting with the moral certainty of one who aspires to high government office. Though Gus might be officially a criminal, his business is conducted with honor and an internal moral system that is consistent and enforced.

Mike

Mike Ehrmentraut is a more clear-cut case, and a classic western genre archetype. His roots, as a law man who turned to crime, of course transcend the Western and borrow heavily from popular crime literature and the genre of film noir that has its roots in Weimar cynicism (Kracauer). Henchmen, in Westerns, are often no more clearly defined than in any other adventure genre. Often they are simply part of the posse of villains that opposes the hero, and the "third bad guy from the left," to use Sir Christopher Frayling's phrase, is no more significant than his horse in terms of idiosyncratic characterization (Frayling, *Sergio Leone*). Later, post-revisionist Westerns such as *Blazing Saddles* (Mel Brooks, 1974), explicitly reference this by having a henchmen admit, "Mongo only pawn in great game of life [*sic*]." But sometimes, henchmen can play an important role as supporting characters for the villain and often providing an effective counterpoint for the hero. Such is the case with Mike, a character firmly within the world of western villains, but one who has his own moral compass and sense of loyalty and honor. Mike takes villainous action, and allies himself with outlaws, but he is also a family man, completely committed to providing love and support, primarily financial, to his granddaughter. What he does might be villainous, but Mike doesn't seem to regard himself as a villain, and this is yet another trope familiar to Westerns. Many Westerns, from the afore-mentioned *The Man Who Shot Liberty Valance* through both versions of *3:10 to Yuma* (dir. Delmer Daves, 1957; dir. James Mangold, 2007) feature family men turning at least partially to lives involving crime in order to defend what they have accumulated for their family.

Mike has long since "broken bad," in the parlance of the show in question, and he is at peace with it. In the end, Mike seems to express, if his family is taken care of by him or some outside force over which he exerts an influence, then all is well. It isn't necessary for him to conform to all the rules of society because, in the logic of the Western, society hasn't completely caught up to the realities of the environment in which the characters find themselves. What the lawyers and lawmakers in "the east" call justice is different from how a self-reliant man of the western frontier uses the term. And even the DEA must have some knowledge that certain great American fortunes (the Kennedys, for example) were at least partially built on the manufacture and trafficking of officially, legally prohibited substances. Therefore, Mike's conscience is clear. He is, in his worldview, allowed to occupy the space that includes "outlaw" and "family man."

Jesse

In terms of the American Western, Jesse Pinkman is also playing an archetype: that of the morally troubled young recruit. Jesse occupies a clear social position but is the least at ease with it. Unlike Mike, for example, Jesse's conscience is assuredly not at peace, and his station in life gives him no end of moral trouble. Jesse actually says early on in the series to his compatriots "Badger" and "Skinny Pete": "I'm like, an outlaw!" and means it (203, "Bit by a Dead Bee"). It's accurate, but very troubling to him. Consider the character of "The Schofield Kid" from *Unforgiven*, played by Jaimz Woolvett. Here we have a character who, unlike Jesse, aspires to be a gunfighter and appears intent on studying that profession and cultivating a tough image even though he is a very young man. He is more enthusiastic than the older ex-gunfighters, played by Eastwood and Morgan Freeman, who express fear and reluctance about reentering back into the profession of bounty hunting. The "Kid," on the other hand, muses out loud about how he's going to perform the killing. Ironically, the Kid does in fact perform a murder during the film and almost immediately regrets it, pulling on a bottle of whiskey and crying underneath a tree, saying to Munny tearfully, "I ain't like you." Jesse, though he never shows quite as much enthusiasm for the business (although in early episodes he is very enthusiastic and his friends Badger and Skinny Pete continue to provide a Greek chorus of enthusiasm for drugs and drug manufacturing throughout the series), follows a similar path into regret. In fact, he follows that path quickly and repeatedly: he realizes by the series second episode, "Cat's in the Bag..." (102), that he "isn't like" Walt and is uncomfortable with the idea of disposing of a human body with acid or torturing and killing another person. Walter, on the other hand, is fine with these acts, or at least accepts their necessity.

Jesse's motivation for this criminal activity is also different from the other characters in the show. If he were a character in a traditional or revisionist American Western, his motivation would be to make enough money to make a name for himself in the world—enough to leave town and never have to look back. Jane, his caring and supportive girlfriend from Season Two, attempts to explain that logic to him and Jesse in turn tries to explain that logic to Walter White who doesn't listen. Jesse may or may not listen to this advice—throughout the run of *Breaking Bad*, Jesse demonstrates great ambivalence, frequent turns of conscience and articulates strenuous objections to the course of the protagonists. It is he who repeatedly asks Walter to "pull over," to take what he has and establish a new life for himself. Jesse, though he self-labels as an outlaw, is really behaving a lot more like a family man, trying to bring order to a lawless environment, trying to cash out and establish a stable life for himself somewhere. Hank and Gus speak in terms of commitment to family (and we see Hank acting on his words in his relationship with his sister-in-law, niece, and nephew) but they are both drawn, fatally, into the swirl of crime and conflict. Jesse, if he is a Western outlaw, is acting much more like an older figure: a late-period Frank James, perhaps, seeking to end the adventures and settle down, rather than the brash young irresponsible cowboy. He chooses the outlaw life but is closer to the family man in his imperatives. But Jesse goes along with the plan and makes money, still participating in the adventure even if it troubles him. In the great "outlaw vs. family man" divide, then, we should place Jesse in the outlaw category even though he might see himself in the latter, though he has every promise of growing into that role with time.

Walter

Walter, when we first meet him in the pilot episode, has clearly made the "family man" choice. When time is not an issue for him, he chooses the path of least resistance: a relatively stable and easy life, not without its financial hardships, but that only makes the Whites quite typical of middle class Americans in the early 2000s. He appears quietly committed to the rules of the house, accepting Skyler's gentle reprimand about using the "wrong" credit card with quiet submission, working a humiliating second job at the car wash, but accepting it all as his station in life. What changes his orientation if not his mind (there may well have been impulses below the surface in Walter that were brought to the fore by circumstances, but they were present to begin with) is the pressure of time. Time is something Walter White[2] doesn't have, just like the hero of the classic western *High Noon* (Fred Zinnemann, 1952). In that film, the main character is literally waiting to be killed for most of the running time, awaiting the arrival of a train that will bring the instrument of his death. The film uses repeated imagery of clocks and references to time to emphasize the immediacy and the symbolic resonance of the motif. *Breaking Bad* does sometimes demonstrate a similar clever use of time, grounding the entire narrative in a very specific span of time between Walt's 50th birthday and his 52nd. Walter's cancer gives him a finite span of time in which he can be active in this plan. Walt's relationship with his disease (at first denying it, then continued denials or expressions of arrogant dominance over it), is really his relationship with time, just as the main character in *High Noon*. Walter expresses a need to manipulate time, to abuse time, to finally acknowledge the passage of time in the Season Five opening episode "Live Free or Die"—but the issue is always present in his Walt's consciousness, driving his decisions. As soon as that metaphoric clock starts ticking on his cancer, Walter transforms from being a family man to an outlaw. Unlike Gary Cooper in *High Noon*, he isn't going to saddle up and face what is waiting for him at the train station, but instead fight against it and try to find a way around it with the naive arrogance that will come to characterize Walter as the series goes on.

A family man, as we have defined it in the vernacular of the American Western, is someone who stands on the barricades against the forces of chaos and natural decay. In the "family man" justification for actions that may seem violent or unlawful, the forces of decay are waiting right outside the door. Walter has very little faith in Skyler, or Walter Jr.'s ability to take care of themselves financially or otherwise without him. Like many breadwinners before him, he has put his work so far above any sort of work that his wife or son could perform that he imagines, if it is taken away, they will be on the proverbial streets, completely helpless against the dangerous socioeconomic forces of the world. In the western idiom, it would take the form of the homestead (or the "ranch" in reference to their ranch house) being overrun by Native Americans or burned to the ground by some other force—be that government or a rival. For a man in that situation, there is no compromise or nuance, only the impulse to be the sort of man who stands heroically against the forces of destruction to maintain the patriarchal family structure. Therefore, Walter chooses the outlaw life but professes it to be for his family, out of necessity.

Spaghetti Westerns and *Breaking Bad*

The American Western is one sort of capitulation of the genre, and a very interesting one, loaded with protestant morality and the apocalyptic imagery of the evangelical movement. But there were always other kinds of Westerns, made in other places, right from the very beginning of the film industry. Europeans such as Karl May had published their own take on the myth of the American West in novels and stories since the 1870s and European Westerns appeared in the 1920s alongside their American counterparts. By the late 1950s, as Westerns in the U.S. were becoming more revisionist and less classical, Italian directors such as Sergio Leone, raised on American westerns and now working in the "pulp" cinema of Italy, created an important sub-genre: the "Spaghetti" Western (Frayling, *Spaghetti Westerns* and *Sergio Leone*).

The term "Spaghetti" Western was actually coined by the American press in the 1960s as a derogatory term, a fact which right away sets the tone for the tension between the two major sub-genres. Italian Westerns were different, and the major difference was in the deconstruction and refinement of the genre. Spaghetti Westerns reflected back to the American audience certain unappealing aspects of their own history and value systems (casual violence, gunplay, capitalist ruthlessness) and (in the most important alteration for our discussion), ignored or eliminated the "family man" character type. There were no clear-cut "good" and "bad" guys in Italian Westerns, rather characters who acted completely out of their own ambition and interests or characters who acted mostly that way, with occasional bouts of generosity. Though this may be closer to the true moral landscape, the effect of seeing it on screen can be jarring, particularly for an audience trained to look for solid "American values" in this genre.

Breaking Bad is clearly influenced by the visual style of Spaghetti Westerns, with their distinctly European sense of humor. For example, in the credit sequence to Sergio Leone's *The Good, the Bad and the Ugly* (1966), the director's name appears on screen in the title sequence fired out of a canon, and after a moment the canon fires again and destroys the cartoonish lettering. The bawdy, "low" humor is set against the majestic landscape with larger mythic themes. *Breaking Bad* emulates this style often, juxtaposing something sublime and menacing like a meth cook in the desert, with the notion of him being dressed only in white underwear. Or the device of the charred pink plush toy from the plane crash so central to Season Three. Or the iconic image of the pizza on the roof of the White's home, hauntingly symbolizing the fraying of their family unit. This visual richness and willingness to combine the profoundly serious with the profoundly silly is one of the most subtle but powerful influences of Leone, and European cinema in general, on *Breaking Bad*.

Leone's understanding of the Western came from a childhood watching government-approved American Westerns (Mussolini enjoyed American Westerns for their upright moral character) and was blended with a love of puppet theatre, Japanese cinema, European landscape painting, and the speed and energy of the Italian *pepla* films on which he worked as an assistant director (Frayling, *Sergio Leone*). As such, his take on the Western genre led to films much different from the American Westerns of the day, even the "revisionist" ones.

Leone's westerns were notable, among other things, for their moral ambivalence. Right in the titles of the films themselves (*The Good, The Bad and The Ugly*), there is a moral ambiguity, a leveling sense of equivalence to the characters. Without "good" and "bad" characters in Spaghetti Westerns, introducing tension or conflict into the stories was a challenge. The solution of Leone's team of writers, which included such future luminaries as Bernardo Bertolucci, was to externalize character conflict and put these morally questionable characters in a competition over some external goal. For example, *The Good, the Bad and the Ugly* is essentially a "treasure hunt," with the three major characters looking for some lost confederate gold. Sometimes they would plug these Western characters into gangster plots, with gangs plotting bank heists while others operate as hired killers for a crime family (this is partially what happens in *For a Few Dollars More*, from 1965). Or sometimes they would lift a plot whole from another film, as *A Fistful of Dollars* (1964) is clearly a direct re-make of the earlier Kurosawa film *Yojimbo* (1961), in which a masterless samurai hires himself out to one powerful family in a small town, then the other, and walks away with the gold of both. The moral ambiguity of *Breaking Bad* could be said to owe a great deal to American crime dramas, which themselves explored moral and legal middle ground in the 1970s. But certainly *Breaking Bad*'s take on the extent to which capitalism can drive men to take extreme actions is straight from Leone's moral universe. All of Leone's Westerns are least in part about the pursuit of money above all other considerations and the moral decay that results from that pursuit. *Breaking Bad*, it seems almost too obvious to point out, covers similar ground.

Finally, the pace of Spaghetti Westerns, particularly those made by Leone, is so remarkably different from American Westerns (and again owes more to the Japanese approach to cinematic pacing). Increasingly towards the end of his career, Leone's films are characterized by long pauses, drawn-out scenes of staring, often with close-ups of the eyes, contrasted with ultra-wide angle shots that take in the entire landscape. This alternation between close-up and wide with little time spent exploring the middle range epitomizes the formal nature of the Spaghetti Western. It is a Western with all the culture, history, and American values pulled out, reduced to renderings of "men on horses with guns" or more often just "men with guns" set against dusty, hot backgrounds, who stare for what seem like endless stretches of film time before quickly, and balletically, killing each other.

Breaking Bad as Western

Breaking Bad shares the Spaghetti Westerns' tendency to reduce a story to a single image, often not explaining the significance of the image until later such as the pink plush teddy bear mentioned previously. Often images are cinematically strong, almost cartoon-like, once again venturing into the deep satirical genre territory of the Italian western as when Walter White rolls his barrel full of money through the desert in "Ozymandias" (514). The show also focuses on silences between characters to an interesting degree, and the collection of studied pre-violence poses throughout is evocative of the world of the Spaghetti Western. In "Ozymandias," for example, we get a powerful scene illustrating Walter's continued amateurish naiveté about his criminal activity as Jack holds a gun to Hank's head and Walt begs for his brother-in-law to be spared. Walter talks and talks in a moment that should properly be one of silent contemplation as in a Leone western. Hank himself comments on this, reminding Walter before he is shot that Jack "made up his mind ten minutes ago." That little exchange demonstrates Hank's professional engagement as opposed to Walt's amateur criminal status even in this late episode but it also shows how much the audience is primed by the experience of Westerns, particularly Italian Westerns, to expect silence at that moment—perhaps punctuated by a few minimalist guitar or harmonica notes, but not overrun with begging and sobbing. In Leone Westerns, as later in his Dirty Harry movies, Clint Eastwood would similarly dispatch his opponents with a minimum of dialogue and a maximum of grim silence. Mike hits an almost identical note when, in "Say My Name" (507), he slowly dies from a gunshot wound and implores Walt to "Shut up and let me die in peace" as Walter keeps stammering on. Silence is important to *Breaking Bad*, as to Italian Westerns.

Leone's *Once Upon a Time in the West*, from 1968, concerns itself with the world that is "to come" in the West with trains and capitalists and civilization being introduced into a landscape previously populated by outlaws and family men. The times of the wild gunfighter roaming the countryside settling scores with his wits and his guns are coming to a close. In the film's final sequence, the two main antagonists, both gunfighters whose time in this mythic landscape is rapidly running out, calmly circle each other in the backyard of a house being built—very much in their own world, isolated from the swirling activity of train construction and other political violence. They are acting out a ritual that feels ancient, just as from time to time, *Breaking Bad* also isolates its protagonists and antagonists from the reality of their situation. Particularly in the meetings in the desert, have a ritualistic quality reminiscent of Leone's cinematic storytelling. Also, the focus on middle-aged characters engaged in brutal violence while life around them goes about its business is terribly evocative of Leone westerns and particularly *Once Upon a Time*. These characters, whether named "Frank" and "Harmonica" or "Walter," "Gus," and "Mike," seem to come from a different era. Hank's use of GPS tracking and Gus's claim to steel-plated technological capitalist efficiency aside, they live in a world with very old rules. As Mike himself states repeatedly to Walter, this is the way things are done. Walter White has the most difficult time adjusting to this ancient world, making the transition from pension funds, lawyers, and scientific professionalism to a much more stratified and socially rigid society as his approach to individuals such as Gus demonstrates. When Gus is "civilized" and "businesslike" to him, Walter makes the mistake of thinking that this means he's incapable of violence, that he is playing by the rules of the surrounding society rather than the ancient rituals of crime and violence.

Breaking Bad, however, doesn't appear to share *Once Upon a Time*'s nostalgia for a simpler time when men solved their disputes with guns and knew the "rules" of honor and warfare, etc. Unlike the Leone films which, with their Japanese influence, commonly allow characters to die discretely "with honor," the deaths in *Breaking Bad* are all horribly real and tend to change the course of the show. From Jane dying in front of Walter, to Tuco Salamanca's death, through the murder of Gus Fring, Hank's death, and finally the death of Walter White himself; death is something tragic and permanent in the world of *Breaking Bad*. In a Leone Western, death comes early and often for many characters, and it is the expected fate of some. "There's something about those guys," Cheyanne says in *Once Upon a Time*, remarking upon the gunfighters engaged in deadly combat in his backyard, "Something to do with death."

Walter's entire approach to death marks him as the least spaghetti-western-type character in the entire ensemble. With his predilection for making "big plans," for never settling for what he has and arrogant tendency to ignore advice and insist, loudly and often, that he is in control of the situation, are not in line with the behavior of a Leone hero or villain. But they are in line with some American westerns, where the "family man" is expected to represent upright moral virtue in that distinctly protestant way. Compare this to Gus Fring, or Mike, who, being seasoned members of the criminal fraternity, have a calmness about them even in the face of death, have practiced what they do for a long time and are very good at it, and are comfortable with the moral compromises that they have made. These characters are straight from the more rarefied and metaphorical world of the Italian western. This is ultimately the disconnect between Walter and the rest of the characters, and an interesting way to view his relationships as a whole: Walter thinks he's in an American western, where everyone is either an outlaw or a family man, as we have discussed, and he is in control. Whereas the rest of the characters know they're in an Italian western, where there are deep and abiding rules of conduct and honor, but there is no safety net, no cavalry that will come and save you. Death is a part of the landscape, and part of the lifestyle. Walter, who fights against death from cancer from the very first episode to the very last, cannot accept that. Believing that somehow he will be different, that making choices and sticking to them regardless of evidence is a virtue, and most of all that he will create his own fate, Walter White is the classic American western figure. His fall, in the end, and the continuation of the drug empire in one form or another, along with the ruin of his family, demonstrate that *Breaking Bad* understands the moral landscape of the Italian western, and represents it, even when its own main character does not. *Breaking Bad* isn't just replete with western texts, it ultimately teaches their importance to its own characters. As a genre meta-exercise, this is yet another admirable and laudable feature of a superbly executed piece of art.

Notes

1. One of the most effective of these featured actor Bryan Cranston reading the poem "Ozymandias" as scenes of a rolling desert vista played on the screen, evocative of a landscape belonging both in the ancient world and in the mythic American West.

2. For a further discussion of *Breaking Bad's* innovative use of time, see Freeley's essay in *Breaking Bad: Critical Essays on the Contexts, Politics, Style, and Reception of the Television Series,* ed. David P. Pierson (Lanham, MD: Lexington, 2014), pp. 33–52.

Works Cited

Frayling, Christopher. *Spaghetti Westerns: Cowboys and Europeans from Karl May to Sergio Leone.* London: I. B. Tauris, 1981.
Frayling, Christopher. *Sergio Leone: Something to Do with Death.* London: Faber and Faber, 2000.
Kracauer, Sigfried. *From Caligari to Hitler.* Princeton: Princeton University Press, 1947.
Schatz, Thomas. "Film Genre and the Genre Film." *Critical Visions in Film Theory,* ed. Timothy Corrigan, Patricia White and Meta Mazaj. Boston: Bedford/St. Martin's, 2011.
Wright, Will. *Six Guns and Society.* Berkley: University of California Press, 1975.

Filmography

A Fistful of Dollars (directed by Sergio Leone, 1964)
Big Trouble in Little China (directed by John Carpenter, 1986)
Blazing Saddles (directed by Mel Brooks, 1974)
Dead Man (directed by Jim Jarmusch, 1995)
For a Few Dollars More (directed by Sergio Leone, 1965)
From Dusk Till Dawn (directed by Robert Rodriguez, 1996)
The Good, the Bad and the Ugly (directed by Sergio Leone, 1966)
The Great Train Robbery (directed by WS Porter, 1903)
High Noon (directed by Fred Zinneman, 1952)
The Magnificent Seven (directed by John Sturges, 1960)
The Man Who Shot Liberty Valance (directed by John Ford, 1962)

Once Upon a Time in the West (directed by Sergio Leone, 1968)
Sanjuro (directed by Akira Kurosawa, 1962)
The Searchers (directed by John Ford, 1956)
Seven Samurai (directed by Akira Kurosawa, 1954)
Stagecoach (directed by John Ford, 1939)
Star Wars (directed by George Lucas, 1977)
3:10 to Yuma (directed by James Mangold, 2007)
3:10 to Yuma (directed by Delmer Daves, 1957)
Unforgiven (directed by Clint Eastwood, 1992)
The Wild Bunch (directed by Sam Peckinpah, 1969)
Yojimbo (directed by Akira Kurosawa, 1961)

• ROUND TABLE DISCUSSION •

The Phenomenon of
"Bad Fans" and "Team Walt"

Participants:
—Bridget Roussell Cowlishaw (BRC)
—Brian Cowlishaw (BC)
—Stephanie Stringer Gross (SSG)
—Susan Johnston (SJ)
—Jeffrey Reid Pettis (JRP)
—Ian Dawe (ID)
—R. Nicholas Gerlich (RNG)

BRIDGET ROUSSELL COWLISHAW: Your essays in this collection cover significant ground in terms of how *Breaking Bad* portrays/critiques contemporary concepts of masculinity but there are a few questions of its reception that we can best address in the form of a discussion among ourselves. The first issue I'd like to raise is that of "Team Walt"—what Emily Nussbaum has called "Bad Fans." Nussbaum describes the Bad Fan as being very like the character Todd: "he arrived late in the story, and he saw Walt purely as a kick-ass genius, worthy of worship." Anyone who has spent any time on a fan website will be struck by the presence of these unconditionally pro–Walt fans, seemingly incapable of understanding the show as anything but *The Adventures of the Great Hiesenberg*. I myself have spent a good deal of time wondering if these fans are simply too poorly socialized to understand that the series is unambiguously critical of Walter (particularly in the later seasons), too cognitively challenged to understand how to have sympathy and yet be critical, or just angry teens who want to vent a free-floating rage for which they use *Breaking*

Bad as a conduit. It was only when I had a conversation about the series with a well-educated, intelligent professional gentleman who told me about his total sympathy with Walt right to the end, along with his passionate hatred of the character Skyler, that I realized this Bad Fan issue is more complicated than a some-people-are-just-ignorant/stupid/crazy dismissal would allow.

So, I throw it out to you: how do you account for the phenomenon of the "Bad Fan"?

BRIAN COWLISHAW: Let me begin my answer by quoting a telling passage from a very smart, insightful article about the show:

> This model of manhood also requires control not only over your own life, but over the lives of others. Think about all of the most iconic moments of the show, the badass lines that made us want to pump our fists: "Say my name." "I am the danger." "I am the one who knocks." "I won." Every single time, it's about dominance—not just about having power, but about taking power away from someone else [Laura Hudson; see my essay's bibliography].

"The badass lines that made us want to pump our fists." This line gets right at the heart of the meaning of the show, in a way typical of the "bad fan" posited in this question. A "bad fan" of this type completely fails to perceive one of the two central points of the show.

Point 1 is that Walter White's life as of the pilot, on his fiftieth birthday, is a shambles, and that much of what's wrong can be diagnosed in terms of lacking masculinity. The pilot episode shows all the ways he is henpecked, underemployed, underachieving, and passive—a "pussy." His terminal lung cancer diagnosis pushes him to turn all that around, to become more masculine. So Point 1 is: Walter White must "become a man." By that standard and none other, yes, the lines quoted above "made us want to pump our fists." Over the course of five seasons (or six, depending on how you want to count them), yes, Walter gains masculinity. He does all the things "a man" is supposed to do: he becomes aggressive, competitive, violent, and effective at "providing for his family." In that sense, true, these moments really are thrilling.

But that is half the story. Point 2 is that this model of masculinity Walter adopts is toxic, dangerous, harmful to him, his family, and society. He becomes a man, but tragically that man he becomes—Heisenberg—is 100 percent a sociopath. One person has made a YouTube video of every single death Walter either orders or performs directly: https://www.youtube.com/watch?v=y-4WGPYJ2gI. There are 22, plus of course the nearly 200 airplane-crash deaths and all those Walter causes secondarily (for example, Combo's). There are plenty of direct reactions dramatized in the show to highlight how horrible the deaths are: the high school gym assembly called for faculty and students to come to grips with their trauma; Jesse's horror and shock at seeing Walt shoot a rival drug dealer in the head after first slamming into the dealer with his car; Jesse's long-term trauma after being pushed into shooting Gale Boetticher; and many others. Not to mention, of course, all the suffering and damage caused by the (literally) tons of meth Walt manufactures during his criminal career.

In short: anyone who unqualifiedly "roots for" Heisenberg (as opposed to Walter) seriously worries me. The whole point of the show is the impossible situation into which Point 1 and Point 2 combined push Walt, our representative man: "be a man" and lose your soul. You can't do the first without also doing the second—that's the hell of it. You don't want to be a pussy, but being macho is messed up too.

The universe of *Breaking Bad* is consistently and overtly moral; any fan of the show would have to watch incredibly selectively to miss its messages about how awful this model of masculinity is. Ultimately, I guess I'm saying that a "bad fan" of this type would be so heavily invested himself in this model that he simply can't see it—and watch out for him!

STEPHANIE STRINGER GROSS: I address this in my essay as well. The conflation of business, scientific discourse, and Machiavellian manhood are so incredibly basic to late capitalism and have filtered down into how we relate to each other in every aspect of our lives, that it is surprising that there are not MORE people fist pumping those moments of hard-ass machismo. One of the things *Breaking Bad* does so beautifully is show the nuances of the double bind most Americans are in. It isn't just men, as Brian says above; women are in this bind as well. We all know the basics, there are few women CEOs, we make less on the dollar than men in similar or equal jobs, etc. But what *Breaking Bad* captures is the moment-to-moment decisions women make: is it better now to speak up? Better to keep quiet? How do I show support? How do I show support without losing my own identity? What is abuse? Where's that line? Those who think Skyler is only a "nag" or that Walt is "henpecked" have indeed bought into a dichotomous view of gender, and bring to their viewing rigid role requirements, whether they know it or not. One of the fascinating things about *Breaking Bad* is how it forces many of us to question our own positions on gender roles. It's uncomfortable.

BRC: Maybe the "Bad Fans" just don't want to do the hard work of looking squarely at that "double bind"?

SSG: I would also say that there's another uncomfortable thing a person has to face if they are to be something other than the "Bad Fan." Walt and

Skyler at first appear to be a couple who have made all the "politically correct" choices for a modern couple: they seem to be partners, they seem to be committed to raising Walt, Jr. without violence, they seem to be putting family first, he seems to support her need and desire to write, and they seem, to me, more like a fairly enlightened couple who clearly came of age with the benefits of second-wave feminism. She's chosen to stay home to have the baby and to parent Walt, Jr. in a way that seems more like a sacrifice for the greater good of the family than her preference. But, again, the lifestyle is subject to greater "Fortune" from outside: the present system pays Walt insufficiently, the health care is abysmal, and the need for two incomes forces all kinds of resentment and choices past the front door into the living room and bedroom. Again, the brilliance of *Breaking Bad*, Gilligan, and its writers is to show the subtle effects of a world in which our range of choices is not particularly good or effective, and, in fact, often aren't real choices at all.

BRC: Perhaps the "Bad Fan" simply wants someone to somehow "win" in this damned-if –you-do, damned-if-you-don't world.

Susan Johnston: Brian and Stephanie have focused on one kind of bad fan, so let me mix it up a little by talking about another kind, "the feminist-minded sucker" Emily Nussbaum recognizes in herself.

BRC: Yes, because Nussbaum does confess to being another kind of bad (or bad-ish) fan: "the Prissy Progressive Fan ... who was all too eager to see Skyler as a pure victim." I'll admit that when I was faced with the well-educated gentleman who was all fist-pumping Team Walt, I felt it was somehow my duty (as a woman? as a feminist? I'm not sure) to make the case for "Skyler's side." When I reflect on it, I know that's not where my own sympathies really lie and yet....

SJ: I could say that I'm yet a third kind, but I will get to that in a minute. I want to say that as long as we are focused on who is dominating who, who is powerful or powerless, we are always being trolled, because from my perspective the show is more interested in questions of personhood than in questions of egalitarianism. The problem is not that Skyler dominates Walt, or that Walt comes to dominate Skyler, from this perspective; the problem is that neither really sees the other as a person in themselves, of themselves, for themselves; both seem to see the other as a means to their own ends, rather than an end in themselves. In my essay I talk about the fairly chilling scene in the pilot episode where Skyler offers Walt what she doubtless thinks of as "birthday sex": perfunctory as it is, Skyler appears to offer it freely and wholeheartedly to Walt, but it is worth noting that what she does not offer is herself. Throughout, she remains focused on the online auction we later discover nets less than the average cost of a pair of jeans. This marriage is not the intimacy of persons, but one in which an other is always reduced to an object.

To give the shortest possible version of the Catholic social teaching which forms my perspective: It's a sin to treat people like objects. It's a sin to treat objects like people. And in this view, the question of who has the power and who doesn't, which is the view both kinds of bad fan Nussbaum talks about take, misses at least some of the point. Spooge's Woman, to pick one of the most powerless figures in the series, nonetheless instrumentalizes everyone around her; Jesse, in both powerful and powerless incarnations, tends to imagine others as persons even as his language of "bitch" and "pussy" wants to deny them that essential dignity, reducing them in the first instance to animals and in the second to mere bodies, not ensouled but unsouled.

The third kind of bad fan? That's me, the fan who is late to the party. Nussbaum has picked out the dangers of a certain kind of naiveté (for to be naïve about privilege is to make one kind of error) but my difficulty is the opposite: having binge-watched my way through all of the seasons after the final episode had aired, I am too knowing. Not for me the sympathetic identification with Walter, gradually turning to horror as I realize I have been of the devil's party without knowing it. My Walter was always a devil, my Skyler always the abused and traumatized wife—and yet, even so, that birthday sex scene [in "Madrigal," 502] chills me to the very marrow of my bones.

BRC: Amen, sister.

JEFFREY REID PETTIS: I think Brian is spot on in saying that anyone who defends Walt's enactment of masculinity as something to be aspired to would have to "watch incredibly selectively." The series is punctuated by moments of Walt enacting his masculinity in moments that make people want to pump their fists, perhaps because these are often moments when he has attained his desires (I'm thinking here in particular of the "Say my name" scene where he seems to come out of the business deal "on top"). But, people continue to pump their fists even when his masculinity is "toxic." I remember reading somewhere, I think it was a quote from Vince Gilligan, that in Season Five we would see what it looks like when Walt is winning, and I didn't appreciate the horror that that statement entails. The bleak tone of Season Five both in terms of its plot and its cinematography should alert the audience that this particular form of winning—becoming a man by the standards Brian outlined—doesn't look very good. The visual evidence alone should be enough to warn us that Walt is a villain rather than something to aspire to; try to count the number of shots where his face is concealed in shadow or where he looms over Skyler or Jesse and the upper half of his body is segmented—his face off-screen.

I'd also like to take another approach at explaining the "bad fans" phenomenon. I should begin by disclosing that I'm not often an active member of online communities. Breaking Bad was an exception, and I was a fairly regular participant on the imdb message board about the show. Anecdotally, I noticed a marked increase in "bad fans" in Season Four and Five. Rather than unique and compelling fan theories and analysis (I had a pretty strong theory, if I do say so myself, about Skyler being poisoned by the ricin back when there was a ricin cigarette and there had been the whole subplot of her smoking— but that's beside the point), there seemed to be a rapid increase in trolling posts and uncritical commentary on the show. One possible explanation is the increased number of fans going into Season Four and especially Season Five. However, the increase in fans cannot alone explain the phenomenon of "bad fans." There's no reason that there would not be both critical and uncritical fans brought in in equal measure. One of Nussbaum's comments, though, might help to explain the issue. With regard to the phone call in "Ozymandias," she says that she took Walt's speech "at face value, for nearly an hour, until I suddenly realized, in a flash of clarity, that it was a fake-out for the police" (my emphasis). Anything that is rich and complex demands a certain slowness of thought, and I think that *Breaking Bad* falls into that category. But, *Breaking Bad* is also the most watched show on Netflix, a place where people notoriously binge watch. I think what made conversation so rich in the early years of the show was that, as far as I know, watching it on Netflix was not yet an option. Those who watched it had to wait from week to week and it gave people time to think, to let things percolate. People who came to the show late and binge watched the whole series may not have had the same opportunity for critical reflection. Maybe there is some connection between how people are watching the show and how they come to think about it.

BRC: I think that's right. *How* people watch seems to make a difference. Lisa Coulthard and Jason Mittel have commented upon the mechanics of time between episodes as opportunity for necessary reflection.

But I did what you would say sets a person up to be a Bad Fan: I binge-watched the series on Netflix, seeing the final episode there a few weeks after it had aired in AMC. Coincidentally, I was watching with the same frame of mind and under the same conditions Susan describes as her "third kind of fan." I don't know if we can attribute Susan and me being Fans of the Third Kind to the fact that we binge-watched as the show was just ending or that we were both practicing Catholics when we watched. OK, here's my confession:

I had avoided watching Breaking Bad for years. My graduate students had urged me "You will love it! It's exactly your kind of thing! It's about moral and ethical choices!" I chose to reply that there was nothing deep to explored about ethics or morality in a show about a high school teacher making meth. The very concept of it turned me off and I find violence really difficult to watch. But my husband decided to watch it because of all the sensation the last season was making. He got through the first season on Netflix and came back to my writing room where I was engaged in Catholic apologetics and told me, "I think you need to see this. I think you'll really like the writing." He lured me to the TV with promises that I would know if it was for me by watching the pilot. I've seen the complete series five times now and my first impression of Walter White is the one I still have: there, but for the grace of God, go I. (I have some pride issues myself, you see.) Again, this brings up the issue Susan suggests which is that those of us who know we are about to watch a show about an individual's moral decline bring to the viewing whatever standard of moral reasoning we already have in place when we watch. I would be tempted to conclude that Bad Fans are what my Jesuit uncle would have called *the unchurched* except that the Team Walt gentleman I have mentioned was raised a Catholic. So was Vince Gilligan. Maybe takes better with some of us than with others.

IAN DAWE: Since everybody else is doing it, let me make *my* confession. I was a Heisenberg fan for most of my first viewing of this show. I reveled in his "cleverness" and his hijinks, wondered why he didn't just get rid of that annoying Jesse character, was irritated by Skyler the nag, enjoyed the "buddy cop" dynamic of Hank and Steve but mostly just rooted for Walter. Then, somewhere around Season Four, I believe it was in response to a distinct look of horror and shock that Jesse gives him over one of his escalating chain of atrocities, that my moral world collapsed. I realized that all this time I had been in the camp of a true psychopath, and not even a "cool, interesting" psychopath like Hannibal Lecter. Walter was everything I had always hoped I wouldn't be: arrogant, insecure, a bragger and a liar, believing himself to be "above" his profession and his social company. Walter was a horrible person, redeemed only by the genre thrills of an adventure-thriller TV show and by the very slender thread of his stated motivation, to earn enough money to support his family.

To those of you who saw that aspect of Walt right from the start, I say in my defense only that I was probably more willing to be seduced. I originally have a background in the sciences, so it was interesting to see the amount of science in a crime drama that wasn't something like *CSI*. I understood how deeply wounded Walter's pride must have been, teaching High School Chemistry (literally the *lowest* profession available to a research scientist). I wanted him to succeed because I saw part of myself in him. I also responded to the fact that he was clearly the main character in the show, and not obviously positioned as the "bad guy," so I went blindly with the flow. It was short-sighted on my part, but I forgive myself for putting my sympathies with such a wretched character.

Let's face it: manipulating an audience's sensibilities and sympathies is one of the oldest dramatic tools in the box. I suspect Gilligan and company *wanted* me to stand out of my chair towards the end of Season Four and say, "Oh my God, I've been wrong this whole time!" By the time Skyler gives her Munch-like scream in the episode Nussbaum references, I was solidly in her camp. And on the second complete viewing, doing research for this book, my eyes were open from the first episode. In fact, it was an almost completely different experience the second time through, in which I was much more emotionally guarded and reserved judgment on all characters. That became a better way to appreciate the brilliance of the show, but an experience with which I struggled a bit in a moral sense.

Nussbaum, in this article and her previous one, suggests that Heisenberg fans are a bit like the character of Todd: amoral, outwardly sociable with good manners but inside sociopathic. This is just the sort of Jekyll and Hyde persona those who would habitually post on message boards or comments sections seem to exhibit. (Wouldn't we all *love* to see Todd's dating profile?) In an environment such as the internet, where emotional distance is prized and giving vent to dark anti-social impulses through anonymous activity is common and almost given tacit approval, Heisenberg fans flourish.

That still doesn't explain or excuse why I was so completely on Walter's side for my first viewing of *Breaking Bad*. It's a disturbing thought. I don't *think* I'm a guy like Todd ... but then again I don't think I'm someone like Walter, either. This is, sneakily, a way of making the simple point that *Breaking Bad* challenges its viewers to consider their own moral perspective, to contemplate who is worthy of their sympathy and a test of how close the viewer is actually watching the emotional levers being pulled. I would like to think that if it can "get" me, it can "get" anyone.

BRC: Actually, Nick and Lori have done quantitative research on this question. We Humanities folks might not be into that but, hey, we owe science a seat at the *Breaking Bad* round table. Unleash it, Nick.

R. Nicholas Gerlich: Ms. Nussbaum makes some valid points about the typical Breaking Bad fan, and that latecomer Todd was actually a stereotype of the hardcore viewer. But her assessment that maybe we (they) have been watching it all wrong may be ... well, wrong. OK, partially wrong. Turns out that, at least in the study my co-author Lori Westermann and I did measuring the levels of fandom among Breaking Bad viewers, there are some pretty interesting differences between viewers.

Like between men and women, which may help explain some of Ms Nussbaum's comments. Our study included 332 volunteer participants from a social media call to be surveyed. The call was issued from Breaking Bad-related Facebook pages to ensure a high degree of interest in the show. The survey was run during September 2013, during the weeks leading up to the climactic finale. The purpose of the survey was to study elements of fandom among viewers of the show.

One particular question asked respondents to indicate their agreement or disagreement with 16 different aspects of the show, using a scale from 0 to 100. These items included technical matters (cinematography, location, script, actors, characters, etc.), opportunities to engage with other fans (fan pages, Facebook groups, etc.), as well as more esoteric elements such as the darkness of the storyline, the plot, and illegal activities. And this is where some significant differences were noted, specifically between men and women. Long live Bad-assery, for it reared its not so ugly head in the results.

T-tests for independent means were calculated using gender as the criterion variable; significant differences at the 0.05 level were found for the following items (with M and F mean scores in parentheses): plot (M=85.8; F=77.8), drug culture (M=43.4; F=36.0), violence (M=48.6; F=38.3), illegal activities (M=57.7; F=43.1), and dark storyline (M=78.5; F=68.9). In each of these five cases, men had a significantly higher mean score than did women.

To be fair, it should be noted that overall means for drug culture, violence, and illegal activities hovered at or below 50, indicating that there was not as much support for these aspects compared to the plot and dark storyline. Still, that men scored significantly higher than did women suggests that Ms Nussbaum's sweeping generalizations must carry an asterisk.

In other words, the stereotypical *Breaking Bad* fan and Todd reflect the male perspective, and not necessarily that of females. For Ms. Nussbaum to assert that we have been viewing all wrong may be the result of watching through her very female lenses. No, there's nothing wrong with this. It's just that our data show men and women saw things very differently. Masculine flight of fancy? Departure from the real world? Maybe so, but I was not the least bit surprised in Todd's retelling of the great train robbery.

Wait. There was a kid down there too?

SJ: So what I'm hearing from you, Nick, is that men and women are each prone to different kinds of bad fandom, but also that bad fandom is the minority report—a loud and insistent report, maybe, but minority nonetheless. I guess that leads us back to what Bridget calls the "what kind of man" question; what happens when you examine significant variables like age, income, place of residence, or—back to my own persistent interests—fatherhood?

I think it is so striking that you mention the kid at the end of the great train robbery; suddenly you are pointing to factors beyond the dichotomy in male and female responses that the survey identifies and opening up the question of kinds of masculinity. I've talked a lot in my essay about the way Jesse responds to children in particular, and the kind of protection and care the vulnerable bring out in him; that's the contrast between him and Todd, who kills just to demonstrate the purity of his allegiance. But it makes me wonder what would happen if you went back to the respondents and asked them to score their responses to Jesse and Todd. To me that would be really revealing, because I think Walt's status as the protagonist and point of view character really does muddy the ethical waters for a lot of viewers. We want the protagonist to be the hero. And he surely isn't.

I wonder not just about what kind of man would think that but what kind of viewer—can we distinguish between support for elements of the show as exciting, thrilling, complex viewing, and support for elements of the show as moral and ethical stances in the world? Let's face it, if Walt is a real person I want him to confess his sins, do penance, and amend his life—but since he is fictional I am pretty happy with the downward spiral. It's compelling viewing. And I wonder what kinds of variables and correlated preferences might let us make those distinctions.

• Intellectual Men •

Masculinity Versus Intelligence

Brian Cowlishaw

Masculinity in America

Breaking Bad provides a thorough, relentless critique of the dominant traditional American definition of masculinity. *Breaking Bad* is, in many ways, a show *about* masculinity. This may well be a key reason for its impressively wide, deep cultural impact.[1] Walter White, the show's central protagonist, is a hapless nerd trying to become a successful, respected man. He does so over time and the results are horrible to see. His gradual transformation dramatizes all the danger—"I am the danger"—built into our cultural definition of masculinity. He forces us to see how, and how urgently, that definition needs to change.

Gustavo Fring's question "What does a man do?" is of vital significance in our masculinity-obsessed culture. As Walter White's gradual moral descent/ masculine ascent demonstrates, to "be a man" turns out not only to be a constant challenge, but a grave decline into sociopathy as well. A "man" as we tend to define one is dangerous, violent, amoral, and generally horrible.

Phrasing the question Gus's way—"What does a man do?" as opposed to "What is a man?"—reveals the show's internalization of current cultural theory. Most cultural critics nowadays[2] reject essentialist, Mars-and-Venus conceptions of what men and women "are" simply by virtue of having been born with particular body parts. Instead, critics such as Judith Butler have shown, "gender proves to be performative" (33). If gender were essential, congenital, then models/standards for manhood would be universal across regions and cultures.

Yet clearly masculinity is shaped by society. Anyone wondering how mutable it is need only look at how differently it is expressed under the Taliban in Kabul or on the streets of Paris.... As anthropologist David D. Gilmore demonstrated in Manhood in the Making, his comprehensive cross-cultural survey of masculine ideals, manliness has been expressed as laboring-class loyalty in Spain, as diligence and discipline in Japan, as dependence on life outside the home in the company of men in Cyprus, as gift-giving among Sikhs, as the restraint of temper and the expression of "creative energy" among the Gisu of Uganda, and as entirely without significance to the Tahitians (Faludi 14–15). Masculinity is clearly not "natural" and "universal," not an instinct every man feels on his Y chromosome. Rather, "[m]anliness is a symbolic script, a cultural construct, endlessly variable and not always necessary" (Gilmore, qtd. in Faludi 15).

A man defines and proves himself as a man by his visible actions. Men define themselves as men, primarily, "not in relation to women but in relation to other men" (Faucette 72), according to how well they live up to "normative models" of masculinity (Butler 33). A "real man" does such-and-so, and does not do such-and-so. Masculinity is fluid, dynamic, always in process. A man must "act like a man" 24/7/365, because a "man" can become a "pussy" (or vice-versa) with any given choice or action.

What does a "man" do? *Breaking Bad* provides examples that are right in line with current cultural theory on the subject:

1. "A man provides for his family. And he does it even when he's not appreciated, or respected, or even loved. He simply bears up and he does it. Because he's a man," as Gus explains to Walter (301, "No Mas"). This is the central task that purportedly makes the others socially acceptable. Without this justification, "a man" is synonymous with "an angry sociopath": "Ken" (with the "KEN WINS" license plate), for example. "In Walt's mind, the measure of a man isn't his relationship to his family, but rather his ability to support them financially. Faced with a terminal cancer diagnosis, and the decision about what sort of legacy he truly wants to leave behind, Walt sacrifices the former for the latter" (Hudson).

2. A man possesses (and if possible, flaunts) visible physical strength. A physically weak man is not really a man. As Laura Hudson points out, the conflict between Hank and Walter illustrates the typical masculine dynamic. Hank, the almost comically masculine man, possesses considerable physical strength; we see him manhandling perpetrators effortlessly

many times during the first season. Walt, the "nerdy chemist," has to rely (at first) on his nonexistent muscle; consequently, he's no threat to anyone (again, at first). Later on, when Walter has built up his empire and his masculinity, he makes up for his lack of physical strength with firearms, ruthless willingness to kill rivals, and technical ingenuity (for example, his rigged gigantic machine gun system).

3. A man stays ready to wreak violence at any time, especially for the purpose of protecting his family. (See #1 and #2.) He commits violent acts as needed. "The masculinity described in *Breaking Bad* is something deeply pernicious.... It promotes violence, retribution, and a hierarchy built upon the backs [of] victims both male and female. Sometimes, it kills them" (Hudson). Protectiveness for his wife Marie is the force that drives Hank to violent madness toward Jesse (307, "One Minute").

4. A man shows no weakness and brooks no challenge to his manhood. "Masculinity in *Breaking Bad* is a brittle thing, one so terrified of weakness that any display of vulnerability must be punished, and any slight against another man's power answered with violence—or else perceived as a weakness" (Hudson). (See #2 and #3.) "We see it in the hyper-masculine culture of both the neo–Nazis and the drug cartel, where the air is always dripping with machismo and vengeance is considered an almost sacred duty" (Hudson). Macho culture involves frequent challenges to masculinity, frequent testing, and that just makes defending it more difficult. A man has to prove it often. Even on a minor scale, see how often, for example, macho Hank jokingly attacks even his friend and partner Steve Gomez's manhood: "You finally got your period?" (407, "Problem Dog"), accusing him of "sit[ting] down to pee" (202, "Bit by a Dead Bee"), and the like.

5. "This model of manhood also requires control not only over your own life, but over the lives of others. Think about all of the most iconic moments of the show, the badass lines that made us want to pump our fists: 'Say my name.' 'I am the danger.' 'I am the one who knocks.' 'I won.' Every single time, it's about dominance—not just about having power, but about taking power away from someone else" (Hudson). One's family, to be sure, but really all others in the environment. "The man controlling his environment is today the prevailing American image of masculinity.... He is to be in the driver's seat, the king of the road.... He'll fight attempts to tamp him down; if he has to, he'll use his gun" (Faludi 10). Walt even resents—and denies—being controlled by his cancer, telling

a fellow patient, "Fuck your cancer.... One of these times, I'm gonna hear some bad news. Until then, who's in charge? Me" (408, "Hermanos").

It's worth noting that, according to Susan Faludi and Michael Kimmel, this dangerous vision of the American man as "frontier wastrel" has historically competed with a softer alternative, in which "the perceived key to masculinity was 'publick usefulness'" (11). *Breaking Bad*, like the culture generally, highlights the "tougher" alternative. The show, unlike the real world, interrogates the validity and desirability of the model. Walter claims he does even his worst actions for the benefit of his family—until he confesses in the final episode, "I did it for me. I liked it. I was good at it"—but he has no concern at all for the general public (516, "Felina"). He begins as a man useful to the public, a self-sacrificing, committed high school teacher, but ends as a nationally demonized public enemy. If he has any public feeling at all for the users of his product, it is contempt for being stupid junkies.

This last requirement of masculinity—controlling everything and everyone in one's environment—effectively imposes a double burden. First, a man's control must be constant: a real man always determines his own course, never falling victim to circumstances. He can never lose, or even slow down. Since the nineteenth century, "[t]o be a man increasingly meant being ever on the rise, and the only way to know for sure you were rising was to claim, crush, and control everyone and everything in your way" (Faludi 11). Who (in reality) wins all the time, forever? Second, being a man means never complaining about your cultural situation. Don't like the confining definition, the "box," that the culture puts you in? Well, the "box is there to showcase the man, not to confine him. After all, didn't he build it—and can't he destroy it if he pleases, if he is a man? ... How dare the kings complain about their castles?" (13).

The Nerd

Competitive, confrontational, successful, violent, strong, tough—but not intelligent. In American culture, a man as we define him need not be particularly bright, so long as he is winning. In fact, gratuitous intelligence generally undermines masculinity. Although in reality, obviously, nothing prevents intelligence and physical strength from coexisting in the same body, our culture's powerful respective stereotypes consider the "nerd" and the macho dude polar opposites. One popular movie from 1984 sums up the binary and the tension neatly, even in its title: *Revenge of the Nerds*. The nerds' nemeses and eventual targets for revenge are the most "masculine" guys on the university campus, the football team and associated testosterone cases. A "nerd," a "geek," a "brainiac"[3]—a male whose most notable personality characteristic is unusually high intelligence[4]—is by cultural definition not really a man. In his half-sociological, half-autobiographical work *American Nerd: The Story of My People*, Benjamin Nugent defines the nerd this way:

> [D]isproportionately male, [he] is intellectual in ways that strike people as machinelike, and socially awkward in ways that strike people as machinelike. These nerds are people who remind others, sometimes pleasantly, of machines.
>
> They tend to remind people of machines by:
>
> 1. Being passionate about some technically sophisticated activity that doesn't revolve around emotional confrontation, physical confrontation, sex, food, or beauty (most activities that excite passion in non-nerds—basketball, violin, sex, surfing, acting, knitting, interior decorating, wine tasting, etc.—are built around one of these subjects).
> 2. Speaking in a language unusually similar to written Standard English.
> 3. Seeking to avoid physical and emotional confrontation.
> 4. Favoring logic and rational communication over nonverbal, nonrational forms of communication or thoughts that don't involve reason.
> 5. Working with, playing with, and enjoying machines more than most people do [6].

"Disproportionately male,"[5] reports Nugent—but not disproportionately masculine. Male but not manly. Masculinity would demand the opposite qualities: not machinelike (frequent displays of anger and gloating); using substandard English (sports or street slang); seeking physical and emotional confrontation; nonverbal, nonrational communication (call it intimidation); preferring the company of people (who can be intimidated and dominated) to that of machines.

The First Fifteen Minutes

Proceeding with these cultural definitions of "man" and "nerd": the first fifteen minutes of *Breaking Bad*'s pilot establish the struggle at the center of that whole episode, the whole first season, the whole run of the show. Namely,

> what, exactly, does it mean to be a "man"? It's a question that sits at the dark, warped heart of the entire series and its anti-hero protagonist. A nerdy chemist whose brains haven't earned him any power or respect from the world at large, the terminally ill Walt decides that he's finally going to get that power and respect through whatever means necessary (and whenever possible, using science) [Hudson].

The pilot's opening shot literalizes two key familiar metaphors. We see Walter's pants floating against a backdrop of blue desert sky, then falling to the dirt roadway and being run over by the out-of-control RV (with panicked, near-blinded Walter at the wheel). Will Walter gain control there in the driver's seat? Will he wear the pants?[6] Early signs suggest that yes, he will: the first teaser ends with him, pantsless but unafraid, grimly assuming a gunfighter's bowlegged stance and steadily aiming a gigantic silver pistol at whatever siren-screeching vehicles approach.

But then minutes 4 through 15 demonstrate that the manly apotheosis achieved so rapidly in the teaser will take a considerable while. What does a man do? Pretty much the opposite of everything Walter is currently doing.

Walter's masculinity languishes in pitiful shape in every way as the pilot's chronology begins early in the morning of his 50th birthday. He lies awake, staring, at 5 a.m. (beginning at 4:00 in the episode), gives up the attempt to sleep, and begins to exercise on what must be the cheapest, saddest bargain exercise machine ever made. Vincent Gilligan's original script ("OS" hereafter) describes the machine like this: "We come upon the source of the SQUEAK-ING. It's Walt balanced on a Lillian Vernon stair-stepper, just three easy payments of $29.95. Walt plods up and down in the darkness like he's marching to Bataan." Lillian Vernon! Ur-source of cutesy, frilly, "feminine" knick-knacks!

While he plods, he looks at plaques displayed on the wall:

AWARD OF MERIT
NEW MEXICO PUBLIC SCHOOL SYSTEM
WALTER H. WHITE

and much more impressively,

WALTER H. WHITE
CRYSTALLOGRAPHY PROJECT LEADER
FOR PROTON RADIOGRAPHY
1985
CONTRIBUTOR TO RESEARCH
AWARDED THE NOBEL PRIZE

We see baby-related items, many of them still wrapped as gifts, stockpiled around the room.

In just these few seconds we learn a lot about Walter's situation, particularly with regard to his flaccid manliness:

1. This room used to be his professional home study, but right now it's being converted into a nursery. (OS: "We pass an empty crib, Pampers, a baby monitor still in its box. There's going to be a new addition to the family.") Walt used to have his own room to do the high-level work with which he supported his family; now that room is becoming a space reserved for baby (girl) and mother.

2. He was a Nobel Prize winner 23 years earlier, but now he teaches high school? How did that happen?[7] (We have to guess or hope even this much for him; the plaque vaguely names only the "public school system"; from this, he could be teaching junior high or even elementary classes.) Also, compare the plaques' wording. In the Nobel plaque, he's a "leader"; he won the world's most prestigious science award; his role is named precisely. As a teacher (?), he received a vague "award of merit," a recognition that likely went to many others too. A securely masculine man always wins and climbs; this one has descended far.

3. He has anxieties on his mind, to give up on sleep and instead exercise at 5 a.m. That point is made even more strongly in Gilligan's OS, in a scene eventually not filmed:

> Walt sits down on the edge of the tub. We're watching his face in the bathroom mirror. He masturbates. Judging by his expression, he might as well be waiting in line at the DMV.
> Walt double-takes, catching sight of himself. Distracted, he examines the sallow bagginess under his eyes. He draws at the loose skin under his chin.
> Staring at himself long and hard, Walt loses his erection. He gives up trying, pulls up his sweat pants [4].

Walter at 50 is both figuratively and literally impotent.

At breakfast, his wife spells out "50" with bacon on his scrambled eggs (at 5:20), apparently following family tradition. This, however, is less a celebratory gesture than another proof of how Walter doesn't wear the pants in his own home with his own family. His wife Skyler is foisting veggie bacon upon him; he limits his rebellion to muttering, to his son Walt Jr., "We're watching our cholesterol now, apparently." (Junior, less beaten down than his father, rejects the veggie bacon, observing that it "smells like Band-Aids.") Junior cheekily asks his father, "How's it feel to be old?" In terms of control, Walt is like another child in the family, and not even the more independent one.

At school (beginning at 7:20), Walter shows his intelligence and passion for chemistry to a class full of students. His delight in the subject plays all over his face as he explains that he prefers to see chemistry not as the study of matter but as "the study of change," an accurate metaphor for what's about to happen. "It is fascinating, really!" he effuses. Right then he's brought back to mundane existence, noticing that one student, Chad, is out of his seat, talking loudly to his girlfriend, and totally ignoring the lesson. Walter directs the boy to his seat; Chad then makes an extended show of his disrespect, noisily dragging his chair from one table to his own, halting the lesson until he's finished. Walter continues—"Ionic bonds. Chapter six"—all his joy and authority sapped. Even his "nerdy" interests can't help him save face or heart.

Underachieving Walter, we discover (at 9:10), has to work a second job at a car wash to pay the bills. He has done so for the last four years (as we find out much later, in Season Four, when he and Skyler angle to buy the carwash). Again, he has fallen far. At the car wash, his boss, Bogdan, regularly runs roughshod over him, taking him from the cash register and forcing him to wipe down cars, keeping him later than he's paid to work. Over breakfast, Skyler had instructed Walt not to let Bogdan keep him late "again." "I don't want him dicking you around tonight. You get paid till five, you work till five, no later." This is a double shot below Walt's belt: a reminder that his boss bullies him, plus some extra bossing from his wife. As Brian Faucette comments, "Her statement shows her concern for the family but also indicates that in effect Skyler is the person who is in charge in the home, which is a situation that as the series moves forward it seeks to destabilize in an attempt to make Walt feel masculine and in control" (77). Hard at work, literally down on his knees washing a customer's tires, Walt finds out that this customer is the same disrespectful student from chemistry class. Chad smugly instructs him, "Make those tires really shine!" and snaps a photo with his cell phone.

Back at home—late after all, for which Skyler duly chides him—Walt has a surprise fiftieth birthday party waiting (10:45). Home, school, second job: at none of those sites does Walt enjoy masculine control and respect, so why would his own birthday party be different? His brother-in-law Hank Schrader,[8] everything a "real man" should be,[9] commandeers the party's attention. First he shows the guests his "daily carry," a large Glock pistol functioning as a stunningly obvious phallic symbol. (The subtext translates as: "Look at my huge 'gun,' wink-wink!") Walt Jr. looks mightily impressed and urges his father, "Take it!" ("Be a man!") Walter does, awkwardly and with noticeable reluctance, remarking, "It's just ... heavy." ("Manhood is a heavy burden that I may not be up to carrying.") "That's why they hire men," blusters Hank, earning a big laugh at Walter's expense. ("Obviously I am a man and you're not.")

Hank ribs Walt, "Jesus, it's not gonna bite you. It's like Keith Richards with a glass of warm milk." ("See how repulsive this guy finds manhood.")

Though it's a secondary characteristic of masculinity, it's worth mentioning here: Hank is persistently vulgar. At the party, he flips Marie and Steve Gomez his middle fingers when they comment that he looks heavier on TV. Hank constantly makes off-color remarks and rude gestures that are generally scolded or shushed by women. The implication is that concern for social niceties, manners, is feminine, while being brashly outspoken and vulgar is masculine.

Hank then grabs Walter's beer right out of his hand (and doesn't give it back) to offer him a most telling toast: "You got a brain the size of Wisconsin. But we're not gonna hold that against ya. But your heart's in the right place, man. Heart's in the right place." Lacking a drink, Walt responds by feebly waving the Glock. Shortly afterwards, Hank pulls the party over in front of the television, which plays a news report of Hank's big drug bust that day, a seizure of about $700,000 and a whole meth lab. ("Look at me, being all manly again!")

The party scene highlights the contrast between Hank and Walter—successful vs. underachieving, in control vs. under others' control, respected vs. not, not clearly intelligent vs. "brainiac": real man vs. nerd. Channeling our culture's typical view of intelligence/nerdiness, Hank refers it as if it were an obvious liability or handicap: "But we're not gonna hold that against ya." Ordinarily, we would hold that kind of intelligence against a male.

Gilligan's OS makes these points about masculinity vs. nerdiness even more directly and powerfully. There, the following conversation takes place between Hank, Steve Gomez, and Walter while they wait for the school bus to clear the neighborhood of their imminent drug bust:

> HANK: I made the mistake of watching "Jeopardy" with this dude one time. He is a stud, Gomez. He's a brainiac. BEEP! "What is E equals MC squared, Alex?" BEEP! "What is, like, freaking ... Shakespeare? Hamlet?" I'm telling you Walt, you shoulda gone on that show. You'da cleaned up.
> GOMEZ: Right on, man.
> HANK (to Gomez): Shit, you don't know the half of it. Two big companies wanted him while he was still in college. He coulda written his own ticket [27].

Walter didn't go on Jeopardy and didn't "[write] his own ticket," for which he is blameworthy. A man succeeds, wins, dominates. Walter "coulda" and "shoulda" put his brain to practical use, but he didn't. His brain would have redeemed his lacking masculinity, as winning/succeeding trumps nerdiness, but Walter didn't apply it appropriately and lost his opportunities. Hank can't understand or countenance a failure of masculinity like this.

Hank says of Walt, "He is a stud, Gomez. He's a brainiac." According to the terms of masculinity in our culture, which Hank and Walt so precisely embody, the second sentence cancels out the first. "He is a stud"—but only in terms of answering Jeopardy questions. "He's a brainiac" every hour of every day—and as discussed above, that means not being a stud. Hank wins at manhood, but/so he feels no shame in being dominated at answering trivia questions. Walter is a stud at that, but in the larger picture that doesn't really count for much. See, for example, the way Hank makes fun of Steve Gomez just for knowing the word "sage" as a term for a specific shade of "green"—in the meth-bust scene that was actually filmed, he repeats the word with stereotypical-gay-femme intonation (101, Pilot).

Along these lines, in Season Four, when Skyler and Walt concoct, rehearse, and tell their fiction about how Walt acquired all his money counting cards at blackjack, Walt Jr. praises him: "Dad, you're such a stud!" (404, "Bullet Points").[10] He's a stud for winning "into seven figures" of dollars for his family, though—not for having a brain powerful enough to beat the system that way. He's a winner and provider despite having a brain "like Rain Man," not because of it (3.9, "Kafkaesque"). Rain Man is hardly a viable model for masculinity: he's super-intelligent but damaged, incapable of normal social interactions, unable to perform basic "manly" tasks such as keep a job, support a family, or intimidate rivals.

Walter would have dominated the Jeopardy game and its buzzer: "BEEP! 'What is E equals MC squared, Alex?'" As a career chemist, Walter truly is at home with machines and delicate high-tech equipment of many kinds. He ably applies that technical/mechanical expertise[11] in several key plot situations: fabricating ricin out of raw beans, and less deadly poison out of Lily of the Valley; making a batch of fulminate of mercury that looks just like crystal meth; creating a makeshift battery for the RV out of coins, washers, and sponges; replacing his own water heater (and the rotten flooring beneath it); bugging ASAC Schrader's office; and finally, rigging the gigantic remote-control machine gun system to slaughter Jack and the other neo–Nazis. See above: comfort and skill with machines is a key signifier of nerdiness.

To return to the final scene of the pilot episode's first fifteen minutes: the bedroom/EBay scene (13:45) concludes that key establishing segment. It showcases Walter's failures to live up to masculine ideals. It is also arguably one of the unsexiest sex scenes ever aired on television. One hand operating her computer—her EBay auction is coming to a close—Skyler slides her other hand under the covers down to Walter's groin, grabs a handful, and unceremoniously starts stroking. Startled, he asks, "What's up?" (Subtext: "Shouldn't I be the one grabbing you?") She informs him, "We are just doing you tonight." ("I make these decisions—and anyway, hands off. No.") She strokes. Meanwhile, she tries to hold an everyday conversation with him, asking him what his plans are for Saturday. The car wash, he answers, then (he hopes) a visit to the Los Alamos museum, where there's "an exhibition on the Mars Rover photographs" he'd really like to see. ("I would like to indulge my intellectual interest; won't you let me, please?") "I reeeeaaaaally need you to paint at some point," she nags. ("You keep delaying fulfilling this promise. Isn't this the kind of thing you're supposed to do as the man of the house?") All this time she has continued stroking, but nothing's happening with him. She stops, lifts the covers, and peeks. "What is going on down there? Is he asleep?" ("Are you a man, or what?") She instructs him—twice—to close his eyes, then resumes stroking. ("I will manage this, too. Wimp.") Judging by his face, he finally starts to respond. "Keep it going, keep it going, keep it going," she urges; but her eyes are locked on her computer screen, and when she exclaims, "YES! Fifty-six!" we realize that she wasn't thinking about him at all, only her eBay auction. She catches herself, looks at him, drops her smile, and looks at his groin, implying that he's quickly lost whatever erection he had going. ("That sure died quickly. Wimp.") As in the unfilmed OS scene, Walter is both figuratively and literally impotent. Skyler doesn't even seem particularly interested in Walt, let alone guided or controlled by him. He's just another child and/or chore for her to manage in the domestic sphere she manages by herself.[12]

Compare the eBay scene with the last scene of the pilot. By that point in the chronology, Walt has made excellent progress toward regaining his dormant masculinity. Creeping into bed late at night, and (predictably enough by then) chided by Skyler for acting oddly and not talking to her, he begins to passionately kiss his wife and then mounts her from behind, indicating that he is now the person in control in the bedroom. Where in the previous scene Skyler was in charge of Walt's sexual satisfaction, Walt shows that he is beginning to transform into a more dominant male figure.

This change shocks and thrills Skyler (Faucette 77). "Walt? Is that you?" she asks, unable to believe the hard evidence. Interestingly, episode 2 begins with the couple breathlessly finishing the act; then, as Walt gets up out of the bed, Skyler asks him, "Are you okay?" This sudden display of manhood strikes her as a symptom that something is wrong with him. (Not that she's incorrect about that.) Clearly, he has considerable lengths to go to prove his masculinity overall.

What has happened in between the EBay scene and the pilot's end, of course, is that Walt has begun to "man up" under extreme duress. Having received the news that he has inoperable lung cancer, he sees that his central task of "being a man"—providing for his family—is one he has very limited time to perform. He must produce lots of money right away. The TV news story about Hank's bust of a super-lucrative meth lab, together with seeing Jesse Pinkman ("Cap'n Cook") in person escaping the scene of a similar bust, gives him an idea. Netflix describes the series's central premise: "A high school chemistry teacher dying of cancer teams with a former student to manufacture and sell crystal meth to secure his family's future." As Walt insists right up to the end, even his most awful actions serve the purpose of accomplishing "what a man does": providing for his family. He has not been acting at all "like a man"; in an instant he sets out to change that.

Unfortunately—and inevitably, the series indicates—to take up that central task of masculinity is to take up all its tasks. What does a man do? He doesn't only provide for his family. Time after time, Walter tries to turn his illegal way of providing for his family into a "professional," safe, rational, discrete task—and can't help but fail miserably. He always finds himself pulled unwillingly into violence, ruthlesslness, deadly competition ("Stay out of my territory"), defense of his tough-guy reputation (sending Jesse off to "handle" the junkies who robbed Skinny Pete), and demands for deference ("Say my name"). This is not merely the effect of his bottomless ambition, the fact that he's "not in the meth business or the money business" but rather "in the empire business" (506, "Buyout"). Walt's problem is that the tasks of masculinity prove to be inextricably intertwined; the definition of masculinity is a list of requirements, not options. To "be a man" is to complete the checklist. And so, Walter the provider becomes a menace to society in his acts originally intended to support and protect his family. Like any "real man" in our culture, he is effectively a sociopath with an excuse. Breaking Bad dramatizes how this is exactly the problem: the definition itself is toxic.

Hank, the show's primary example of effective manhood, gets around this problem by means of his career with the Drug Enforcement Agency. His job provides a legitimate channel for all his potentially destructive masculine energy. Violence? Ambition? Direct it at the "bad guys"; the public good is served and Hank can "be a man." Hank's masculinity serves his family (by earning them a living, supporting them), himself (by providing a productive outlet for his competitive strivings), and society (by removing drugs and violent criminals from its midst). Walt's masculine actions tear down society, his family, and himself; Hank's build them up.

Extreme Cases

Probably the most efficient way to test the accuracy of the polar-opposite stereotypes "man" and "nerd," and how they function in Breaking Bad, is via obviously extreme examples. Because cultural pressures to "be a man" are so strong, and American culture is so obsessed with masculinity, its signifiers can easily slide below our awareness. The opening joke in David Foster Wallace's speech "This Is Water" illustrates how that works:

> There are these two young fish swimming along and they happen to meet an older fish swimming the other way, who nods at them and says "Morning, boys. How's the water?" And the two young fish swim on for a bit, and then eventually one of them looks over at the other and goes, "What the hell is water?"

Wallace explains: "The point of the fish story is merely that the most obvious, important realities are often the ones that are hardest to see and talk about." In other words, we're so accustomed to living in this manhood-obsessed environment that we can't really see it. It's so familiar that it comes to seem like "just the way things are." But an exaggerated example helps us see what has been right beneath our noses the whole time.

Breaking Bad handily supplies one of each, "man" and "nerd": "Ken," presumably, the obnoxious businessman with the "KEN WINS" license plate on his BMW; and Gale Boetticher, Walter's hapless, short-lived lab assistant.

Ken only spends about a minute total onscreen, a few quick scenes scattered through one episode, but he makes a strong, 100 percent odious impression (104, "Cancer Man"). Everyone remembers and loathes him. If a standard-issue man is a sociopath with an excuse, then Ken is a sociopath without an excuse. He seems not to have a family with which he could justify his obnoxious behavior: he only talks about himself, we only see him alone in his BMW, and he wears no wedding ring (we see his left hand clearly as he shuffles papers in line at Walt's credit union). Apparently, everything he does, he does purely for his own gratification.

He steals Walt's parking space at the credit union, ignoring Walt's angry honk. In line, he blusters loudly on the phone, for the whole building to hear, about how pitiful his ($40,000) quarterly bonus is—"I'm not gonna sit here

and be disrespected"—so he should quit and go work somewhere else—
"They'd make me a partner at Goldberg Wayne just for walkin' in the damn
door, that's how ecstatic they'd be." He mocks his phone partner's choice of
sexual partner, advising him that "we're talking major barnyard boo-hog," and
he should "roll her in flour and look for the wet spot before you hit that. That
kind of stink does not wash off," drawing deathly glares from Walt and several
of the cashiers. Later, at the gas station, Walt sees Ken honk at a senior woman,
then shout "C'mon, move your ass!" while nearly bumping her with his BMW.

In just that minute of screen time, Ken illustrates an extreme/concen-
trated version of "what a man does"—except for that central requirement that
justifies the negative edge of those actions, doing it all to provide for his family.
He is the very embodiment of selfish obnoxiousness. He dominates his environment, ignores others' needs, acts aggressively, puts down women, and grabs
as much as he can. His (supposed) business/money-making prowess stands in
metaphorically for literal muscular strength—as it arguably does in the larger
culture. Money swagger looks and works much the same as muscle swagger.
Critic Laura Hudson sees the connection as integral: "Money and masculinity
are deeply linked in the series. Not only does money signify the value of the
person who earns it, but also the control and self-sufficiency that comes [sic]
along with it."[13] In any case, as the series shows us repeatedly, an awful lot can
be justified under the heading "I did it for my family." But not everything, nor
is the justification an automatic universal pass. For example, see the conversation between Skyler and her lawyer: [Skyler] "Maybe what he did…" [Lawyer,
interrupting] "…He did it for the family. Right? Well, guess what? That is one
enormous load of horseshit." [Skyler, whispering meekly] "Okay" (3.5, "Mas").
In any case, again, Ken lacks even this standard excuse. He's in it only for himself, and to hell with the rest of the world. Ken brings to mind the "publick good"
model for manhood: utterly uninterested in public good—he doesn't even
seem to notice other people unless they interfere with his goals, at which time
he just pushes right through them—and contributing nothing to the public
good, he shows the crying need for it. If Ken were the effective norm for masculinity, rather than an exaggerated version of it, society would suffer. Life
would be most unpleasant. Imagine dealing with Kens everywhere all the time.

Walter, seeing his chance to take revenge on Ken—to knock this car-
toonishly macho dude down a couple pegs—short-circuits the BMW's battery
with a wet windshield cleaner. The car blows up satisfyingly while Walter,
enacting a stereotypically macho cinematic moment, walks away from the
explosion without looking back or reacting. Two satisfying things happen with

Walter's revenge. First, speaking literally, Walter gives a jerk exactly what he deserves. That in itself feels like poetic justice. Second, Walter achieves two desirable effects in the process of administering this justice: he asserts his own manliness (using his knowledge of science), punishing someone who had wronged him and others; and in doing so, makes an exaggeratedly macho specimen suffer for having behaved anti-socially. Put another way: Walt moves up from his low nerd position into acceptable manhood, simultaneously cutting down an obnoxious uber-male. Walt enforces the limits of what a man can do before that man becomes a detriment to society. The action feels doubly satisfying for the audience: good for Walt, twice over!

Ken at least lives within society's basic requirements, though he does not serve society nor act politely: he holds down a job, he breaks no laws (as far as we can see), he wears a suit, he commits no actual violence. Tuco Salamanca is literally insane, possibly as a result of his meth use: he believes he can see the future with his special mental powers, and rages frequently at the urgings of an extreme paranoia. Except for his diagnosable insanity, which disqualifies him as a viable example, he could almost serve as this discussion's extreme example of masculinity. Unlike Ken, Tuco provides for his family—in his case, primarily his Tio Hector Salamanca. He doesn't care about others' families: when Walter objects that he can't accompany him to Mexico to cook meth, and just abruptly leave his wife and family, Tuco offhandedly replies, "We'll get you another one." Tuco loves the idea of Walter's family, but only so they can serve his (Tuco's) purposes: seeing a family snapshot in Walt's wallet, he gloats, "I like doing business with a family man. There's always a lot of collateral" (202, "Grilled"). Tuco's family will commit violence on his behalf, too: see for example his cousins,' the twin assassins,' impatience to kill Walter, and their near-hit of Hank in substitution. Hector (in a flashback) told the two cartel killers when they were boys, "La familia es todo"—family is everything—and in his own ultraviolent way, Tuco lives up to that ideal. Tuco himself is a violent time-bomb, ready to explode on anyone at any moment. He protects his manhood from all potential slights, even perceiving grave slights where there are none—for example, his henchman's reminder to Walter and Jesse, "Just remember who you're working for" (107, "A No-Rough-Stuff-Type-Deal"). That earned the henchman a beating to death (and then afterwards too). Tuco certainly does dominate and control all people in his environment. Danger hangs around Tuco like his own personal stormcloud. Following the letter (but not the spirit) of our culture's definition, and disregarding the important element of societal acceptability, he's more of a man than anyone else in the series.

The character Gale Boetticher provides an exaggerated example of a nerd, up against we can gauge Walter's initial nerdiness. Gale even applies the "nerd" label to himself. He and Walter have a wonderful first day working together in Gus's superlab. Sipping something red and bubbly in celebration (cold duck?), they discuss their deep, abiding love of chemistry. "I love the lab! Because it's all still magic," Gale enthuses. Walter totally understands: "It is magic. It still is." Gale then recites from memory the Walt Whitman poem "When I Heard the Learned Astronomer"[14]; seeing Walter's sympathetic, admiring response, Gale proudly proclaims, "Yes. I am a nerd" (306, "Sunset"). Jesse dubs Gale "Captain Nerd" after giving him only the briefest once-over in his (Jesse's) introduction to the superlab.

All the available evidence supports this definition. Gale certainly possesses the central, defining characteristic: unusually high intelligence. In terms of applied intelligence, or expertise, we can almost quantify this exactly; it's just a hair short of Walter's. If we use the purity of their respective meth cooks as measurement, Gale's 96 percent very nearly reaches up to Walter's unbelievable 99 percent+ (401, "Box Cutter"). However, in terms of "pure" intelligence, of wide-ranging curiosity and intellectual voraciousness, Gale has Walter beaten by a mile. Walter has no real hobbies or interests outside chemistry. The few times we see him read, he's either not really reading (leafing through a magazine in agitation, then dropping it) or reading Leaves of Grass, the book affectionately signed to him by Gale—the book primarily serving the purpose of trophy. (One of the creepiest Heisenberg moments of the series comes when, long after Gale is dead, Walter picks up the book and smiles nostalgically. His untroubled expression suggests a thought along the lines of: "Ahhh, that's right, I had that guy killed. Good times" [504, "Fifty-One"].) But Gale reads a lot, and widely. His apartment has books on many subjects set on all available surfaces and piled in the corners—books on Marxism, existentialism, Jane Austen, tribal cultures, and many other subjects, plus fiction by Stephen King. He collects antique cameras, tribal masks, and rugs from around the world. He has a telescope and a potato-powered clock. He listens to, and sings along with, the song "Crapapelada," an "old Italian swing song" (Nardi 183).[15] When Jesse comes by to shoot Gale, Mike's warning phone call is drowned out by a Chinese-language song, "Man Chang Fei," which is sung in what Jesse later describes as "squeaky voices." Later, after Hank becomes involved in Gale's murder investigation, we also learn that Gale expertly performed Thai karaoke, practiced veganism, and knew all about recumbent bicycles, plus who-knows-what-all. All kinds of scraps of scattered knowledge are recorded in his lab notebook along with formulas and equipment schematics (episodes 313, "Full Measure"; 401, "Box Cutter"; 404, "Bullet Points").

Gale fits "the nerd"'s other standard characteristics as fully as the primary one of super-intelligence. "[P]assionate about some technically sophisticated activity that doesn't revolve around emotional confrontation, physical confrontation, sex, food, or beauty" (Nugent 6): Gale is passionate about many such activities, as just described—and exclusively such activities, it seems. That is, we don't see him going to current mainstream movies, listening to bubblegum pop, or watching some stupid sitcom on TV. What time could he possibly have left over for such mainstream activities?

Gale is sexually neutral: there's no evidence of a sexual partner (current, past, or desired), a romantic interest, or really even sexuality at all. Is he heterosexual, gay, or what? We can't answer with any certainty; he appears asexual.

He speaks Standard English in full sentences. He's not pedantic, though, as Walter can be sometimes, early on, with Jesse: "Red phosphorus in the presence of moisture and accelerated by heat yields phosphorus hydride—phosphene gas"; "What I'm trying to say is that [Krazy-8]'s a distributor, right? He's a businessman. He's a man of business. It would therefore seem to follow that he is capable of acting out of mutual self-interest, yes?" (101, Pilot). A normal man doesn't talk like these quotations by Walter—write, in some situations perhaps, but not talk. Gale's speech usage is dialed down one notch below Walt's pedantry, but up a notch more formal than most men.

Gale is at least as comfortable around machines as Walter is. It's Gale who ordered and assembled all of Gus's superlab equipment, and Gale who was slated to be Gus's meth cook there. The cold open to episode 401, "Box Cutter," shows Gale talking himself out of a job, accidentally persuading Gus that Walter's 99+ percent meth purity was "a tremendous gulf" better than Gale's own 96 percent. "Real men" constantly seek competition and strive for dominance; Gale's behavior here is the opposite of that—self-deprecatory, meek, admiring, submissive, beta.

The one part of the nerd stereotype that does not fit Gale, nevertheless does establish him in the series' terms as the opposite of masculine: he deeply feels and openly expresses a wide range of emotions. In Gale's short time onscreen—around twelve minutes—he shows awe (for science's "magic"), fear, desperation, giggly joy (taking high-tech lab equipment out of its boxes), stunned admiration (for Walt's 99 percent+ meth purity), and silliness (at home singing "Crapapelada"). He breaks into tears when Jesse points a gun at him and he suddenly understands why (313, "Full Measure"). Only a few strictly limited emotions are socially sanctioned for "real men," but tears are never allowed. See, for example, the neo–Nazis' disgusted reaction to Jesse's confession video: "Does this pussy cry through the whole thing?" (515, "Granite State").

"Bitch"

This masculine value—keeping one's emotions reined in—remains central throughout *Breaking Bad*. As in our culture at large, the only emotions men are socially sanctioned to feel and express are anger and pride/gloating.[16] Walter struggles constantly to maintain the appearance of stoic strength. Jesse suffers from being pulled both directions, being himself (a person with actual feelings) versus "being a man."

Jesse is highly aware of the very narrow cultural script for being a man, and certainly knows how to act it out. This is a guy who feels perfectly comfortable grabbing his crotch and telling Walt to "speak into the mic, bitch!"[17] But despite his flaws and his posturing, he's always been a good guy: compassionate, caring and even sensitive. Deep down Jesse is more creampuff than criminal, unable to take part in the sociopathy of the people around him and deeply traumatized when forced to commit violence. (Walt, meanwhile, just whistles.) We see Jesse cry on more than one occasion, and he has a particular soft spot for children, both very stereotypically feminine traits (Hudson).

In addition to grabbing his crotch, Jesse constantly uses the taunt "bitch" with other men. The real-world actor who played Jesse, Aaron Paul, says he is asked to call people that all the time when they meet him in person. It has become his trademark. Jesse does not apply the word to women, only men.[18] The word in this context takes on a very specific meaning:

> When you call a woman a bitch, you're saying that she's difficult, unaccommodating. By that standard, Walter White would be possibly the biggest bitch of all. Of course, that's not the way it works. When we apply a female slur like "bitch" to a man, something strange happens. It stops meaning that someone is difficult or unpleasant—words that for men more easily [are] seen as signs of strength—and instead becomes an indicator of weakness and cowardice.
>
> In short, calling a man a "bitch" is designed to diminish his power by comparing him to a woman. It implies that women are weaker and less powerful, and also that they are to be used and dominated. "Bitch" is linked to exploitation, to submission; if you make someone your bitch, you force them to submit to your will, in one way or another [Hudson].

Jesse, who calls other men "bitch" out of mostly false bravado, finally becomes the neo–Nazis' bitch, forced to make meth for them as their slave. Ironically, the male with the word "bitch" most constantly on his lips—becomes one.

Masculinity, Intelligence and Expertise

This Venn diagram represents the relationship between masculinity, abstract intelligence, and expertise as these qualities are dramatized in *Breaking Bad*.

A key and explanation are in order here.

"Masculinity" here represents the concept as defined above. That means it is culturally constructed, not essential.

"Intelligence" and "expertise" represent related but different concepts. Intelligence here—representing intelligence as portrayed in the show—is inherently abstract, unapplied, not useful: pure "smarts." That abstract quality

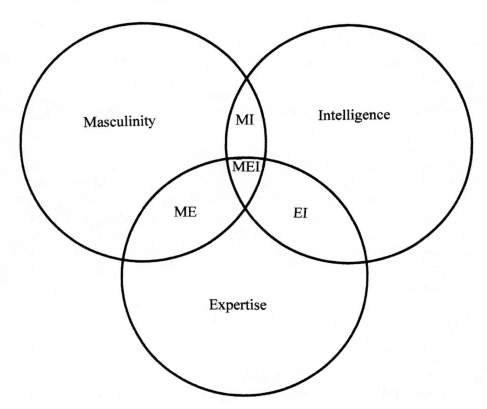

is what distinguishes it from expertise. Expertise here represents technical ability, skill, applied know-how. Accordingly, making super-pure meth requires expertise, but not really intelligence—ability, not raw IQ. That is why by the end of the show, Jesse can make meth that is very nearly as good as Walter's. He will never be as intelligent as Walt, but he can and does learn considerable expertise from him. That is another important distinction: expertise can be taught and learned, whereas intelligence is congenital.

The intersections of the three spheres represent realms where both qualities come into play.

ME = those realms involving both masculinity and expertise.
MI = those realms involving both masculinity and intelligence.
EI = those realms involving both expertise and intelligence.

Masculinity and expertise overlap, but not much. Competency at certain activities confers and/or signifies masculinity: for example, Walter's installing his own water heater and subfloor, and putting together a working battery under duress out of materials at hand. The test for whether a given task requiring expertise is masculine could be: Is this activity of practical use—say, good for making money or fixing things? If so, then it's masculine; if not, then not. By this rule, home and car repairs, which require expertise but not much pure intelligence, qualify as ME. Gale's ability to quote Walt Whitman at length, and his skill at performing Thai karaoke, indicate intelligence but not masculine expertise.

Masculinity and intelligence overlap only the slightest bit—considerably less than the ME and EI realms. A smart man is not therefore considered masculine, nor vice-versa. It is possible to be both, but only just. When Walter achieves some practical success, in reality or in Hank's predictive imagination, he occupies the tiny sliver of MI territory. Junior calls his father a "stud" when Walt (supposedly) wins a fortune counting cards at blackjack: MI. Hank (in Gilligan's OS) says Walt would have won a fortune on Jeopardy: MI. In limited activities such as these, the element of success/achievement trumps otherwise emasculating intelligence.

Intelligence and expertise overlap, but not much. The stereotypical academic male is a good illustration of the principle here: utterly brilliant in his incredibly narrow area of specialization, but unable to change his own car's oil. Elliot Schwartz, and even more so Walter White as chemist (as distinct from Walter as violent meth kingpin Heisenberg) inhabit the small EI area: they are brilliant, brimming with intelligence, and have managed to turn enough of that brilliance into practical channels to succeed and thrive at their respective chosen practical pursuits.

Walter's overarching goal in the series, his nearly impossible challenge, is to hit the tiny, elusive sweet spot where all three qualities intersect. As discussed above, his dominant personality characteristic is intelligence, which coexists quite uneasily with masculinity. He lives deep in I territory every day. His masculinity has been dormant, or fading, for a long time. He has considerable expertise, but it too has been in hiding for quite some time; it resurfaces to serve him in hard times (for example, being stuck in the desert with no way to start the RV). He knows E territory, or did know it, but he has to refamiliarize himself with it. Having received his cancer diagnosis, he instantly begins moving from intelligence (also near expertise) toward masculinity. Arguably, he reaches the sweet spot at the moment of his death. He has always been intelligent; now he also achieves success at expertise (rigging up his machine gun system) and masculinity (building a vast meth empire, providing for his family, visiting revenge on those who have wronged him) at the same time. The faint smile he wears in death, in the company of the chemistry machines he loves and has mastered, amid the bodies of his slain enemies: that expression registers his deep satisfaction—"I hit the spot."

A Nerd Is Not a Man

This essay establishes above how "nerd" and "masculine" are cultural definitions in polar opposition. A couple of key scenes from Breaking Bad exploit and reinforce these definitions.

First, Hank and Jesse break in to a chemical storage warehouse to steal methylamine (201, "Seven Thirty-Seven"). Walt's encyclopedic knowledge of chemistry suggests a "McGyver"-type solution: collect the thermite from several Etch-a-Sketch-type toys and use it to fry the building's massive lock. But then he doesn't have enough sense to roll the barrel away.[19] Hank and Gomez chuckle at the surveillance tape: "What, they didn't think about stealin' a hand truck? Hey, try rollin' it, morons! It's a barrel! It rolls!" The combination strikes Hank as strange: "Pseudo's in short supply, so these two make do by changin' up the formula. That and the thermite—I'd say these two know their chemistry." (Hank incorrectly ascribes to both men equally the intelligence that only Walter has.) Gomez: "But rankin' 'em as burglars?" Hank: "Yeah, I wouldn't trust these two to break into the Special Olympics! They got book-learnin,' but no street skills." That last sentence describes Walt in a nutshell.

(At first.) It could legitimately be considered, and reworded, in the language of masculinity: "book-learnin,' but no manliness."

Second, Hank experiences a bout of temporary mineral-mania. After suffering a horrific third round of trauma—the cartel brothers' unsuccessful assassination attempt—accompanied by severe post-traumatic stress disorder, plus (literally) crippling spinal injuries, bedridden Hank becomes obsessed with collecting, examining, researching, and cataloguing minerals. Most of his masculinity has been stripped away: his physical strength, his self-sufficiency, his ever-advancing, highly successful career. Lacking his usual strengths and usual path, miserably stuck in bed, he becomes a temporary nerd: he sets about immersing himself in gratuitous, inapplicable knowledge. Unable to use his body in masculine fashion, he uses his mind instead. As he has no particular application for his studies in geology, his hobby is arguably a metaphorical form of masturbation—masturbation being an activity he also indulges in literally. But once Hank becomes interested in the Gale Boetticher/Heisenberg case—and probably not coincidentally, as his physical state improves—he takes up his more familiar work and drops his interest in minerals like ... a rock. He begins as a "man's man," loses that status, becomes a nerd for a while, then over time regains his manliness.

All of this—Hank vs. Walt as opposed models of masculinity, masculinity vs. intelligence, real man vs. nerd, strength vs. weakness—comes together in Hank's death scene (514, "Ozymandias"). Walt wants him to beg for his life, but Hank refuses to oblige. Hank wants to die like a man—self-sufficient, prepared for the worst, asking no quarter. "My name is ASAC Schrader, and you can go fuck yourself," he spits at neo–Nazi crew leader Jack. To Walt, pleading with him, he observes wryly, "You're the smartest guy I ever met, and you're too stupid to see, he made up his mind ten minutes ago." To Jack, with steely resolve: "Do what you're gonna d"—BLAM. Hank really does die like a man.

If masculinity could be graphed, then Hank's path would describe a U-shape: it starts super-high at Walt's surprise birthday party; dips after Hank shoots Tuco (and consequently develops PTSD)[20]; dips again after the exploding–Tortuga incident in Mexico; bottoms out after the assassination attempt; then climbs gradually to its original position. Hank is as much a man in death as he is when we meet him. Walter's masculinity follows a fairly straight line: very low at the beginning, then a gradual, steady climb to the end. In his own way, Walt too dies like a man: knowingly, by choice, after taking revenge on the men who had robbed him of seventy million dollars; having rescued Jesse from slavery; having finally been honest with Skyler, and said goodbye to her and Holly; and, the key task, having made arrangements to provide for his family after he's gone.

Walter White, nerd, has become a man in full. That is the profound tragedy, and nuanced cautionary tale, of *Breaking Bad*.

Works Cited

Beggs, Scott. "Read the 'Breaking Bad' Pilot Script and Watch Aaron Paul Audition." Film School Rejects. Face3. 30 Sept. 2013. Web. 6 June. 2014.

Butler, Judith. *Gender Trouble: Feminism and the Subversion of Identity*. New York: Routledge, 1990.

Faludi, Susan. *Stiffed: The Betrayal of the American Man*. New York: William Morrow, 1999.

Faucette, Brian. "Taking Control: Male Angst and the Re-Emergence of Hegemonic Masculinity in *Breaking Bad*." *Breaking Bad: Critical Essays on the Contexts, Politics, Style, and Reception of the Television Series*. Ed. David P. Pierson. Lanham, MD: Lexington, 2014. 73–86.

Gilligan, Vince, prod. *Breaking Bad*. AMC Network, 2008–2013.

_____. "Pilot." *Breaking Bad*.

Guffey, Ensley F., and K. Dale Koontz. *Wanna Cook? The Complete, Unofficial Companion to Breaking Bad*. Toronto: ECW Press, 2014.

Hibberd, James. "*Breaking Bad* Series Finale Ratings Smash All Records." *Entertainment Weekly*: Inside TV. CNN/Entertainment Weekly Inc. 30 Sept. 2013. Web. 3 July 2014.

Hudson, Laura. "Die Like a Man: The Toxic Masculinity of *Breaking Bad*." *Wired Magazine*: Opinion. Conde Nast. 13 Oct. 2013. Web. 6 Jun. 2014.

Kimmel, Michael. Manhood in America: A Cultural History. Oxford: Oxford UP, 2011.

Nardi, Carlo. "Mediating Fictional Crimes: Music, Morality, and Liquid Identification in *Breaking Bad*." *Breaking Bad: Critical Essays on the Contexts, Politics, Style, and Reception of the Television Series*. Ed. David P. Pierson. Lanham, MD: Lexington, 2014. 173–89.

Nugent, Benjamin. *American Nerd: The Story of My People*. New York: Simon & Schuster, 2008.

Wallace, David Foster. "David Foster Wallace, in His Own Words." Kenyon College Commencement. *The Economist*: Intelligent Life. The Economist Group. 19 Sept. 2008. Web. 6 June. 2014.

Notes

1. There is practically universal agreement among American and European news sources that the show belongs among the top five best television series ever aired; a quick Google search shows that. Those same newspapers, magazines, and wire services generally consider *The Wire* and *The Sopranos* to be *Breaking Bad*'s toughest competition.

Even the way the show was aired is now being copied. *Breaking Bad* famously split its final season into two halves, with almost a year in between, to create buzz and anticipation for the last eight episodes. The gambit paid off handsomely: according to Entertainment Weekly, *Breaking Bad*'s viewership increased 442 percent between the season 4 finale and the series finale. *Mad Men* chose to split its final season similarly, openly crediting *Breaking Bad*'s precedent.

The "Netflix effect" has been significant, too, especially in combination with the split final season: people heard the buzz, then binge-watched earlier seasons to catch up in time for the last episodes. So now series such as *Orange Is the New Black* and *House of Cards* are releasing whole seasons at a time via Netflix, banking on and encouraging similar binge-watching.

See, too, the ubiquitous *Breaking Bad* memes for a measure of how much the show is on the public's mind. "I am the one who knocks," "I am the danger," Jesse's calling people (generally men) a "bitch," "Better call Saul," Hank's insistence that "it's not a rock, it's a mineral," and Walt Jr.'s love of breakfast have become general household pop-cultural references.

2. Although critics generally agree on this, the general lay public hasn't quite come to that understanding yet. For example, the day I'm writing this, a popular Facebook quiz is circulating widely, purporting to calculate to a precise percentage "What gender is your brain?" Father's Day

is coming up in a few days, and nearly every advertisement for Father's Day items employs rhetoric about how dads work hard for their family but, underneath, live for golf and/or to lounge with beer in their "man caves." As a hater of golf and beer, and a man with no "man cave," I feel very much the odd man out.

3. I'm using these terms synonymously. To attempt differentiating between them seems like the surest way to prove myself all three.

4. That is, pure/abstract) intelligence as opposed to technical ability or expertise; unapplied, not-practically-useful, excessive braininess. This distinction is discussed further at the end of this essay.

5. As with all stereotypes, this proves inaccurate in the real world. There are plenty of "nerd girls"; only the stereotype itself is "disproportionately male."

6. Both Jesse and Walt eventually use this metaphor explicitly, as a taunt. After Skyler goes to Jesse's house to warn him not to sell Walter any more marijuana—and nearly catches him dragging Emilio's corpse—Jesse jabs at Walter, "Good job wearing the pants in the family" (1.2, "The Cat's in the Bag"). Walt, forced by Jane to bring Jesse his $480,000 in a bag, throws back, "Nice job wearing the pants" (2.12, "Phoenix").

7. Before long we get confirmation that Walter feels embarrassed by his professional decline. At Elliot's birthday party (1.5, "Gray Matter"), some guests are impressed to find out he's the "White" in the company name. "So, you run the company with Elliot?" "I gravitated toward education." "What university?" [No answer; Walter drinks his wine to evade the question.]

8. Even his name is arguably extra-masculine compared to the official form "Henry." "Hank serves as the uber-masculine counterpoint to Walt" (Hudson).

9. Gilligan's OS: "The teenager worships his fire-pisser uncle" (12). Also: "Hank is everything Walt isn't: bold, brash, confident" (12)—in a word, masculine. The show, much more than OS, makes Hank and Walt good friends. OS has the tension you'd expect between polar opposites: at the ride-along drug bust, after Hank goes inside, "Walt's pleasant demeanor fades. Spending time with Hank is hard for him" (27).

10. Walt Jr. can't help buying into the masculinity system heavily, being a teenager deeply concerned with establishing an acceptable masculine public identity. All the more so, considering his physical disability; see, for example, the kind of teasing he would have to endure every day, as delivered cruelly by the three teenage boys in the clothing store (Pilot). Junior "worships his fire-pisser uncle" all the way to the end of the show—*over* his own father. This dynamic surfaces, and irritates Walt terribly, frequently. For example, at the celebration for Walt's cancer's remission, Walt pours Junior a drink; Junior looks to Hank for an okay, and Walt can't stand that, demanding, "What are you looking at *him* for?" Then later to Hank: "MY SON! MY BOTTLE! MY HOUSE!" (2.10, "Over"). When Walt calls Junior from New Hampshire, desperate to hear his voice, Junior absolutely rejects him because: "YOU KILLED UNCLE HANK!" (5.15, "Granite State"). Walter and Hank function as opposites in the unforgiving terms of masculinity. Hank is everything (macho) that Walter is not; Walter is everything (weak and nerdy) that Hank is not.

11. Again, see the end of this essay for a discussion of the distinction between abstract intelligence and applied technical expertise.

12. Ordinarily, anyway. On a few occasions Walt does some cooking—an occurrence so rare it prompts Walt Jr. to jeer, "I didn't know you were allowed to touch the stove." Walt makes breakfast a few consecutive mornings when he's trying to jolly Skyler out of wondering why he has a second cell phone—a tactic she eventually calls him on. And Walt is just finishing up dinner preparations on the night Skyler comes home and bluntly informs him, "I fucked Ted." In terms of masculinity, Walt's doing "woman's work" at home is a bad, bad sign, associated with some of the hardest blows to his manhood. He does such work in order to control Skyler and her emotions, but this strategy backfires badly—quite possibly because he's employing a "feminine" tactic in the "feminine" sphere of the kitchen.

13. Another way of making this point is to observe that our culture's masculine ethic and business ethic overlap considerably. That would explain why Walt increasingly spouts business jargon as his empire grows: "What does that [map of Albuquerque] look like to you, hmm? Opportunity! Golden, that's what that looks like!"; "We lack initiative"; "Exponential growth, that's the key here!" (2.7, "Negro y Azul").

14. Other critics, including some in this book, have commented on this poem's meaning in the context of the series and this episode. I understand it to express a preference for a personal, mystical, emotional understanding of science over a mathematical, cold, cerebral understanding. That is, the poem artistically expresses Gale's and Walter's joy in the "magic" of chemistry.

15. This song seems merely amusing and eccentric on first hearing, but details about the song demonstrate that Gale would have to know a lot to know it so well:

The song 'Crapapelada' was composed by Gorni Kramer (music) and Tata Giacobetti (lyrics) in 1936, therefore during the fascist regime, while the version used in the series was recorded in 1945 some months after the Liberation. The title of the song is the equivalent for 'bald head' in Milanese dialect and allegedly was a way to make fun of Mussolini while avoiding censorship. (Nardi 187)

16. Possibly a bit of lust, too. Upon meeting principal Carmen, for example, man's-man Hank can't help grabbing his crotch, then observing to Walt, "Damn! That chick's got an ass like an onion. Makes me want to cry" (106, "Crazy Handful of Nothin'"). We also eventually find that Hank, fitting the macho stereotype, likes "girl on girl" porn, and he frequently expresses his sexual fantasies about Shania Twain.

17. Along these lines, note how often in the series a man makes this gesture to another man. All the time, it's "Wipe down this!" and "I got you a Fat Man in my pants, *bitch*!" (Pilot; 207, "Negro y Azul").

This also brings to mind Tuco's necklace. It may be boxing gloves(?), but it looks for all the world like he's wearing a pair of bright platinum testicles around his neck, which would of course fit this hypermacho, violent, intimidating character.

18. The single exception: his own mother, as she's evicting him from his aunt's house (204, "Down").

19. Neither does Jesse, but: (a) he's pretty thick-witted most of the time early in the series, besides being high much of the time, and (b) the series is much more centrally about Walter's masculinity than Jesse's. Jesse, for example, never responds to taunts to his manhood, whereas Walter *always* does.

20. Just before those symptoms start to show, Marie fatefully says on the phone to Skyler, "You know Hank. He's indestructible" (2.3, "'Bit by a Dead Bee'").

• Business Men •

Breaking Bad's
Best Business Practices

R. NICHOLAS GERLICH AND
LORI WESTERMANN

Walter White's only prior business experience was with Gray Matter, but it could hardly be described as embodying the traditional business disciplines of accounting, production and marketing. Following his cancer diagnosis, though, and subsequent association with Jesse Pinkman, Walter morphed into BusinessMan. Suddenly, Walter found himself speaking the language of business: distribution channels, supply chain, manufacturing, raw materials, profit margins, risk, and dealer networks. Never mind that it was all illegal.

Within this drug business culture, Walter was surrounded by other men. He quickly learned about pecking orders, power and partnerships. Walter may not have known it at the time, but his ascendency had begun, his star was rising, and he was quickly learning how to maneuver himself upward in a precarious hierarchy. Cooperation and extermination were cards played deftly by Walter as he plied his trade and built his kingdom. It was a culture in which men, at least stereotypically, tend to play well and play hard.

The show ultimately portrayed women in business roles, though. By Season Four, Walter's wife Skyler had unwittingly become complicit in the drug business. Following Fring's demise, Lydia Rodarte-Quayle emerged as a force with which to be reckoned. But both of these women were also cast as neurotics, for all intents and purposes negating the legitimacy of their roles as businesswomen.

In the end, even in death, Walter was king and CEO of a patriarchical empire, one he built of his own design, and one in which women were viewed as users at best, and basket cases at worst.

Business versus Consumer

Business has always been a male-centered occupation. Although the feminist movement in the 1970s helped initiate change in this regard, the domain of business is still decidedly masculine. While the demographics of the American workforce started to change after World War II, the types of jobs each gender seeks (and finds) are decidedly different. According to Grant Thornton International Business Report (IBR), a mere 20 percent of management roles were held by women in 2013 which brings the number close to the level it was in 2010. This puts the United State in the bottom eight countries in the world for women in senior management. It is within this context that Walter found himself once again entering the world of business. It was a subject of which he knew little but it was a man's world. While his chemistry genius may have once allowed him to create valuable proprietary processes that became the signature of Gray Matter, his tenure there was short and not pertaining to actual business operations. While Walter was a neophyte in the business world, he never let his lack of training deter him, nor the illegality of his new moonlighting. It was as if Walter were a recently minted business major from the University of New Mexico, one of the guys, the brotherhood of businessmen.

And if ever a TV show could lend itself to there being a Business case study written, it is Breaking Bad. The show is a tour de force of all the major topical areas in a Business curriculum. Walter quickly embraced the principles of management, and required his equal partner Jesse (perhaps more in name than fact) to adhere to his mandates. In short order, Walter had evolved from amateur cook to CEO. He wore it well, understanding the nuances of raw materials procurement, quality control and human relations. He understood theoretical economics when he announced to Jesse that they should "corner the market ... raise the price." He grasped the concept of cash flow and target returns on investment. He knew the implications of having too much tied up in receivables. Finally, he embraced the 4Ps of Marketing: Product, Price, Promotion, and Placement (i.e., distribution). And he ruled with an iron fist, heartless in his determined resolve to maximize his profits. Mild-mannered high school teacher Mr. White was a tame shrew compared to his alter ego CEO Heisenberg. Business can be cruel; it is, within the context of capitalism, a take-no-prisoners concept. Profits are to be maximized, competitors beaten down or gobbled up. It is only the fear of anti-trust prosecution that competitors are allowed to remain at a safe distance, lest the federal government intervene. It was in this environment that Walter excelled. Walter made it his business to not just make money. He realized that he was in the empire business. He was not satisfied with only covering his family's long-term financial needs. No, he wanted to dominate the Southwest. His power hunger epitomized the male mystique; he was not satisfied with merely winning the pennant. He wanted to win all 162 games. His attention to detail in all of the business disciplines demonstrated his method-driven legitimacy to ascend to the top. But it was his bullets-to-barrels method that helped instill fear among his peers and associates. It was a no-nonsense type of business that helped him dominate men in a male-dominant field.

As for street drug trafficking specifically, the prevailing masculinity of the drug overlords and associates stands in stark contrast to the demographics of their users. In Breaking Bad, all of the significant players plying the trade are male: Walter, Jesse, Gus, Don Eladio, Declan, Uncle Jack. But in the real world of drug users, things are actually much different. Among meth users aged 18–25, a full two-thirds are women (Matthews). While cartels of testosterone-fueled manufacturers, distributors, and kingpins fight for market superiority and territorial rights, they are also in fact fighting for a market that is their exact opposite. Young women use meth for a variety of reasons, chief among them being for energy to work multiple part-time jobs while also caring for a family—with the side benefit of weight control (Matthews). They are thus using the drug to better conform to perceived societal norms for females, in spite of the long-term effects often being very unflattering to one's appearance. Worse yet, some of these female users wind up in prostitution to support their habit, and wind up working for onerous males who market their services.

The cycle of repression makes another revolution. The boys make the product the girls want; the girls use it, become hooked, and then take on a secondary role to support the first. In the process, they become doubly subservient to men. It is a cycle of which Walter had no clue when he found himself in the drug business. That he started manufacturing meth may be of coincidence only, it being a convenient way to make money fast. It could just as easily have been widgets or whatchamacallits, but like a shrewd businessman, he quickly sensed the market opportunity. Demand exceeded supply (especially with the DEA beating down doors), the margins were good, and Walter's proprietary knowledge and expertise gave him strategic advantage. Yes. This was business. Big business. He built his brand. And meth was simply the shortest and fastest reach for a desperate man.

The Business of Branding: What's in a Name?

In the world of business and marketing, there is little debate, however, about the power of a name. A study by Adam Alter and Daniel Oppenheimer indicates that investors choose stocks based upon their names, the shorter, easier to pronounce ticker name, apparently, the better. Countless celebrities, brand names onto themselves, change their name to reflect the image they want to portray. Archibald Alexander Leach doesn't convey the leading man attributes nearly as well as the name Gary Grant, nor does Caryn Elaine Johnson seem quite as appropriate for a comedian as Whoopi Goldberg. A recent study by economists Bentley Coffey and Patrick McLaughlin revealed that female lawyers in South Carolina were more likely to become judges if their names were more "masculine" (Alter).

As the impact and lore of Heisenberg spreads, the name alone begins to wield a Svengali power over its audience. The name Heisenberg becomes inextricably associated with the much sought after blue meth and soon associated with a mysterious bald man in a black pork pie hat. A product with distinct visual appeal, a readily identifiable mascot, and a strong name recognition; the Heisenberg moniker has developed true brand equity. But, as with any brand name, it's not enough to have a strong out-going marketing message. In the age of audience engagement and brand ambassadors, authentic endorsement must ultimately come from the mouths of the customers. It is only fitting, therefore, that Walt tests his brand's name recognition in the final season. While Walt is negotiating a methylamine deal with Declan he brazenly takes credit for being the creator of the blue meth, as well as the killer of Gus Fring. Sensing full recognition in Declan's eyes, Walt utters the infamous demand, "Say my name," to which the only response is, "Heisenberg." The verbal acknowledgment uttered with both respect and understandable fear.

In the world of *Breaking Bad*, no one is given a name by accident. As Alberto Brodesco has examined in detail, the name Heisenberg itself is appropriately associated with the randomness of the universe and the slippery rules of the *Breaking Bad* universe as well. Pinkman represents the constant tension of masculine (man) and feminine (pink) forces with which Jesse struggles. And Gray Matter Technologies is a clever combination and double meaning of the founders' last names (Walter White and Elliot Schwartz, German for black).

In the first episode of Season Five, a bearded Walter White shows the Denny's waitress his ID to confirm his birthday. The driver's license now, however, identifies him as Mr. Lambert, the alias Walt assumed during his exile in New Hampshire. The fact that Walt uses Lambert, Skyler's maiden name, as his alias, leaves one to wonder if his selection of this specific surname is a final homage to his wife and a recognition of the role she would continue to play in what would be left of the White family. If names are so important in the world of *Breaking Bad*, one must take note when key characters are assigned generic names or given derogatory descriptors. Skyler's normal role is as a caretaker, but it is when she dares to step outside of that approved position that she loses the right to her name.

The first time Skyler displays her business acumen is in Season Three when she learns of Walt's meth involvement. In response, Walt's lawyer, Saul, announces, "We may have a wife problem." Which is company code for, there's no room for a meddling woman in this business model. Undeterred, Skyler campaigns against Saul's idea to buy a nail salon to launder Walt's drug money, and instead suggests buying the car wash where Walt used to work. Later when Walt explains to Saul the logic of buying the car wash, Saul ridicules him by asking, "Is that you or Yoko Ono talking?" (A direct reference to Yoko Ono's perceived control over John Lennon's career that ultimately led to the breakup of The Beatles.) After compiling a detailed expense analysis, Skyler approaches Bogdan directly and makes a calculated offer to buy the car wash. Bogdan counters with an exorbitant price of $20 million, in part because Walt has disrespected him by sending "his woman" to do his business. The only other time the term "his woman" is used is to identify Spooge's female accomplice, who is repeatedly referred to as either "just his woman" or "skank." Although she is the figure that ultimately outsmarts Jesse by knocking him out, she is assigned no identity apart from being Spooge's woman or the boy's mother, roles which clearly have limited significant on the bottom-line business structure. Skyler finally receives the go-ahead and hatches the plan to trick Bogdan, Walt's former boss, into believing the car wash must be closed for expensive repairs. Having done her research, she uses a bluetooth device to feed the fake inspector exactly what to say to convince Bogdan that his carwash is in violation of emission standards. It is a telling scene to witness Skyler literally talking through one male to address another one.

One might question, then, how Lydia, the Madrigal executive, gets away with playing hardball with the boys and maintaining the right to be called by her name. The secret may lie in the name itself. Lydia Rodarte-Quale is the only female character given a hyphenated last name. In most cultures a hyphenated name is comprised of the last name of both the husband and the wife. Unlike the other females in the show who have acquiesced and taken their husband's surname, Lydia's last name may reflect a remnant of her independence, and refusal to totally surrender her identity (Scheuble and Johnson). Regardless, *Breaking Bad* is a textbook case study on the skillful use of names to both ascribe value and take it away when the masculine business setting demands gender-faithful style.

Man with Two Hats

Walter was a man with two hats: the Hat of Family, and the Hat of Heisenberg. We know which one won in the end. And lost. As the show opened, Walter found himself caught in the eddy of responsibility, with scant likelihood of ever breaking free. Whatever oats he had sown during his youth had been plowed under. Skyler, his attractive wife ten years his junior, was his last conquest. Making it through another month without going broke was his only goal.

Many years prior, Walter had made a conscious decision to step away from Gray Matter. For reasons unclear, he had terminated his relationship with Gretchen (who went on to marry Elliott), and Walter sold his one-third stake in the company for a meager sum. Rather than pursue any other business or technology interests, Walter became an educator. Financially, these decisions cost him dearly. The National Center for Education Statistics (NCES) reports that "the average salary for public school teachers in 2011–12 was $56,643 in current dollars (i.e., dollars that are not adjusted for inflation). In constant (i.e., inflation-adjusted) dollars, the average salary was about 1 percent higher in 2011–12 than in 1990–91." The teaching profession is one that is distinctly characterized as being the female domain. According to the NCES, "in 2007–08, some 76 percent of public school teachers were female, 44 percent were under age 40, and 52 percent had a master's or higher degree." That Walter's science specialty is male-dominated is of little consequence, as he is but an island in a sea of femininity. While math and science teachers are in short supply (likely because of higher demand in industry for people with these skills), teaching salaries at the K-12 level are based on years of service rather than market demand. The Houston Chronicle reports that, "according to the 2011 salary survey of degrees released by Georgetown University, [science] teachers earned a median $43,000 per year. About 58 percent of these degree holders were female, but they made lower annual medians of $39,000. Males earned a median $50,000 per year.

Further complicating matters is that the teacher's salary is hardly one on which to lead a family of four, especially given that Skyler was not employed at the time. The house in which they lived is appraised at $214,000 in real life (per Zillow, 2014), hardly affordable for someone earning $43,700. Even when Skyler returned to work after Holly was born, it was not enough. Toss in Walter's chemotherapy treatments, and suddenly the financial picture turns dark.

Domesticity and Businessman war within Walter very explicitly in the series' second episode episode 2. As much as the gun battle at To'hajiilee found Walter channeling his repressed masculinity, he quickly found himself tugged by domestication. After Jesse botched the disposal of Emilio via chemical disintegration, Walter had to lead the clean-up, a stereotypically female household chore: mops, buckets, hands-and-knees. But he also had to tend to Krazy–8, secured via bicycle lock to a downstairs pole. Walter tended to him like he would a sick child by bringing food, water, even a beer. The scene of Walter dutifully preparing a sandwich, and then methodically trimming the crust, speaks to his years of domestication. Walter's nurturing was put to task shortly though when Krazy–8 seized an opportunity to stab Walter with a piece of broken china. At that point, the kill-or-be-killed imperative of the drug industry took over.

If the Walter's inner conflict was evident throughout the expansion of the empire (he was in the *empire* business, remember?) via his insistence on cleanliness in the lab which demonstrated a certain feminine preference (in the name of chemical purity, of course) while not hesitating to don the Hat of Heisenberg to dispatch uncooperative thugs with near reckless abandon, his boss Gustavo Fring demonstrated the same traits to an exaggerated degree. His almost prissy mannerisms and attention to personal appearance (e.g., obsessively straightening his tie, impeccable style, etc.) was offset by his steely, silent resolve (ten minutes of wordless Clark Kent-to-Superman transition in disposing of Victor with a box cutter). From Fring, Walter learned that business is business, and even though Fring may have had what can be termed feminine personal traits, they did not interfere with the business of meth.

Throughout the two calendar years that unfolded in the series, both Skyler and Walt Jr., saw the emergence and evolution of Walt's macho Heisenberg side, a side that was not needed in the mundane life of a chemistry teacher living in the suburbs with his family. In Walter, we saw a man tugged by opposites, two hats vying for position atop his shaved head. As the series evolved and neared its end, we saw Walter inside his house in a cold open (episode 509)—the house vacant, an urban explorer's dream, a graffiti artist's canvas. He paused momentarily as if in remembrance of the domestic realm he once inhabited but Heisenberg quickly retook the helm and attended to the task that sent him there in the first place: retrieving the ricin.

Family Business: I'll cook. You clean

Every family has a certain set of expectations or "house rules." In the business environment, these expectations are called corporate protocol. They dictate management style, employee etiquette and community relations. Walt's rapidly growing drug dynasty is no different. From Walt's first partnership with Jesse, we see clear operational rules emerging specifically in regard to the cleanliness of their workspace, the intricacies of the cook, and even the cleanup routine.

Throughout history and across cultures, cooking and cleaning are seen as domestic roles normally assumed by females (Anderson). We are somehow comforted, therefore, when the pilot episode brings us into the modest kitchen of the White family. We think nothing unusual when Walt's wife, Skyler, cheerily cooks him a plate of bacon and eggs, as their handicapped son, Walt, Jr., finishes up a bowl of wholesome cereal and milk. Skyler conscientiously arranges the veggie bacon in the shape of "50" to commemorate Walt's birthday. It is here, within this domestic tableau, that literal and figurative breadcrumbs lead us to reconsider what it means to bring home the bacon; the result of too many cooks in the kitchen; and whose job it is to clean up the mess. Skyler's stove-top creation becomes both message and metaphor for the scrambled story about to unfold. The bacon is really just processed vegetables. Walt is, in all likelihood, consuming egg-substitutes. And within the week, Walt will come to view his existence as an artificial replacement for someone of his potential. Every dramatic element seems to beg the question, "Is anything what it seems to be?"

Once receiving the diagnosis of his terminal lung cancer, and subsequently learning how much a methamphetamine lab can make, Walter decides to use his chemistry knowledge to *cook*. From this pivotal moment on, we rarely see cooking in the same light again, as the male protagonists take over the kitchen duties. For much of the series, cooking obviously refers to the manufacturing of meth. And, although Walt is fond of donning an apron, nothing about this repurposed cook says hearth and home. Consider the places Walt and his sidekick, Jesse Pinkman, create their custom blue meth. Their first cooking attempt takes place in a Winnebago RV that has been converted into a mobile meth lab. Their kitchen comes to rest in the remote "no-man's land" of To'hajiilee. The isolation proves effective for keeping their operation clandestine, but it also almost ends their partnership before it begins. The next kitchen pops up in the dank recesses of Jesse's basement, followed by Gus Fring's superlab operating beneath a commercial laundry. Walt's final cooks take place under the guise of Vamonos Pest Control and inside other people's homes. In an odd sense, cooking still maintains its original purpose of sustaining those we care about. The men of *Breaking Bad* just seem to do it a little differently.

Even when we see men in a traditional kitchen, there is generally something sinister or apologetic about the experience. On two different occasions, Gus Fring, the owner of Los Pollos and mastermind behind the meth distribution, cooks dinner in his home, once for Walt and once for Jesse. Interestingly, he cooks the same thing for both guests; Paila Marina, a sophisticated Chilean fish stew. (In regard to Gus serving stew, it is interesting to note that Keefe reports in the *New Yorker*: "Many viewers were repulsed when Walt and Pinkman used acid to melt a body in an early episode, but this is such a common disposal technique in Mexico today that it has acquired a nickname—the guiso, or 'stew.'") Close up camera shots reveal Gus's hands forcefully chopping the vegetables with expert precision. Each smack of the stainless steel blade sends a reminder of who's in charge. One wonders if the main ingredient, fish, is a reminder of who is the big fish in this pond. Even though the meal itself is by its cook's description a "peasant" dish, by the time Gus finishes chopping up the ingredients and pouring the wine, one feels as if a sophisticated death sentence has been passed.

In episode 204, we watch Walt unleash his (food-based) culinary skills three different times. He takes his first turn behind the stove and cooks up pancakes for Skyler and Walt Jr. after recovering from his fugue state disappearance. While his son eagerly accepts the morning treat, it's clear to Skyler that his cooking display is an effort to distract her from her growing concerns about his mysterious second cell phone. By the end of the same episode Walt's unusual behavior and evasive actions have made both mother and son eerily suspicious. So much so, that when Walt surprises them with another breakfast, this time plates of omelets, they both pass on the offer, signaling the first of many futile attempts where Walt's cooking efforts fail to truly provide for his family. By the end of the episode, Walt finds himself offering up one last breakfast under unusual circumstances. Walt becomes irate when he sees that Jesse has parked the mobile meth lab down the street from his house. Walt refuses to give him any money and the two engage in a one-sided fight that ends only when Jesse releases Walt's neck and refuses to pummel him as he would like. Inside the house, Walt succumbs and divides up the money. After passing Jesse his stack of the earnings Walt asks, "Want some breakfast?" Jesse agrees and the episode ends as it began, around the family table with Walt at the stove. Walt's offer to cook for his partner could be interpreted as a conciliatory olive branch, or the acceptance that the only family that he will be breaking bread with from now on will be his business associates.

It's not just the cooking that the male leads transform. From a traditional perspective, cleaning is one of those feminine duties that nobody really wants to do, but must be accomplished in order to maintain a proper work or business environment. (Sanchez) So it is with their male counterparts. And, as Walt and Jesse learn from their first time in the meth kitchen, the cleanup process can be a very unsavory business. Instead of rinsing off dirty dishes and sweeping an occasional floor, "cleaning up" for Walt and Jesse means the disposal of incriminating evidence, usually a dead body. The first "clean-up" job takes place in Jesse's house. As determined by the flip of a coin, Jesse must dispose of Emilio's body while Walt is left to clean up the problem of Krazy–8. Walt's knowledge of chemistry comes to his aid as he instructs Jesse to dissolve Emilio's body in a plastic tub with hydrofluoric acid. Unable to find a tub large enough, Jesse reasons that the upstairs tub will serve as a suitable replacement. What Jesse doesn't realize is that that the chemical eats through ceramic, and before long what's left of the tub and the body comes crashing through the ceiling. To Walt's dismay, a simple chemical process becomes a gut-wrenching mop-up job that forces both men to bloody their hands with the first of many attempts to cover their tracks.

The next time Walt and Jesse are assigned cleanup duty is inside Gus Fring's underground superlab where they've found themselves at the end of Gus's patience and his box-cutter blade. As a statement and a business decision, Gus instead slashes the neck of his assistance Victor. Although the lines between guilt and innocence have long since blurred, it's clear that the blood on Walt and Jesse's sponge should have been their own.

The most tragic clean up chore is undoubtedly when Todd shoots a young boy on his motorcycle whom unintentionally witnesses their train heist (episode 505). Sadly, by this time in their business history, the protocol has become effective with repetition. The size of the tub is precise. The amount of chemical exact. What was once a revolting proposition has become business as usual for everyone but Jesse. The company line has been toed, the corporate protocol observed.

Management Style

Although Walter White never fancied himself a manager, he quickly found himself thrust into a position that required leadership. As high school chemistry teacher, all he had to do was show up and teach his classes. While standing in front of students and maintaining decorum implicitly requires some degree of managerial skill, it was a decidedly different environment from that of running a business, whether it be a legal or illegal one.

Walter's classroom leadership was a mixed bag. In the Pilot, we saw him engage and entertain his students with his eloquent definition of chemistry ("it's the study of change"). But in that same episode, cash-strapped Walter was working at the car wash, only to be spotted by a well-off student driving a fancy car. The student mocked and ridiculed Walter, this showing of disrespect no doubt reflecting the weaknesses of Walter's classroom management.

Stereotypic behaviors of males and females in business differ considerably, especially when it comes to leadership style. The literature confirms these expectations are in fact reality; men tend to lead less with a democratic or participative style than do women, and with a more autocratic and directive style. Writing for the popular press, Eagly and Johnson concluded that the "masculine mode of management (is) characterized by qualities such as competitiveness, hierarchical authority, high control for the leader, and unemotional and analytic problem solving." Loden asserts that "women prefer and tend to behave in terms of an alternative feminine leadership model characterized by cooperativeness, collaboration of managers and subordinates, lower control for the leader, and problem solving based on intuition and empathy as well as rationality."

Burke and Collins, in examining accountants, found that females tend to lead more with an interactive style that they termed transformational leadership, and males less so. Melero concluded that women managers have a more democratic style, and rely on interpersonal and interactive relationships. Walter White fit these stereotypes perfectly. If anything, he was the epitome of extreme masculine leadership. Autocratic. Directive. Unforgiving. Nonempathetic. Cold. Whatever business skills Walter may have been lacking in his early years with Gray Matter or as a teacher, he more than compensated for in business—and quickly. By episode 107, Walter challenged Tuco and metaphorically kicked dirt in his face. He was nonplussed in episode 201 at the junk yard when Tuco tried to instill fear in Walter and Jesse by killing No Doze, his own henchman. Walter managed with an iron fist. He also knew that, in order to get anywhere in the drug business, he had to systematically remove the people above him. Kill or be killed. He paid lip service to Gus Fring, but he did not trust him, ultimately disposing of him in episode 413. In episode 507, Walter calls Declan's bluff and intones perhaps the three most famous words ever spoken in the series: "Say my name." Such was the case in an industry run by men, huffing and puffing, beating their chest, exerting dominance with impunity.

It is interesting to note that the thread of male management predominated the series until Skyler, and later Lydia, were brought into the fold. It is uncertain whether these women were written into managerial roles to appease critics that the show was exclusively masculine, or this was the plan all along. In any regard, the contrast between stereotypical male and female management styles has likely never been made more apparent than in this series. Both Skyler and Lydia were cast as emotional loose cannons, irrational, testy, and—in street lingo—bitches.

Both women dressed to the nines in their managerial roles, both in business suits and high heels. Lydia raised the bar with her red-soled Christian Louboutins. And in both cases, they used their appearance to try to demonstrate power. Never mind that what came out of their mouths spoke very differently from what they wore. This is in stark contrast to how the male managers in the show dressed. Gus Fring, who could be accused of being decidedly feminine in mannerism and attire, dressed impeccably. Ted Beneke dressed in business casual. And Walter was decidedly pedestrian, usually a long-sleeve patterned shirt atop khakis, a school teacher for so many years that he forgot how to dress up.

While it is not clear whether these female managerial roles were tokenism, their scripted behaviors stand in stark contrast to the managerial styles of males in the show. Anna Gunn alluded to this in her *New York Times* piece in which she discussed how much her character Skyler was hated by viewers. To be certain, this hatred was more about her general character throughout the run of the series, but her transition into management did nothing to alleviate such perceptions.

Furthermore, few if any shed a tear when Walter taunted Lydia by phone in the final episode (episode 516) that the reason she was feeling flu-like was because of the ricin. Her sex appeal may have lured Todd toward the end, but neither Walter nor Jesse cared for her, nor did Mike before Walter dispatched him. They saw her as someone to be tolerated at best. She was a woman in a man's world, the world of drugs.

Risky Business: From Pissing Contests to Power Plays

Descriptors of the world of commerce are replete with metaphors. According to Boers, the most popular metaphorical themes in economics are: machines, animals, fighting, warfare, and sport. Of these traditional masculine metaphors, most business references draw heavily from the animal kingdom. A good market is a bull, a bad one's a bear, and the market leader is the 800-pound gorilla. A competitive environment is a dog-eat-dog world, which operates according to the survival of the fittest and leaves only the last man standing. It stands to reason, therefore, that the male dominated world of *Breaking Bad* would reflect a certain animalist agenda undergirded by physicality and sexual aggression. According to social theory, the control of social capital is used to produce an advantage in the social hierarchy and to enforce one's own position in relation to others (see Calhoun).

Chief among the ways that individuals, particularly males, attempt to assert their superiority is through the act of the taunt. Long before Michael Jackson repurposed the crotch grab as a signature dance move, or professional athletes made the act synonymous with pro baseball, the grabbing of one's nether regions was largely interpreted as a cross-cultural taunt and sign of aggression. It seems only fitting therefore, that Walter White chooses this display of masculine defiance to announce his newfound virility. After receiving the news of his terminal cancer, Walt reconsiders many of his life choices, including his after-hours job at the car wash. When his boss tells him to wipe down the cars again, Walt explodes, grabs his crotch and yells, "Wipe down this!" With one decisive act, Walt single-handedly announces to himself and the world that he is reclaiming his "man card" and all rights thereby associated. In her book *Engendered Lives*, Ellen Kimmel analyses the current culture in which the masculine lens defines the world by naming, evaluating, containing and invading it. One such framing example is the use of the term "pissing contest" to describe an aggressive competition. The term originates, of course, from the instinct in most animals to mark their territory, either to entice mates or ward of others by establishing dominance. On more than one occasion, *Breaking Bad* male protagonists engage in a pissing contest of sorts in which their urine is simultaneously a sign of disrespect and a marking of their territory. In Season Four, a flashback returns to 1989 and a Mexican hacienda, where Gustavo Fring and his associate Max Arciniega are meeting with the Cartel boss, Don Eladio. A much younger Hector Salamanca is featured as Don Eladio's right-hand man and, as such, is responsible for coordinating Eladio's business deals. When Gustavo and Max attempt to talk business with Eladio without Hector's prior consent, Hector displays his disapproval and supremacy by intentionally urinating in the pool in front of them. Soon thereafter, Hector makes his stature secure by shooting Max in the head. Decades later, an aged Uncle Tio, as Hector is referred, still resorts to urination as a show of macho disrespect. In Episode 413, the wheelchair bound Tio who cannot walk or speak, lures Hank to his nursing home claiming that he has information for the DEA. In reality, the only message Tio has for Hank is a few vulgar demands (sexual in nature) spelled out with the help of a communication board. He ends the session with an unceremonious grunt and puddle on the floor, as if to say, "You may take my family and my livelihood, but you will never have my respect." After being allowed to return to the family home, but not the bedroom, Walt awakes on the floor of Holly's nursery when he hears her crying in Skyler's room. Walt asks if he can help, but when Skyler doesn't respond, he asks if he can use her bathroom. When she still refuses to answer, Walt defiantly makes his way to the kitchen and relieves himself in the sink. Walt may not possess the words to confront his wife about his request, but he certainly has the obligatory equipment to display his distaste for her refusal.

Psychoanalyst Ethel Person asserts, "The cultural stereotype of male sexuality is a kind of phallic omnipotence and supremacy, a phallus invested with the power of mastery." Throughout history, rulers have carried scepters to symbolize the power they wield over their domain. In the *Breaking Bad* enterprise, a different kind of staff identifies those worthy to be the king of their castle. DEA officer and Walt's brother, Hank Schrader, displays a testosterone-infused lexicon as part of his daily business proceedings. Although his tough-guy exterior seems to mask a sea of insecurities, he toes the macho line with frequent sexual references intended to either bolster his masculinity or call into question someone else's. His wife, Marie, seems to adhere to this perspective and displays it in an unexpected challenge in episode 312. After Hank has spent weeks in recuperative hospital therapy, Marie becomes frustrated with his unwillingness to leave the hospital and general attitude of despair. While giving Hank a sponge bath, she attempts to lift his spirits by playfully betting that she can arouse him with her hand. Certain that his paralysis in complete, he agrees to return home if she succeeds. "You've got one minute," he says. The next time we see the two, Marie is victoriously wheeling Hank out of the hospital. No explanation is required. Marie has grasped the obvious, and a bit more, as she affirms the cultural assumption that a man's worth and well-being is only as healthy as his sexual virility.

From a psychological standpoint, this observed behavior is a textbook example of what Mosher and Sirkin define as hypermasculinity, the exaggeration of male stereotypical behavior that emphasizes physical strength, aggression and sexuality. One of their first studies quantified this "macho personality" with three variables:

(a) "callous sexual attitudes toward women,"
(b) "the belief that violence is manly," and
(c) "the experience of danger as exciting" (150).

It is not surprising, therefore, that the hypermasculine male often exhibits sexual aggression after the rush of surviving a dangerous experience. Even an early version of the usually mild-mannered Walter White exhibits a victorious chest-beating behavior after arriving home from his first death-defying meth cook. When questioned by Skyler about his absence, he responds, not with a deceptive explanation, but rather with an unexpected display of sexual aggression. An apparently stunned, but pleased, Skyler asks, "Walter, is that you?"

As Walter's confidence in the meth world grows, so does his confidence in his sexual virility. After having shaved his head and blown out the office windows of meth distributor, Tuco, Walt sits calmly at a parent-teacher meeting. As the principal discusses the disappearance of the chemistry lab equipment, Walt becomes distracted and brazenly begins to fondle Skyler under the table. The rush of risky behavior culminates in the parking lot with unbridled sex in Walt's Aztec. "Where did that come from? And why was it so damn good?" asks Skyler. "Because it was illegal," replies Walt. By Season Two, however, Walt's spontaneous sexual appetite loses its novelty and Skyler begins to have deep-seated concerns about his motives. Walt is seen idly clicking through TV channels and choking back tears in response to his feelings of emptiness. To bolster his ego, he attempts to force himself on Skyler. She resists his advances and finally resorts to shouting stop to end his unwanted advances. The urgent sex, like the illicit profits, begins to ring hollow.

Whereas males are usually portrayed in the series as using sex to assert themselves, female characters are more often seen using it as persuasion or outright currency. No character more vividly illustrates female sexuality as commerce, than Wendy the Meth Whore, who openly supports her drug habit by prostituting herself. Even Walt's wife, Skyler, displays her feminine charms in the workplace. When she applies for a data entry job at Beneke Fabricators, where she used to work, she selects an uncharacteristic black velvet dress as her interview outfit. The alluring bodice simultaneously catches the eye of her former boss, Tedd Beneke, and raises the eyebrows of the other women in the office. The fact that Skyler is in her third trimester of pregnancy, makes the sexual undertones of her outfit all the more incongruent. Skyler's apparel selection proves effective, as she not only gets her old job back, but with it, a new sense of confidence. Gone are the frumpy post-baby frocks. Instead Skyler wears form-fitting suits and stiletto heels. Her ample cleavage stays on display until the final season, and takes center stage when she dons a plunging black neckline and performs a sexy rendition of "Happy Birthday" to Beneke at his request. Her office flirtation eventually leads to a short-lived tryst with her boss. The affair can be seen as Skyler's attempt to gain a modicum of control in her rapidly unraveling life. She just happens to use her body to do it. According to several recent studies, Skyler might have been on to something. A University of Florida study found that for every inch of height, a worker can expect to earn an extra $789 per year (Judge & Cable). A 2010 study found blonde women earn greater than seven percent more than female employees with any other hair color (McWilliam). And a study in the *American Economic Review* announced that women who wear makeup can expect to earn more than thirty percent more than non-makeup wearing workers (Etcoff).

Skyler later uses well-played gender assumptions to help get Beneke out of serious legal trouble. The IRS eventually catches up to the irregularities in Beneke's books and threatens him with prison time. During Ted's meeting with the IRS representative, Skyler unexpectedly shows up wearing a revealing black dress and overly teased hair. She plays the role of the blonde bimbo so well that the IRS agent assumes the accounting errors are a result of her ignorance. In her book *Sex and the Office*, Julia Berebitsky provides the first historical examination of sexuality in the workplace. Her research examined archival sources, personal papers and individual accounts. Despite notable transformations over the years, her findings generally support the *Breaking Bad* business hierarchy where gender, power and desire are used for negotiation and advancement.

One could argue that Lydia's management position with Madrigal makes her immune to using sexuality for business purposes. However, in episode 513 she begins to sense that Todd has a crush on her. When he apologizes for not cooking up the blue color of meth her European buyers desire, she uses this knowledge to her advantage. While Todd's hand is resting on her shoulder, Lydia implores him to make the cook better ... for her. Her intentional feminine ploy is palpable. Lydia's strategy is one which social scientist, Catherine Hakim would applaud. In her 2011 book *Erotic Capital: The Power of Attrac-*

tion in the Boardroom and the Bedroom, Hakim argues that women should use every ounce of "capital" (flirting, fashion sense, and charm) to get what they want. A study published in *Personality and Social Psychology Bulletin* confirmed that chatting up men gets women a better deal in zero-sum negotiations (Kray, Locke, & Van Zant).

The *Breaking Bad* business culture seems to reflect with surprising accuracy the reality that the modern work environment continues to be infused with gender expectations; a competitive arena in which women who expect to play with the boys must understand the rules of exchange.

Business as Usual: Secretaries and Interns

The first glimpse into the role of women in the *Breaking Bad* corporate structure occurs before Walter has even considered entering the drug business. The pilot episode clearly introduces us to Skyler as the family's administrative assistant. Whether she is making sure that everyone has their breakfast for the day, doing background checks on Walt Jr.'s friends, or coordinating carpool chores and family gatherings, she easily fulfills traditional secretarial job duties. Her administrative skills kick into high gear shortly after Walt receives his cancer diagnosis. As an efficient assistant, it is Skyler who locates and schedules Walt an appointment with a top-rated oncologist. As the specialist explains various treatment options Walt begins to zone out, unable or unwilling to take in the reality of his condition or the enormity of the treatment bill. In contrast to her "boss's" passive state, Skyler, with notepad in hand, takes detailed dictation, reflective of her personal assistant status.

The most recent U.S. Census reveals that such relegation of females to secretarial roles in fact reflects current employment trends. Of the four million workers who identified themselves as secretaries or administrative assistants, a whopping 96 percent of them were female. In 2010, the most popular job for American women was secretarial, the same as it was in 1950 (Kurtz). When Skyler decides to supplement the family income, it is a telling decision that she applies for a data entry job at Beneke Fabricators where she used to work. Her former boss, Ted Beneke, ends up giving her old job as a bookkeeper back to her. Before long, Skyler is wearing nicer outfits, but still taking notes, managing a man's assets, and attempting to fix the problems that have resulted from another boss's poor decisions.

But Skyler is not alone in the *Breaking Bad* typing pool. She is joined by her sister, and Hank's wife, Marie Schrader. Although we are told that Marie works at a radiology clinic, we never actually see her at work. Instead, we witness her meddling in the lives of those around her and giving in to her kleptomaniac tendencies. Although she would likely rebuff the thought, by Season Three Marie too assumes a secretarial role when Hanks becomes partially paralyzed by a gunshot. It becomes evident that the female counterparts are allowed decision-making roles only when their male superiors are in some way incapacitated. Realizing the severity of Hank's injuries, Marie, like Skyler, aggressively assumes the reins of her support position. She scours research for the best medical options available, overseas Hank's physical therapy routine, ensures he's taking his meds as prescribed, and coordinates the hiring of various physical therapists. At one point, Marie insists that Hank participate in an expensive therapy treatment that their insurance won't cover. Undeterred, Marie goes behind Hank's back and secures the needed funds from Skyler and Walt. The administrative assistant role in the workings of Breaking Bad is as necessary as its counterpart in corporate America. However, like the thankless midcentury secretarial typecast, the position is governed by rigid expectations and swift criticism when those boundaries are overstepped. Once Hank moves home from the hospital, the slow recuperation progress begins to take a toll on him. He exhibits signs of depression, and begins purchasing box upon box of mail-order minerals. At one point, Marie finds herself questioning Hank's demands that she check every box for damage, because in her words, "they're rocks." Hank erupts, "Jesus Christ, Marie, they're minerals!" and yells at her to leave his presence. Were it the 1950s, one could almost see an angry boss exploding at his secretary over the temperature of his coffee. Similarly, when Skyler steps out of line in Episode 102 and confronts Walt about his relationship with Jesse, Walt puts her back in her place with the demand, "Climb down out of my ass! Can you do that for me, honey?" Regardless of age, the males make it clear that there is a strong disapproval when the feminine support character appears to be exerting undue influence in a given setting. At one point, Walt Jr. misinterprets his father's red eyes "like he's been crying" (episode 302) and blames Skyler for trying to keep his father away from him. "Why do you gotta be such a bitch?" he demands. Such is the reward for attempting to provide nurture and protection in the man's world of Breaking Bad.

The final female character that assumes a prominent role in the storyline is Lydia, Head of Logistics at Madrigal, the German firm responsible for supplying methylamine for Gustavo Fring's meth operation. Although she is given the title of management, her actions are anything but executive office. As with Marie, we never actually see her workplace. Instead she is most often pictured in an upscale eatery, alternatingly swirling a packet of Stevia in her tea or wringing her hands in anxiety. At times when she does execute a tactical business decision, it is never far from the protection or involvement of a male. Arguably her most lethal decision was when she directed Jack's gang to take out the meddling Declan crew to eliminate the competitive threat they posed. Although, Lydia might have been the one to create the plan, she has no part in meting out the sentence. In fact, she is pictured cowering in the recesses of an underground meth lab while the real business takes place overhead. Even when the gunfire has ceased, she is unwilling to survey her victory. Instead, she is helped up the ladder and shielded from the dead bodies by none-other-than Todd Alquist—a clear case of more brawn than brain. Apparently even the sole female at the top of corporate meth ladder must rely upon a man to get her job done.

If females are cast in secretarial roles, Jesse Pinkman is an intern at best. He is assigned this role not because of his lack of skill, but rather due to his feminine traits. Traditional female characteristics include being emotional, intuitive, nurturing and indecisive (Putnam and Heinen). In this male-dominated workplace, any player who habitually exhibits these traits is relegated to a support role. This is where Jesse Pinkman finds himself, in the company of every female character. Jesse displays his nurturing instincts during his first meth cook with Mr. White. After a labor-intensive session in the RV meth lab, Walt is overcome by a coughing fit and ends up coughing up blood. Although Jesse first reacts in anger over the fact that Walt did not reveal his delicate health, he quickly offers practical support. Jesse explains how Walt should apply an icepack to his head during his next chemo treatment, a therapeutic technique he witnessed his aunt use during her battle with cancer.

But it is in the presence of children, the ultimate innocents, that Jesse's vulnerable compassion is most evident. In Season Two, Jesse's search for the money and meth taken from one of his dealers takes him to the rundown house of a junkie named Spooge. Jesse breaks into the house and plans to wait until the perpetrator returns. But his plans are thrown off course when he discovers a half-dressed five-year-old boy amidst the squalor. Instead of lighting up a joint to wait out the addicts' return, Jesse plays a game of peek-a-boo with the child and prepares him something to eat. When the druggie and "his woman" arrive home, Jesse carries the boy to a bedroom to avoid seeing him attack the couple. Later the boy reemerges and begs Jesse to resume the game of peek-a-boo. Although not in Jesse's best interest, he relents and the woman quickly knocks him out while his eyes are closed, sending a clear message that a sympathetic instinct is rewarded with swift and painful consequences. Ultimately, however, the couple's own ineptness is the undoing of them as the ATM containing Jesse's money falls on top of Spooge and "his woman" succumbs to the drugs and passes out on the couch. Although making a fast getaway would be the obvious "best business practice," Jesse calls 911 and carries the child outside to avoid him seeing Spooge's dead body and his strung-out mother. Jesse makes the boy promise not to go back inside and flees only when the sound of sirens assures him that help for the child, is finally on its way. Jesse repeatedly displays his affinity for children and the protection of the uninvolved. And repeatedly it is met with unproductive outcomes. It is Jesse who argues against the original train heist plan because it would take the life of the innocent crew. It is Jesse who tries to stop Todd from shooting Drew Sharp, the young boy who witnessed the heist. And it is Jesse who, in time, tries to convince Saul to give his money to Mike Ehrmantraut's granddaughter and Sharp's grieving parents.

Jesse's caretaking soft spot becomes his ultimate Achilles heel. By episode 3, Jesse becomes very attached to Brock, his new girlfriend's son. Concerned that he could be putting mother and son in danger, he breaks the relationship off but continues to provide financial support to help them move out of their neighborhood and hopefully into a better life. This attempt at protection and provision proves anemic, as Walt later poisons Brock as part of an intricate scheme and Todd gains control over Jesse by shooting Brock's mother. It is only when Brock's life hangs in the balance that Jesse resigns himself to the slave labor meth manufacturing that Jack's crew demands. Whether it is playing peek-a-boy with a five-year-old or doing magic tricks for Andrea's son, Jesse displays a childlike optimism that ultimately has no place in the high stakes drug business.

Within the business playbook of *Breaking Bad*, maternal characteristics are generally seen as a weakness and often used for barter and control. Even the less-than-admirable character of Wendy the "meth whore" maintains her protective maternal instincts. When Wendy balks at helping Walt and Jesse poison her drug dealers, they remind her that these are the same people that use children as part of their drug operation. Having a child herself, Wendy reconsiders, another example of the vulnerability that comes with maternal inclinations. Throughout the storyline we see Skyler resigning her principles and making deals to secure the safety of her children. Most poignantly in episode 505 when she demands that the children not return to the house as long as Walt is involved in the drug business. "You agree to that and I will be whatever kind of partner you want me to be," she vows. Even the ice-queen Lydia seems to show her sole vulnerability when she thinks that she is about to be killed. Her one request is that her body be left inside her home so her daughter doesn't have to live with wondering what happened to her.

It is out of the unlikely mouth of Jane, and the hand of Jesse, that we are introduced to an alternative view of women. Jane is Jesse's recovering addict girlfriend, and as a tattoo artist she becomes intrigued with Jesse's childhood sketchpad. Of particular interest to her are the recurring images of a character Jesse calls Kanga-Man, a kangaroo superhero who carries his sidekick in his pouch. To Jesse's dismay, Jane makes the astute observation that Kanga-Man is actually a woman, since the female kangaroo is the only one equipped with a pouch. As Jesse protests that the character is "definitely a dude," Jane observes, that in fact, all of the superhero characters look like him. "I wonder what a shrink would say if he saw them?" Jane questions.

It is that question that serves as an underlying theme in Breaking Bad. The same question that hovers over break rooms and boardrooms today. Are the prevailing masculine assumptions of traditional business models the most effective system? Will those who rise to the top, do so only by appealing to prevailing masculine expectations? Or, is there room, as Jesse appears to grasp, for both male and female traits to coexist in a leader? Can the superhero stereotype embody the duality of both gender strengths? As a distraught Jesse speeds away from the Neo-Nazi compound, one is left to wonder why he alone escapes an enterprise in which only the strong survive.

Works Cited

Alter, Adam. "The Surprising Psychology of How Names Shape Our Thoughts." *The New Yorker*. June 2013. Web. 28 June 2014.

Anderson, Bridget. *Doing the Dirty Work? The Global Politics of Domestic Labour*. London: Zed Books, 2000. Print.

Berebitsky, Julie. *Sex and the Office: A History of Gender, Power, and Desire*. New Haven: Yale University Press, 2012. Print.

Boers, Frank. "Enhancing Metaphoric Awareness in Specialized Reading." *English for Specific Purposes* (1 June 2000): 137–147. Print.

Brodesco, Alberto. "Heisenberg: Epistemological Implications of a Criminal Pseudonym." *Breaking Bad: Critical Essays on the Contexts, Politics, Style, and Reception of the Television Series*. Ed. David P. Pierson, Lanham, MD: Lexinton, 2014. Print.

Calhoun, Craig. *Social Theory and the Politics of Identity*. Hoboken, NJ: Blackwell, 1994. Print.

Coffey, Bentley, and Patrick A. McLaughlin. "Do Masculine Names Help Female Lawyers Become Judges? Evidence from South Carolina." *American Law and Economics Review* (August 2009): 112–133. Print.

Eagly, Alice H., and Johnson, Blair T., "Gender and Leadership Style: A Meta-Analysis." Center for Health, Intervention, and Prevention. 1 January 1990. Web. CHIP Documents. Paper 11. August 2014.

Etcoff, Nancy. *Survival of the Prettiest: The Science of Beauty*. New York: Random House, 2011. Print.

"Fast Facts." National Center for Education Statistics. 2012. Web. June 2014.

Gilligan, Vince, prod. *Breaking Bad*. AMC Network, 2008–2013.

Hakim, Catherine. *Erotic Capital: The Power of Attraction in the Boardroom and the Bedroom*. New York: Basic Books, 2011. Print.

Judge, Timothy A., and Daniel M. Cable. "The Effect of Physical Height on Workplace Success and Income: Preliminary Test of a Theoretical Model." *Journal of Applied Psychology* (June 2004): 428–441. Print.

Keefe, Patrick Radden. "The Uncannily Accurate Depiction of the Meth Trade in *Breaking Bad*." *The New Yorker*. 13 July 2012. Web. August 2014.

Kimmel, Ellen B. "Engendered Lives." *Psychology of Women Quarterly* (December 1993): 547-549. Print.

Kray, Laura, Connson C. Locke, and Alex B. Van Zant. "Feminine Charm: An Experimental Analysis of Its Costs and Benefits in Negotiations." *Bulletin of Personality and Social Psychology* (19 July 2012): 1–15. Print.

Kurtz, Annalyn. "Why Secretary Is Still the Top Job for Women." *CNN Money*. 31 January 2013. Web. 24 June 2014.

Loden, Marilyn. Feminine Leadership. New York: Crown, 1985. Print.

Matthews, Dylan. "Here's What Breaking Bad Gets Right, and Wrong, about the Meth Business." *The Washington Post* 15 August 2013. Online. August 2014.

McWilliam, Erica, Alan Lawson, Terry Evans, and Peter G. Taylor. "'Silly, Soft and Otherwise Suspect': Doctoral Education as Risky Business." *Australian Journal of Education* (August 2005): 214–227.

"More Women Making It into Senior Management Roles—but Mature Economies Lagging Behind." Grant Thornton International Business Report. 8 March 2013. Web. August 2014.

Mosher, Donald L., and Mark Sirkin. "Measuring a Macho Personality Constellation." *Journal of Research in Personality* (September 1993): 150–163. Print.

Person, Ethel S. "Male Sexuality and Power." *Psychoanalytic Inquiry* (20 October 2009): 3–25. Print.

Putnam, Linda, and J. Stephen Heinen. "Women in Management—Fallacy of Trait Approach." *MSU Business Topics* 24.3 (1976): 47–53.

Sanchez, Laura. "Gender, Labor Allocations, and the Psychology of Entitlement within the Home." *Social Forces* (December 1994): 533–553. Print.

Scheuble, Laurie K., and David R. Johnson. "Married Women's Situational Use of Last Names: An Empirical Study." *Sex Roles* (July 2005): 143–151.

Machiavellian Men

How Walter White Learns "Not to Be Good"

STEPHANIE STRINGER GROSS

"Uncle Hank said, 'The good guys never get ink like the bad guys do.'" Walter White, Jr.

The Power of (Mis)Interpretation

One of the many startling turning points in the complex narrative of *Breaking Bad* is when Hank finds the copy of Whitman's *Leaves of Grass* on the back of Walt's toilet and makes a connection between his brother-in-law Walter, the murdered chemist Gale, and Heisenberg (508, "Gliding Over All"). Whitman's poem, "When I heard the learn'd astronomer," is not only a key clue to the mystery of Walter White's place in ASAC Schrader's investigation, but is an articulation of the speaker's objection to a discourse of science which obfuscates rather than clarifies, and which privileges the arcana of scientific reason over an ability to experience that which is outside that reason. The poem is a kind of metonymic signifier of the struggle between the cold hearted rationality that drives Walter White, and the humanistic tenderness he professes but does not actually embody, or at least not often. Whitman writes, and, in "Sunset" (306) we hear Gale recite:

> When I heard the learn'd astronomer,
> When the proofs, the figures, were ranged in columns before me,
> When I was shown the charts and diagrams, to add, divide, and measure them,

When I sitting heard the astronomer where he lectured with much
    applause
In the lecture-room,
How soon unaccountable I became tired and sick,
Till rising and gliding out I wander'd off my myself,
In the mystical moist night-air, and from time to time,
Look'd up in perfect silence at the stars.

Just as Hank has added up the evidence and studied the charts and diagrams, but now suddenly apprehends the whole from a new and shocking perspective with the very presence of the book of poetry in his hands— instead of a theory about its meaning— the careful viewer comes to understand that both the poem and book it is printed in have been misinterpreted and mistaken as a reification of the power of science and scientific discourse over more basic human concerns— by both Walt and the unfortunate Gale, and even by Hank in a different context. Hank has seen the evidence of such a book before, but his primary instinct is to dismiss Walt, as a scientist, from an association with a book of poetry. The inscription: "to W.W.—my star, my *other* perfect silence," shows how Gale has misinterpreted the poem, and, in his adulation of Walter White, has encouraged Walt in his pride. By flattering Walt as a scientist, and a perfectionist, (and, perhaps, even as God-like), Gale has steered Walt's interpretation towards one which feeds his ego and Walt is even less likely to read the poem as a challenge to his choices. While Walt interprets the poem as validating his choices, Hank reads it initially as the kind of humanism that just does not connect with what he knows about Walt.

    While it might seem odd to think of science as "arcana," because its outcomes are supposed to be objective, verifiable, repeatable, and "true," science also can represent an impenetrable maze of facts, statistics, and conflicting studies. Indeed, the very nature of science refutes any firm and transcendent "truth" because its method is observation and discovery of the unknown based on hypotheses that by their very nature must be altered with each new discovery. "Science" therefore is not a set of fixed truths or mere verifiable facts, but a process, always becoming. The scientific discourse that surrounds the scientific method, and the reasoning which informs it, has nonetheless ascended to a place of hegemonic discourse in ways that obfuscates the value of art, philosophy, vulnerability, love, compassion and whatever insight a poet like Whitman might find in that mystical night air away from the proofs and figures, charts and diagrams. The discourse of scientific rationalism furthermore clams its power from "truth," that is, "certainty" including the certainty of scientific laws, how they function, and the materialist certainty that this world is all there is of reality. As Darryl J. Murphy argues in "Heisenberg's Uncertain Confession," Walt's refusal to address the 0.111958 percent discrepancy between the intact human body and the body's chemical footprint reveals him as a materialist. But the missing percentage above points to a hole in the materialist theory: and Murphy and other philosophers might argue for the "soul" (an hypothesis Gretchen offers in the flashback where she wears stars on her shirt and speaks of "the soul" while Walt insists upon "chemistry" i.e., sex) or "free will" that enables the kind of autonomy of action and identity that Walt will ultimately employ as he adopts the Heisenberg identity. Murphy argues, and I agree, that Walt's dilemma is at least partially one of not wanting to feel guilt (16, 20). He wants the spoils and redemption too.

This is, of course, why Niccolò Machiavelli, as far back as 1539 when *The Prince* was first published, exhorts his prince with the adage that one has to "learn not to be good." Learning how to deal with an inconvenient conscience and the need to redefine "morality" is foregrounded in *Breaking Bad* from the first episode in season one and continues as a theme through the Krazy–8 debacle, the deaths of Combo and Jane, the airline crash, Hank's demise, and Jesse's various hospitalizations and eventual slavery. With free will comes a lack of determinism, a hole in Walter White's materialist viewpoint, and with that comes the possibility that Walt can always turn it around, leaving him with a deluded sense of control. Nonetheless, the audience watches Walt resolve repeatedly to get out, to be honest with his family, to walk away— only to see him give in to the enticements of his own sense of empowerment and ego.

Walt not only has to learn how not to be good, he has to deal with his early blunders, and must adopt a new identity and "morality" in order to learn how to build his own empire. In doing so he employs the explicitly Machiavellian "male" methods of acquiring power. Machiavellian methods and discourse are, by the era of late capitalism, so deeply embedded and so unchallenged they seem unassailable, even necessary if one is not to be perceived as naïve. David Mamet has addressed this in his first film, *House of Games,* when the con artists are pulling in a mark in a staged poker game and she sees what they are really up to, her objections are met with a round of voices (many unattached to any identifiable figure in the room) chanting, "It was only business," "It was only business," "Nothing personal," "It was only business." *Breaking Bad* interrogates, among other things, the Machiavellian morality underneath the business of empire building (including controlling the means of production and distribution), the bribery (and worse) connected to these, the exploitation of international law, and the reality of "collateral damage." In the Machiavellian discourse of autonomy, pragmatic cruelty, and violent attack on "Fortune" (married to the hegemonic discourse of science and business), we see Walt find a path forward. But the writers brilliantly use literature and the arts of film and music to critique the claims of a mostly unchallenged discourse of "science" in the service of such Machiavellian business strategies.

Scientific discourse, and the instrumental reason which accompanies it, has historically been the province of the few—those entrusted with its secrets and passed down through many centuries in a variety of ways and in secrecy for a variety of reasons. Before its current centrality in the age of scientific rationalism that followed the Enlightenment, it was particularly embedded within the secrets of states or societies—especially when it challenged official institutional (often religious) doctrine. What the poet Whitman's narrator is finally led to, however, are the *limits* of scientific discourse—its inhibiting schematism, its impulse to dominate, quantify, and explain. These limits are what Wordsworth called our urge to "murder to dissect" things like experience of the sublime, existential and humanistic truths, life itself; that which cannot be divided, measured, and added up into anything tangibly material but which holds just as much value as the quantifiable. These values, ironically, are what Walter White tells himself he is working for, and what his methods are helping him to achieve. Thus, the humanistic "mystical" experience confronts the "mystery" of scientific arcana, used for practical, often brutal ends.

Whitman's speaker only looks up "from time to time" at the stars in his escape from the lecture hall of instrumental reason. He does not always hold his object of study in view but rather holds "perfect silence" in the "mystical moist night air." At such moments, he allows emotion, unstructured thought, and a sense of the sublime—not irrational but extra-rational— to envelop him. Despite adopting the Heisenberg name, with its connotations of uncertainty, Walter White reads Whitman much differently. His identification with the poem comes from its individualistic move, the "gliding out" and wandering "off by myself," not into contemplation (as I contend Whitman suggests), but into a place where the learn'd and he can "master" the secrets of nature. It is a fantasy of gathering accolades as a rugged individualistic practitioner of the truths of science with access to its secrets. As Gale recites the poem, we see Walt's ego investment, his pride (that first of all mortal sins) in his reaction. Both men misinterpret Whitman's meaning and this blind attachment to a faulty interpretation can help us understand Walt's metamorphosis into Heisenberg. His inability to read the art of Whitman, to understand the humanistic discourse which confronts the hegemony of an urge to dominate nature and to rely on scientific certainty leads him further into a masterful, possessive, competitive, ego-driven masculinity that is reinforced—even required—by the dominant discourse of science. With no apparent ability to reflect[1] on literature and art, Walt more easily adopts Machiavellian traits of power-seeking. He is already eager to learn the arcana of science and state secrets. It is his second nature to employ scientific rationalism. He slips easily into the histories of those men who embody a perverse notion Machiavelli terms "*virtù*." Rather than reading about the "good guys," as Hank encourages Walt Jr. to do by giving him a history of those who brought down the notorious drug lord Escobar, Walt studies the histories and methods of Machiavellian-type heroes, or "excellent men of *virtù*." Walt models himself after the World War II men whose artillery gun could hit a target 23 miles away when he uses thermite. He styles himself after the KGB assassin who uses ricin against a Bulgarian journalist. He learns from Tuco Salamanca to strike with no warning (significantly, while the soundtrack plays Gnaris Barkley's "Who's Gonna Save My Soul Now?" [107, "A No-Rough-Stuff Type Deal"]). This shows nowhere more clearly than the day he comes home and cries on Skyler's shoulder, but then quickly moves to mask his own fear and self-contempt by moving to sexual dominance. The near-rape of Skyler in the kitchen is a disturbing moment for many reasons, but what we see is an internal encounter between the Walt who has rejected machismo as a product of his education and the effective modeling of machismo he has just witnessed watching Tuco kill No-Doze in the junkyard. He is fast concluding that yes, it is, as Machiavelli says, "better to be feared than loved." Not only is it a strategy for staying in business, building or keeping an empire, but is a defense against feelings of powerlessness. We watch his face as he struggles between the choices, finally opting for violence against his own pregnant wife. He lifts Gus Fring's cautious hiding-in-plain-sight strategy and negotiating strategies: ruthlessly play people, and always have a backup plan. He learns from the Cartel actors (the Cousins and Don Eladio) who employ horrifying yet bathetic, over-the-top symbolic statements like "Tortuga." Finally, Walt, thinking he has learned enough and mastered the game, employs Nazi skinheads as his mercenary proxy army (both in "Gliding Over All" and, accidentally, when Hank is killed) benefitting from their philosophy of ruthlessness but, ultimately, no match for it.

Learning from history is exactly what Machiavelli tells his would-be princes to do. In 1539 he advocated a hard realism and efficient, pragmatic action that could not afford idealism. A prince should "read histories and consider in them the action of excellent men." A would-be prince should "examine the causes of their victories and losses ... and imitate the former. Above all he should do as some excellent man has done in the past who found someone to imitate" (60). Among Machiavelli's most basic premises is his belief that it is "more fitting to go directly to the effectual truth of the thing than to the imagination of it." In a direct challenge to Plato and others' "imagined republic and principalities that have never been seen or known to exist in truth," Machiavelli requires this kind of realism because

> it is so far from how one lives to how one should live that he who lets go of what is done for what should be done learns his ruin rather than his preservation. For a man who wants to make a profession of good in all regards must come to ruin among so many who are not good. Hence it is necessary to a prince, if he wants to maintain himself, to learn to be able not to be good, and use this and not use it according necessity [61].

Even Mike can see that Walt is a problem for everyone and that Walter's way of interpreting events (and his own place within them) is flawed. It's clear that Walt's knowledge of when to use strategies and when not to is pretty sketchy and an early clue to Walt's problem becomes apparent when we see him confronted with interpreting the poem. Walt, and of course Machiavelli, depend on the notion of individual autonomy and Whitman's poem does not threaten that. But the way Walt negotiates an interpretation of Whitman's poem is skewed towards reification of the power of the scientist and science itself, something Mike never buys into the way Jesse does. Walter simply does not possess the humanist's ability to read the poem's (very humanist) critique of power and the arcana which nourishes that power. Likewise, Mike sees that Walt has no ability to "read" scenarios and reality either. For Walt, as for Machiavelli, there is no world but this, no ideal community or republic, just whatever brutal realities surround us. Walt's reliance upon scientific and instrumental reason and his lack of humanistic sensibilities provide him no balance, no compass, and underscores his belief that even if his reality is not under his control, the solutions are available to be reasoned out by intellectual effort. Mike is probably the first to see that Walt's *hubris* is downright dangerous, not just a nuisance—and, of course Mike pays the ultimate price for Walt's lack of humanity. Read correctly, Whitman's poem could point Walt to the possibilities of things other than ego-invested applause for accomplishment. But this is not how Walt understands scientific discourse or science's power. While "Heisenberg" may signify the uncertainty principle, one thing Walt is certain about is the exact, stable nature of science and the power it provides the individual initiated into its arcana. Like a certain ex-president in a flight suit on an aircraft carrier under a victory banner, Walt's announcement to Sky-lar that "I won" is premature, misguided, and shows a profound misunder-standing of complexities that instrumental logic just cannot contain.

Magic, Mystery and Scientific Arcana

Walt of course denies that he has a personal stake, other than money, in his alchemy. He tells Gus in "Mas" (305), "You think I must have a selfishness about my own formula—an overweening pride that overwhelms my judg-ment." Gus is, of course, perceptive enough to be correct about this, but Walt is nowhere near ready to acknowledge it to himself, demonstrating his limited capacity for self-reflection and honesty. The bottom line, he tells Gus, is that "the chemistry must be respected." The science has an objective place outside humanistic concerns and, for Walt, it has laws of its own that are immutable. Only a master can know these laws, and only a master can utilize them and make them manifest. This self-delusion also grants Walt a sense of security as he goes down an increasingly chaotic and unpredictable road.

The arcana of "science"—importantly, defined variously throughout his-tory as natural philosophy, magic, alchemy and the rigorously objective scien-tific method outlined by Leonardo—and its use as a means to power can be found, of course, as far back as Asclepius. In *The Golden Ass*, the wrong potion turns Lucius into a jackass instead of an owl (Apuleius 71). Much the same happens in alchemical fables and fairy tales right into the early modern and Romantic periods of literature with characters such as Victor Frankenstein and Faust. It's not a stretch to claim that the science that Walt practices is a sort of alchemy. Like Gretchen and Elliot, Walt is turning dross into gold. Though we are never told explicitly what Walt did at Los Alamos, two very significant things have happened there: cancer research and weapons research. Science is associated with power over life and death in this lab, and whatever role Walt played while there could only have reinforced his sense that science is the key to most anything. As the gun and vest dealer in the back of the truck acknowledges to the Cousins, "Science is a mystery!" (307, "One Minute"). Gale and Walt are even more explicit. After they meet in the lab, and just before Gale recites Whitman, Walt brings up the question of how Gale ended up doing what he's doing instead of working in a legitimate lab:

> **GALE:** I love the lab, because it's all still ... magic.
> **WALT:** Yes. It *is* magic. It still is [306 "Sunset"].

The context for this conversation, and the poetry recitation, is of course a discussion of criminality, as well as Gale's frustration with the business of science as opposed to the practice of it in academia. But, as it has for centuries, magic legitimizes what the two are doing; it has its own secret, and often illicit, rules. (Ironically, Gale's libertarian politics take care of the collateral damage, he thinks).[2] And the scientific rationalism that allows them to continue on in the name of science, magic and mystery also has its rules. Before further examining Walt's descent into Machiavellian manhood, it's worth looking at the notion of *arcana imperii* and its discursive history, as context for Walt's rationale and rules for building his empire.

After Machiavelli's *The Prince* was put on the Catholic Church's Index and banned, there were a number of somewhat surreptitious attempts to rehabilitate his ideas.[3] As one of a multitude of followers of Machiavelli, Gabriel Naudé, a century later, in his *Considerations politiques sur les coups d'etat* (published 1639) takes the notion of a *coup* and extends it beyond the blatant violence often advised by Machiavelli. In doing so, as Peter Donaldson argues, the idea of *coups d'états* "encompass[es] any extraordinary act by which a state, a religion, or a constitution is established" (141). It can, in this formulation, mean law-giving (such as Moses receiving the Law or Muhammad his *Suras*), the founding of Rome by Aeneas, or the Hebrew nation by Abraham—but it can also occur "whenever extraordinary or surprising means are employed to *maintain an existing state*" (141 emphasis mine). The notion of *coups d'états* during the Renaissance and its contemporary meaning have connotations of "intrigue, violence, and conspiratorial amorality" (142). Donaldson notes that as Naudé interprets Machiavelli through an ancient line of secrets of state, these "*arcana imperii*" and *coups d'états* actually work as synonyms, with "links to sacral kingship" as well as "to magic, hermetism, and the 'ancient wisdom' of Renaissance occultism" (142). The arcana of state secrets amounts to an ancient form of scientific reasoning, one formerly reserved for kings, gods and goddesses, or other mythical or legendary figures, and lays the foundation, Donaldson argues, for Machiavellian action as a kind of "mystery of state" to which the "magi" have access and the public should not. Naudé's view includes the notion that truth is obscured, and

> [his] history of thought is based upon [an] opposition between intellect and error. Wise men have often had to teach secretly and make a mystery of their learning so as to avoid persecution by an uncomprehending multitude ... caution was still necessary and always likely to be. The Renaissance itself is thus a flowering of ancient and secret intellectual traditions, which now can be made partly, though not completely, public [Donaldson 144].

Naudé's claim is that the early natural philosophers (here he includes Pythagoras and Socrates) were "magi" in a metaphorical sense, and out of cautious necessity taught "by cabal and tradition, secretly and to disciples, not daring to divulge their doctrine to the people who were, in all eras, convinced that only rash and impious men would investigate the reasons for all the extraordinary effects that depended upon the immediate will of their gods," and that the "Philosophers wished to demonstrate in Nature" the causes attributed to the gods (Donaldson 145).

An assumption underlying these claims is that the Middle Ages was a time of superstition and intellectual darkness from which men were only beginning to emerge (religious spirituality being another form of superstition for Naudé, as well as for his hero Machiavelli), though a few "spirited men" like "brilliant stars" shown but were invariably persecuted. As Naudé claims,

> Before the humanities and good letters had been rendered common and available to everyone by the felicity of our last century [the 16th], all those who delighted in cultivating and polishing them were reputed grammarians and heretics; those who penetrated further into the understanding of natural causes passed for ... irreligious, and those who researched mathematics and the less common sciences were taken for enchanters and magicians, although this was a pure calumny, founded on the ignorance of the vulgar or the envy it always bears toward great people [qtd. in Donaldson 145–46].

Thus, even as the Renaissance progresses towards the Enlightenment and beyond, the need for "educating" in secrecy remains. Donaldson outlines how Naudé accepts that "secret wisdom is passed on in disciplic succession" but sees that wisdom "as knowledge of natural rather than supernatural causes." Donaldson demonstrates that Naudé exchanges "the vocabulary of magic" with "terms like *mystere d'etat*, *secrets d' etats*, and *arcana imperii*" and that he who practices these is "set apart from the common people, [and knows] how supernatural manifestations may be simulated by natural means, *uses his knowledge to gain political control over others, and has the boldness and moral courage to use it despite the taboos, moral hesitancies, and superstitions that keep others from using it*" (183 emphasis mine). Donaldson claims, "Machiavelli's founder of new modes and orders, too, is a natural magician ... and creates fictions of the supernatural." Furthermore,

> Machiavelli is sometimes read as if he were the originator of a technology of politics, or a positive science, in which effective procedures for achieving political ends are explored without reference to the kind of person one would need to be to use them. But Machiavelli's interest in the moral or psychological aspect of his subject is signaled in many ways [184].

In fact, Machiavelli never discusses "technique in isolation from moral and psychological questions." A person like Walt must ready himself to take on such methods—particularly since Walt, like *Breaking Bad*'s audience, lives in a world which ostensibly believes in justice, in moral imperatives, and in humane behavior, if not always in divine law. Machiavelli believes in none of these things. For Machiavelli and his successors, science becomes arcana and takes on the mystique of those magi who have access to it (147). Science, as the persecuted stepchild of the intellect, is rife with knowledge that is not just powerful, but dangerous. Scientific knowledge becomes conflated with power and the secrets of state—right down to Walter White.

The arcana of alchemical forces and the more modern arcana of charts, diagrams, and quantitative data is, by the nineteenth and twentieth centuries, a scientific rationalism that holds hegemonic cultural power. It trumps the humanistic and qualitative forms of knowledge. By the twentieth century, science has somewhat shed its mystical, imaginative and less linear approaches to problems and ethics (there are notable exceptions to this of course). Our more modern version of science (widely critiqued since its inception and vilified by postmodernists and religious fundamentalists alike) still holds the promise of a quintessential, autonomous freedom for Walt. It is an odd but real legacy from Machiavelli and later Renaissance thought. Walt's hubris is thinking he can, as a modern scientist following the scientific and *arcana imperii* of Machiavellian tactics, through reason alone, fully self-fashion. Walt becomes convinced that he can enact Machiavellian arcana, rely on the secrets both of state building and science—imitated, transmitted, and enacted in secret—and somehow prevail against Fortune, as if he were one of Machiavelli's princes or excellent men of "virtue." It behooves Walter to believe in that chemical "hole" in the calculation of the human since it could turn out to be the polar opposite of fortune: free will. Free will offers him the possibility not only of self-fashioning as a kingpin, an empire builder, but also a way back to a kind of goodness.[4] But, intriguingly, Walter also is discomfited by this choice. At times it is easier, much easier, to blame "fortune," or fate, and he does so when he looks for absolution, to shed responsibility, or to rationalize what he "had to do." Blaming "Fortune" is actually a very medieval move.

Fortune Is a Woman

Walt's transition to Machiavellianism is not easy, nor is it as quick as it may seem to some viewers. Reason often leads him to murder, but will not absolve him, and Walt remains shaken. In flipping a coin to determine who will kill Krazy–8, Walt initially (as he will throughout the course of *Breaking Bad*) tries to avoid responsibility by conjuring Fortune (fate) to absolve him. By attempting to make himself a mere victim of chance (for instance when he and Jesse are locked inside the RV with Hank outside) Walt gets Saul to do the dirty work of calling Hank's cell phone with the news of Marie's "accident." But Walt can also credit "Fortune" (this time "good" luck) when the owner of the lot happens to know and confront Hank with the law. Walt again plays with Fortune when he frantically tries to convince Jesse that he (Walt) had no responsibility in the poisoning of Brock, rhetorically placing himself as a victim of circumstance, just as Brock is. And worse, Walt removes himself from the ethical consequences of the murder of Gale, shifting that responsibility onto Jesse. He stands by and lets Jane die, setting into motion circumstances that will kill hundreds of people and traumatize many hundreds more. More fundamentally, Walt blames Gretchen and Elliot for his fate as a high school "overqualified" teacher, living paycheck to paycheck. He ignores the fact that he has chosen to refuse their money and insists that fate pushing him becoming a drug manufacturer to "providing for his family." In each of these situations, Walt manages to convince himself and/or others that he is somehow the victim of (mis)fortune. He speaks of "choice" during the Talking Pillow episode, and with his psychiatrist at the hospital, but he imagines that choice only one way: the way that will build his adrenaline and ego. It will be some time until Walter White is ready to commit to the choices he has made by accepting responsibility for them.

Ironically, as the coin toss in the second episode in season one shows, Walt feels as if he has gained some control by *giving up* control to fate—or an abstract "Fortune" as Machiavelli terms it. Walt seizes upon the idea that his act of murder is only self-defense when he discovers the missing piece of pottery, Krazy–8 has pocketed. The act of murder then takes on a different moral significance: it had to be done "to protect his family." It is now out of Fortune's hands, and Walter, like Machiavelli, has essentially redefined virtue—as Peter Donaldson cogently names it, "revers[ing] the moral sign" (viii). He must do this again and again in his attempt to build up his "virtù." Fortune sets the stakes, but Machiavelli is quite clear about the extent of Fortune's power: Machiavelli "judge[s] that it might be true that fortune is arbiter of half of our actions, but also that she leaves the other half, or close to it, for us to govern." Here he uses the idea of "free will" which God has given us (in other words, he coopts the religious rhetoric of the time and turns it back on itself) in order to justify men's ability to take hold of their own fate. Fortune, he claims, acts like a violent, "enraged" flood and one must, when things are quieter, provide dikes and dams: "It happens similarly with fortune, which demonstrates her power where virtue has not been put in order to resist her and therefore turns her impetus where she knows that dams and dikes have not been made to contain her" (99). Machiavelli has just effectively wrested God's will out of His hands and put it in the hands of "a woman." Clearly, a woman is what cannot be controlled and contained. In *Breaking Bad*, we could see this applied to cancer, to finances, to health care, to a stunted career, the law, a broken down RV that won't start in the desert, to whomever seems to have power over Walt (and the list gets longer): Tuco, Gus, the Cousins, Skyler, Hank, Mike, Lydia, young dead boys and their killers, Uncle Jack— even Jesse.

But, these proactive provisions Machiavelli mentions, analogous to the "virtues" men hold in order to gain "glories and riches," may be different for each prince depending upon circumstances. "The prince who leans entirely on his fortune comes to ruin," but others are happy and successful regardless of how they proceed, whether cautiously, through violence, art or patience, so long as each uses the tools, *virtù*, fit for the "quality of the times" (99). Therefore, an ambitious man like Walt must adjust to the times in order to succeed. He may not remain the same: a man, claims Machiavelli, is ruined when "he cannot deviate from what nature inclines him to or also because, when one has always flourished by walking on one path, he cannot be persuaded to depart from it" (100). We see this change reflected in Skyler's shock as she learns what Walt has been up to and in Gretchen's interrogation of Walt when they meet in "Peekaboo" (206). Gretchen asks, "What happened to you? This isn't you." Walter has indeed adapted. He has learned Machiavellian masculinity: to cultivate "arms," to become ruthless, and to forge a new identity complete with a new morality in order to beat Fortune. He must be aggressive, not passive, and must "command" her rather than let her call the shots.

Machiavelli ends this section on how much fortune can do in human affairs with the famous exhortation to be "impetuous" rather than "cautious," because (naturally),

> Fortune is a woman; and it is necessary, if one wants to hold her down, to beat her and strike her down. And one sees that she lets herself be won more by the impetuous than by those who proceed coldly. And so always, like a woman, she is the friend of the young, because they are less cautious, more ferocious, and command her with more audacity [101].

Whatever *ressentiment* Walt carried for the previous years has been tamped by a repressive lid which blows under the pressure of his diagnosis. In Season 2, Episode 3, "Bit by a Dead Bee," Walt describes his Fortune to the hospital's psychiatrist, after his supposed fugue state:

> Doctor, my wife is seven months pregnant with a baby we did not intend. My son has cerebral palsy. I am a vastly overqualified high-school chemistry teacher who makes 43,700 dollars a year, when I can work. All of my colleagues and friends have surpassed me in every way imaginable, and, in eighteen months I will be dead. And you me ask why I ran?

This is, of course, only a half-truth, and another of Walt's attempts to blame Fortune for his decisions, but at some level it may be the truth underlying all the other reasons to run that Walt's escapades up to now have created. Walt knows he can count on masculine norms embedded in manly rhetoric to influence how the psychiatrist will respond to such a plight. Walt knows he can count on the male psychiatrist to understand that "he just couldn't be in that house another minute." This does not necessarily mean Walt is telling the truth; we know why he's been out of the house and stripping off his clothes in the market. But, the norms of modern masculinity are so strong that both these educated men know this is a plausible excuse; Walt enough to play it, the doctor—and the audience— enough to at least admit the possibility that Walt is telling "the truth." Domesticity is what kills the masculine spirit, makes him "effeminate," in Machiavellian terms, and therefore Walt must find a way to control his fate. If Fortune is a woman, then it is time to face her head on and beat and strike her to hold her down. Walt may sometimes mistake Skyler for Lady Fortune, as he does with Gretchen, but he is fighting something larger which comes not from the restrictions of his marriage, but from modernity's masculine norms. The injunctions of this masculine ethos will devour every male in the series in some way: Hank, Gomez, Jesse, Tuco, Hector, Gus, Todd, even Andrea's little brother Tomas. A man doesn't just provide, as Gus would have Walt do, a Machiavellian man has to assert his will. Fortune has dealt Walt some pretty tough blows, and he needs a strategy to strike her down.

The "Real" Walter White?

One of the ironies of *Breaking Bad* is that Walt, before we see him with Jesse, seems to have made peace with his fortune (his career, his marriage, his son's disability) even if he is frustrated and worried about money. Before his transformation into Heisenberg, Walt seems patient, attentive and kind. He seems to have chosen, for the most part, to operate outside the hegemonic norms of macho, Machiavellian masculinity. That does not, of course, mean that he is unaware of them. The pressure to pursue wealth, to compete, and to win is always on and takes the form of the "indestructible" Hank (who also feels these pressures, in some ways more because of his success). But Walt's masculine role in the family seems to have been what the late 20th and early 21st centuries have deemed more enlightened: more partner than patriarch, a caring teacher, a "good man" by all accounts, someone Hank doesn't fully relate to but respects as "the smartest guy I know." The pressure though, is what leads him to rebel in "Ken Wins," and it's what leads the audience to cheer him on. We all know that obnoxious guy with the Bluetooth and the fancy car who is rude to everyone but especially anyone he deems beneath him (pretty much everyone). Not only do we know him, we hate him but we also chafe at the idea that we should somehow be working to *be* him. And, if we aren't, we "should" be. We may not envy his personality or his morality, but we sure want his stuff, because that's the spoils of a postmodern, capitalist war of all against all. Machiavelli championed this and in fact, helped legitimize it, over five centuries ago. Our *ressentiment* aligns quite closely with Walt's here, as we are all products of the conflicting messages that make up modern capitalism.

Given Walt's former ability to create himself as father, husband, and teacher against many of the traditional codes of masculinity inherent in the culture, the viewer is of course encouraged to wonder who Walt "really" was/is as his transformation happens before our eyes. Was he a good guy? Really? Even as theorists like Teresa de Lauretis and Judith Butler argue that gender is performative, theatrical, and not essential, without origin, only enactment; we can actually see the roots of this idea much earlier in Machiavelli's idea of agency. Before we meet him, Walt had chosen to enact his masculinity in the ways that he did, perhaps under an illusion, Machiavelli would say, that he had less autonomy to change things that he thought. He bought into the perception that he was subject to Fortune and had forgotten where free will could take him. But if there is no "essential" Walt, then there are few barriers to him moving into a new identity, performing an all-too-recognizable form of masculinity by following an age-old formula. Walt must, as Machiavelli exhorts, "learn not to be good."

Besides enabling him to impressively blow things up, chemically disincorporate bodies, make the perfect blue crystal, or pull off the great train robbery, Walt's scientific accomplishments are more than chemical transformations: they are the fulfillment of all magical fantasies, the ultimate in alchemical abilities. But to turn chemical science into gold regardless of the cost to the larger community or to his own family requires him to also reinvent himself and by modeling his methods on the Machiavellian mystery: the *coups d'état* secrets of state building All the while, he must suppress and beat down the woman, Fortune. Michael Palmer argues that from his point of view

> Machiavelli is a radically revolutionary thinker who breaks with classical political thought in both its pagan and its Christian forms, breaks with so-called Renaissance humanism.... My Machiavelli is an atheist. He is, moreover, more anti–Christian than antipapist, anticlerical, or antireligion, above all, he is radically anti–Christ. Machiavelli is the thinker who introduced the modern "truths" that Nietzsche takes to be so deadly: the sovereignty of becoming over being; the fluidity of all concepts; the lack of any cardinal difference between man and animal [80].

Palmer asserts that this is an irrevocable and *positive* turn into what we now consider modernity. This kind of ability to self-fashion is underscored in Machiavelli's advice: one should break free of religious idealism and remake himself according to circumstance. Palmer sees this fluidity of morality and identity as ultimately optimistic, giving humans a new sense of agency. But Machiavelli's methods depend utterly upon a bleak view of human possibility and human nature in general. Machiavelli sees his prince (or any prince) in the position of "trying to protect his interests in a dark world filled with unscrupulous men" (Skinner 42). Rationality and morality are often incompatible in this world (as Walter White has found out early in the series) and Machiavellian amorality is a specifically *realistic* justification for a man to acquire what he needs. Machiavelli writes, "And if all men were good, this teaching would not be good; but because they are wicked and do not observe faith with you, you also do not have to observe it with them" (69).

We have already seen Walt try to use reason to determine his morality: resorting first to a list with two columns in a kind of moral calculus and then flipping a coin. Walt moves from "what ought to be done" to "what needs to be done" in "reality" as if he has taken control of the situation. However, the extreme close-up shot of the coin in "Cat's in the Bag" also marks Walt's turn to Fortune both as a way out (an evasion of responsibility) *and* a commitment to making money at whatever cost (to "provide for his family"). Yet by continuing to blame Fortune ("I can't be the bad guy" [302, "Caballeros si Nombre"]), Walt will not acknowledge his Machiavellian move. When using reason alone doesn't bring him to an acceptable moral conclusion, he paradoxically redefines himself over and over as a victim of Fortune, thereby alleviating his conscience but at the same time preventing himself from taking real control of his situation. In effect, what Walt faces in "Cat's in the Bag" and many other episodes throughout *Breaking Bad* is the most basic, inescapable dilemma Machiavelli has articulated for those who would be a new prince: he must "not depart from good, when possible, but *know how to enter into evil*, when forced by necessity" (70).

As the series progresses, Walt is in flux, and his identity becomes more and more negotiable as his life plays out and "necessity" forces him to "enter into evil." His actions show that he is giving up ideals which arguably had previously defined his masculinity and is facing Fortune head on. Walt has shocked himself. He's also been shocked and traumatized by what he has seen and he is utterly terrified and anxiety ridden. The overhead shot of the industrial wasteland surrounding Walt and Jesse in the junkyard where they've witnessed Tuco's rage against No-Doze's perceived insubordination is a stunning picture of the remnants of a civilization built on carnage. The extreme overhead long shot of Walt and Jesse wandering through the desert after fleeing Hank at Hector's, after their abduction by Tuco shows us the amoral wasteland the two have entered, more hellish than they'd signed up for. They try to pick their way back to a familiar road with no landmarks, no sense of direction. The junkyard in particular resembles a pillaged medieval village at the same time it resembles a post-apocalyptic ruin. The desert, on the other hand, is a postmodern wilderness much, much bigger than Walt but Walt has decided to play by the rules and, as Saul says to Jesse, "go with the winner." The refashioning of his masculinity will be lucrative, at least for a while, and will be a validation for Walt's ego once he lets go of his "good." After Walt leaves the hospital to sneak into his own house to hide his money, he needs to catch a bus back. Sitting in the shelter, he spots one of the "Missing" flyers Walter Jr. had printed. The camera shows Walt gazing at it, and as we see it from behind and through the glass, we know that Walter himself wonders if he's gone missing.

Walter White: Man of Machiavellian Virtue

Michael Palmer claims, in *Masters and Slaves: Revisioned Essays in Political Philosophy*, that in order to understand Machiavelli, the "fortune-versus-virtue–dichotomy ... proves to be fundamental to the deepest teaching of *The Prince*" (80). Besides Machiavelli's contention that the "desire for acquisition" is a "very natural and ordinary thing" (Machiavelli 14) and that it is preferable to strike first, with deadly force (Machiavelli 37) than to turn the other cheek, Machiavelli also redefines virtue as a quality that those acquire not by Fortune but by arms (i.e., the means to violence and the use of violence). In effect, Machiavelli equates virtue with the proper use of arms (Palmer 82). Virtue is also attainable by being in a constant "state of war," thinking about and planning for war. Those who acquire a state by inheritance or through other Fortune are not particularly virtuous—they have not demonstrated their excellence through arms and violence. In Chapter 8 of *The Prince*, "Of Those Who Have Attained a Principality through Crimes," Machiavelli describes Agathocles, who "kept to a life of crime at every rank of his career; nonetheless, his crimes were accompanied with such virtue of spirit" that he is considered one of the most excellent men. It is in Machiavelli's passage above that the distinction between crime and virtue breaks down. Michael Palmer gives a reading of this passage, which does not equate the "glory" of such a man with betrayals or denial of mercy. But, Palmer claims, "Machiavelli's point is that Agathocles was, in fact, 'virtuous,'" even if not "glorious," "but the prevailing modes of moral discourse do not 'permit' his virtue to be 'celebrated.' This mode of moral discourse is what Machiavelli intends to change.... To effect this change, Machiavelli must introduce a new mode of moral discourse to replace the prevailing one" (Palmer 83). Machiavelli points out that Agathocles and those like him, despite cruelties and betrayals (which exclude them from the category of "glorious men") could live securely since theirs were "cruelties well used" and "done at one stroke" even though it may not be "permissible to speak well of evil" (Machiavelli 37–8). The fact is, Machiavelli does speak well of such evils, and conflates "one's own arms," "virtue," and "savage cruelty and inhumanity" (Palmer 83). Unlike Plato and others who have imagined ideal Republics and focused on the law which should govern them (drawing on the natural and philosophical sciences), Machiavelli intends a hard realism, and focuses his attention on arms: how to get them, who should use them, and how to use them effectively to acquire and to maintain one's principality, state or empire. Surely, by "Gliding Over All" Walter White has learned not to be good: he has become a man, not glorious, but capable of the inhuman cruelties Machiavelli attributes to his version of virtuous men. However, once again, Walt will claim that it "had to be done"—that an external force of some kind is determining his choices. His distancing himself from the action is not a simple act of legal self-protection, it is also an emotional and ethical self-protection. Since it clear that Gus makes decisions based on cold calculations such as Machiavelli propounds, and that Walt is learning from Gus, even as he fears him, it's safe to say that Walt is still learning as we go into Season Five. He still has not been able to fully take responsibility for his decisions and actions. Gus, ever the business man, negotiates, strikes hard and fast when necessary, uses children if need be to send a message or control a population, but he never pretends to be anything other than what he is to himself, so far as we can tell. In another mirroring scene, when Walt loses his argument with Uncle Jack to not shoot Hank, we see Walt in the pose we once saw Gus in, with his partner at Don Eladio's (on his side, face against the ground, weeping) after his friend had been shot by Hector Salamanca. It's the only time we see Gus helpless and Walt mirrors this when he finally faces the fact that he has destroyed everything he thought he cared about.

Machiavelli is of course writing advice to a prince—Lorenzo de'Medici—and those who would be princes: builders of states and empires who begin their efforts in a variety of circumstances. Walter White's empire building, his first attempted *coups d'états*, begins first as an infiltration, then as a takeover of an existing "state," first Tuco and his Tio Hector Salamanca's drug empire. His second, of course, is Gus Fring's. Then he must try to maintain what he has usurped before deciding to build an empire of his own, larger than either of those he has managed to infiltrate, destroy or acquire. In order to succeed in each of these cases, Walter discovers he must utilize Machiavellian strategies. He must reinterpret the idea, as Machiavelli famously does, of virtue, and he must become a specific type of "man"—one who knows

> how to avoid the infamy of those vices that would take his state from him and to be on guard against those that do not [have qualities that are deemed good]. And, furthermore one should not care about incurring the fame of those vices without which it is difficult to save one's state; for if one considers everything well, one will find something appears to be virtue, which if pursued would be one's ruin, and something else appears to be vice, which if pursued results in one's security and well-being [62].

Walt's attempt at a moral calculus, an actual two- columned list very much like the charts of Whitman's "learn'd astronomer," is his rational, and instrumental, approach to deciding whether or not to murder Krazy–8, and this inserts us into the Machiavellian dilemma early on in *Breaking Bad*. If we haven't yet realized that Walt is a man who has had some kind of moral conscience before, by "Cat's in the Bag," (S1 E2) it is unambiguous.

The Man in the Mirror

As Walter has shown his chemistry class in a lesson on mirrored isomers, transformation can happen even when things look identical; underneath appearances are secret forces at work for which we cannot always account. Walt's transformation to a darker consciousness takes place visually in "Cat's in the Bag." The *mise-en-scène* depicts Walt on his descent down, into Jesse's basement where Krazy–8 is locked to a pole. On the way down the stairs, Walt's shadow looms behind him, much larger than Walt himself, and both figure and shadow move from right to left, against our visual tracking conventions, pulling the viewer into a sense of foreboding while watching Walt project a darkness much larger than his actual person. Walt may be bringing Krazy–8 sandwiches with the crusts cut off to convince himself of his residual humanity, but the looming shadow of him in the background signifies that he is negotiating the boundaries between how he should act and how he might decide to act. In other words, we see Walt begin to redefine virtue and vice as those actions which either do or do not result in his self-preservation—a precept Machiavelli unapologetically posits as the basis for the success of his prince. We see Walt's cough mimics Krazy–8's and then, as Krazy–8's gets better, Walter's gets worse. Walt then begins to adopt the characteristics of the criminals he encounters. He begins to cut the crusts off his own sandwiches (in imitation of Krazy–8). He wears a yellow shirt like Gus' in "Gliding Over All." He folds a towel to kneel on while vomiting in his bathroom after he's back on chemo—a bit of mirroring that leads him to discover his volume of *Leaves of Grass* has gone missing. Walter White learns Machiavellian masculinity and follows the advice given to princes to imitate those who have come before. As even Jesse can see, once Tuco is dead, if they want to profit by selling their signature blue meth, "We've gotta *be* Tuco" (205, "Breakage").[5] In his mirroring of Machiavelli's self-defined "excellent men" Walt is attempting to learn how "not to be good."

But Walt also has a kind of internal mirroring. As *Citizen Kane's* Charles Foster Kane walks past an infinite regress of mirrors after his second wife leaves him, never even glancing into the depths, we often see Walter White catching sight of himself in some reflective surface. While normally this might signify a kind of inner questioning, an act of self-reflection, Walter's reaction is often anger at what he perceives. We see this in several ways: in the doctor's office washroom when he gets good news about his remission he unexpectedly and violently punches the towel holder when he sees his reflection in it. This could signify that he has realized he's been impetuous and gotten in over his head for no real reason, or it could signify his anger at being deprived of his rationale for continuing to cook. We are left with the ambiguity. Later, he sees the same towel holder with the damage to it still intact, and he examines it, as if he realizes there is no going back to a time when he had some kind of actual choice, a possibility he had not realized he had earlier. Walt also catches sight of himself in the double closet mirror, just as he makes contact with Todd on the phone. This moment begins the downward slide for Jesse and Hank—the moment which decides the fate of his place in the family. Walt turns away from his image as he dials Todd, as if to show his turn from what he has been into a kind of unknown, even more unrecognizable creature. There are times during the series when he cannot look at himself in the rear view mirror and even turns it away. As Walt turns into Heisenberg alternately revels in it and is violently repulsed by it. *Breaking Bad* has the guts to show us the double bind of those who come from within a culture that is at once founded on Judeo-Christian values (even if unofficial) and the Protestant work ethic, yet are pushed to sweep aside our consciences as we strive to succeed at all costs under (mostly) unarticulated and unacknowledged Machiavellian rules.

As Walter White learns by imitation and takes up arms, per Machiavelli's advice, he still finds himself without a real "army." As he attempts to consolidate his power towards the end of Season Five, his use of Uncle Jack and his gang of Skinheads as mercenary forces suits him. But Machiavelli warns against mercenaries. Machiavelli thinks that Italy has been ruined by "mercenary soldiers" and that one should be the "total owner of one's own arms" for greatest success (Palmer 84). At first, though, the grisly plan of the prison murders seems to work, and the soundtrack for "Gliding Over All"—"Pick Yourself Up" by Nat King Cole and George Shearing—in the montage reinforces the Machiavellian move.

At the end of Chapter 12 of *The Prince* (which concerns mercenary soldiers), Machiavelli exhorts "human beings to assassinate—to decapitate— God" (84). The notion of "good" becomes negotiable, and "appearances" of good are all that matter—as a strategy, not a moral imperative. In Chapter 18, Machiavelli discusses law and force in his famous "Foxes and Lions" passage and, as part of this, he observes the qualities that are useful—noting that not everyone will have all of them:

> Thus, it is not necessary for a prince to have all the above-mentioned qualities in fact, but it is indeed necessary to appear to have them. Nay, I dare say this, that by having them and always observing them, they are harmful; and by appearing to have them, they are useful, as it is to appear merciful, faithful, humane, honest, and religious, and to be so; but to remain with a spirit built so that, if you need not to be those things, you are able and know how to change to the contrary. ... he should appear all mercy, all faith, all honesty, all humanity, all religion [70].

This is a lesson Gus Fring has clearly learned, as he "hides in plain sight" among the DEA agents and hospital staff and the larger community. Walt must appear to have most of these to his family (including and especially his brother-in-law) in order to first survive as a cook and criminal, but later to ensure their cooperation. But in infiltrating Gus's empire enough to help bring it down, he resorts mainly to violence. With Jesse, however, Walt always needs to appear "all faith, all honesty, all humanity" in order to manipulate the younger man.

Even in Walt's final moments at the end of the entire series, his allegiance is to science and what he has accomplished through it: it has provided whatever meaning he takes with him to his grave, and it provides his ego the validation it requires—though he has lost everything else. Alternatively, to look up "in perfect silence" at the unattenuated stars, to let them speak, might offer a glimpse at the sublime and, therefore, some perspective—might hold the potential of igniting Walt's imagination in a way that isn't culturally mediated through a lens of scientific power. Instead, Walt caresses the cold stainless steel equipment before he succumbs to his wounds. Only lying on the ground in his final moment does he look up into the night sky, into that mystical moist night air.

Notes

1. Bryan Cranston has spoken to this issue in an interview conducted here: www.http://ohno theydidnt.livejournal.com/90146723.html
2. Aaron C. Anderson and Justine Lopez discuss Gale's politics, and Mill's "On Liberty" in an essay called "Meth, Liberty, and the Pursuit of Happiness" in *Breaking Bad and Philosophy*.
3. Some are also contemporary and not surreptitious at all. See, for example, Michael Palmer (quoted extensively above from his *Masters and Slaves: Revisioned essays in political philosophy*, and Robert A. Kocis in *Machiavelli Redeemed: Retrieving his humanist perspectives on equality, power, and glory*. Bethlehem: Lehigh UP. 1998.
4. Again, credit must go to *Breaking Bad and Philosophy* author Darryl J. Murphy's discussion of this.
5. And, interestingly enough, Jesse mirrors Walt when he strangles Todd in" Felina." This brings the narrative to something like full circle. We also witness Walt's murder weapon, the bike lock, left behind after Jesse's scooter has been stolen implying, of course, that the lock has reminded Jesse every day of the crime but nonetheless must be put to practical use. The leveling up of criminality, even for Jesse, has entered the mundane realm and has become entangled with anything previously thought of as "normal" life.

Works Cited

Apuleius. *The Transformation of Lucius, Otherwise Known as The Golden Ass*. Tran. Robert Graves. New York: Farrar, Straus and Giroux, 1979.
Donaldson, Peter. *Machiavelli and Mystery of State*. New York: Cambridge University Press, 1988.
Gilligan, Vince, prod. *Breaking Bad*. AMC Network, 2008–2013.
Machiavelli, Niccolò. *The Prince*. Trans. by Harvey C. Mansfield. Second edition. Chicago: Chicago University Press, 1998.

Mamet, David. *House of Games*. Screenplay. New York: Grove Weidenfeld, 1987.

Murphy, Darryl J. "Heisenberg's Uncertain Confession." *Breaking Bad and Philosophy*. Ed. David R. Keospell and Robert Arp. Chicago: Open Court, 2012.

Palmer, Michael. *Masters and Slaves: Revisioned Essays in Political Philosophy*. Lanham, MD: Lexington, 2001.

• ROUND TABLE DISCUSSION •

Skyler-Hating Online

Participants:

—Bridget Roussell Cowlishaw (BRC)

—Robert G. Weiner (RGW)

—Jeffrey Reid Pettis (JRP)

—R. Nicholas Gerlich (RNG)

—Stephanie Stringer Gross (SSG)

—Brian Cowlishaw (BC)

—Ian Dawe (ID)

BRIDGET ROUSSELL COWLISHAW: Given Anna Gunn's complaints about her "character issues" in her New York Times piece (*New York Times*, 24 August 2013), how would you explain the phenomenon of Skyler-hating? (For more on this issue, please see the annotated bibliography entries for Sarah Burke, Brendan Foley, Leigh Kolb, Amanda Marcotte, and Stephen Silver.)

ROBERT G. WEINER: I think the fact that so many have posted online that they hate Skyler is just indicative of certain aspects of the "dark" and immature side of online culture. It is NOT representative of all *Breaking Bad* online fans by any stretch. It reminds of me of the recent controversy surrounding comic book editor Janelle Asselin who argued that the cover of *Teen Titans #1* was basically a bad comics cover and sexist as well. For this, she received death and rape threats and some of the most horrible internet hate comments and mail imaginable. I think people are just so enamored with the character of Walter White that anyone who stands in his way is considered suspect especially his wife. Skyler is seen as an impediment to Walter's goals and ambitions. Despite the fact that he does bad things, we all root for him and not for Skyler.

JEFFREY REID PETTIS: This is an alarming phenomenon. I admit that after watching the first two seasons a few times I didn't care for Skyler (hate would be far too strong a word, though). I think part of the issue is that, as an audience, our focus is primarily on Walt, particularly in the early moments of the pilot. We see a series of vignettes right off the bat that illustrate how disempowered Walt is and how pathetic his life has become. At least in some ways, he is a relatable character. So, we like to see him empowered, but he empowers himself at the expense of others, and this is a fact that "bad fans" neglect when voicing their vitriol against Skyler and Anna Gunn.

BRIAN COWLISHAW: My essay pinpoints all the ways in which the pilot, and especially its first fifteen minutes, establish Skyler as emasculating. She is presented as a hefty percentage of Walter's problem; he needs to take back his manhood from her. Since Walter is our central protagonist, our Everyman to whom we relate, we can't really help seeing Skyler negatively. If we don't exactly *hate* her, we sure don't like her much at first. Any character introduced this way would have a lot of negative ground to make up from the beginning.

R. NICHOLAS GERLICH: Comments directed at Ms Gunn, though, may be more a veiled compliment than insult, attestation to her acting skills and character development as the show evolved. As she said in her Op-Ed piece, she knew going in that her role as Walter's antagonist would not make her the most popular person on the show. She did a great job, though, and her 2014 Emmy is proof.

RGW: Right. She is not presented in a very sympathetic light although acted very skillfully by Anna Gunn. Her character does not really attempt to understand Walter or his motivations. Looking at this from ethical standpoint one is faced with the question of whether she even should attempt to under-stand him. He is putting their whole family at risk by manufacturing meth and associating with dangerous people. She really doesn't care about money and is seen by many as the "ultimate nagging bitch." What should she do? That is a tougher question to answer. If you were a mother and your husband had lied to you for months, living the life of Walter White, how would you react? Get a divorce? Go to the DEA? Live your life in fear? It's difficult to say how any wife would act in that type of dilemma. People project that Skyler is horrible precisely because she doesn't support Walter. Perhaps she should have just divorced him and gotten off the show, but *Breaking Bad* would have been less rich for it. The hate mail and personal attacks that Ms. Gunn received is going way too far and in the words of *Mystery Science Theater 3000*, "It's just a show. We should really just relax."

STEPHANIE STRINGER GROSS: I don't think Skyler is annoying. Maybe that's because I see her as dealing with things she doesn't want to deal with (like thinking about the money on the credit cards—somebody has to in their situation). I see her trying to help the family by making the best of a not-so-great situation. No one calls Walt a nag when he complains about anything at home. *Breaking Bad* shows the imbalance between the gender roles quite well, and I think even shows sympathy for Skyler's dilemma. In some ways, even Lydia seems stuck (there's her child to think about, for instance). The women have no room to employ their power, which is why I take exception to the idea that Walt is "henpecked." There are times when I think she is blind to what Walt may be experiencing, and sometimes she sees that too late to make a difference, but I forgive her for focusing a bit on herself. She is, after all, pregnant and her husband has taken to disappearing without explanation. I actually think she's pretty patient.

RNG: The pervasiveness of Skyler-hating is surprising given the demographics of viewers. Lori and I conducted a nationwide survey of *Breaking Bad* viewers in September 2013, during the climax leading up to the finale. While both our study and the letters and comments directed at Anna Gunn were voluntary, the level of hating is inconsistent with an enlightened, educated viewership.

Our results showed viewership to be 60 percent female and 40 percent male, with 55 percent married, a mean age of 40.3, and 95 percent having completed at least some college. Politically, respondents were decidedly middle-of-the-road (36 percent) or Democrat (37 percent). Household incomes skewed high, with 24 percent earning over $100,000. Christianity was the primary religious preference (30 percent), but a nearly equal number (27 percent) had none. The fan base was primarily white (73 percent).

Not so surprisingly, participants identified most with the two male leads, either Walter (22 percent) or Jesse (19 percent). Hank and Mike both scored 4 percent. Among female characters, Skyler was highest with 8 percent, followed by Marie (3 percent) and Lydia (0.3 percent).

Given that 60 percent of the sample was female, and only 11 percent most closely identified with any female character, leads me to conclude that the Skyler-hating may just as easily have occurred among women as it did men. Although our survey did not specifically address this issue, open-ended responses did show some negative biases toward both the character and actress.

Without knowing the gender of the persons sending negative comments, it is not possible to make gender-specific conclusions. Our data, though, show that failing to identify with Skyler was an equal opportunity option among participants. To be fair, 21 of the 22 people identifying with Skyler were female. But among the 63 identifying with Walter, 18 were women, and of the 53 identifying with Jesse, a surprising 37 were female.

Only two men identified with any female character (one each for Skyler and Marie). This may reflect an inability among men (or perhaps unwillingness) to identify with a woman. Women, though, were far more likely to identify with a male actor, perhaps attesting to differing cultural expectations of males and females, as well as the social acceptability of a female identifying with a male.

BRC: Well, I certainly found myself identifying with Walter. If women couldn't identify with a male protagonist we wouldn't be able to properly enjoy most literature and film. There's plenty of scholarship on that phenomenon and conflicting ways of interpreting it. But, since we're speaking informally here, I'll counter Stephanie's view by saying Skyler *did* annoy me—more than I wanted because I came to the series late enough to have been told about the fan hatred of Skyler and I *so* wanted to be a good feminist. But the writers did this, I'm convinced.

BC: Yeah, in *Breaking Bad*'s male-oriented universe, a certain amount of Skyler-hating is almost a given. That is, the primary struggle as I see it is, how does a man—Walter—act "like a man" without also losing his soul? (It's a diabolical trick question—there is no way, the series suggests.) Women have no viable place in a world so preoccupied. They are going to be judged primarily according to how well they facilitate or hinder their guy's "being a man." So a nag, which Skyler is in the pilot, is a problem, an annoyance. But what different, viable position could there be? She would have to be the recipient of her man's providing for the family, ask no questions about how he came by those resources, and mutely support everything he said and did. That's an extremely restrictive, traditional role to play.

RNG: Still, in our study, Skyler did not rate very highly among a sample that was skewed heavily female. There was opportunity to identify with an entire cast of characters, and women overwhelmingly chose men. That the show was about two men and their illicit activities may weigh heavily, but the opportunity was there. Maybe Vince Gilligan and Company also did such a good job in crafting her character that they unwittingly set up Ms. Gunn for some degree of failure in the public eye.

This may suggest that enlightenment about the genders may be a more complex issue than popularly thought, and that we may all have some growing to do. Few if any would doubt the skills that Ms. Gunn brought to the show, nor her delivery thereof. On the other hand, even among a sample that is highly educated, of solid economic means, and of political open mind, Skyler just wound up being the annoying bitch wife. Some things are hard to change.

BC: Even the show itself seems to acknowledge that. For example, when Hank is temporarily stripped of most of his "manly" qualities (physical strength, a successful career, his ability to provide), he takes out his frustrations on Marie. For some time, she passively, uncomplainingly bears the cruelty— and we have tremendous sympathy for her. We can see in her face and body the pain she's feeling as a result of living that traditional "feminine" supportive role. We can countenance her real-life real-estate playacting, and her shoplifting habit, because obviously she needs some relief. It's a huge relief when Marie begins talking back to Hank, and even more of one when he recovers and begins treating her kindly again.

All of this is to say that the show makes it difficult to feel *positively* about Skyler. But Skyler-*hating*? I wouldn't say the show goes so far as to justify that— merely that the very male-focused universe simply doesn't provide a good place for women, since they are defined as secondary and therefore ultimately beside the point.

JRP: In my essay, I discuss how Walt is always subject to surveillance and how that is one of the primary tensions in the show. Skyler in particular is insistent on finding out the "truth" about Walt. Consider how many times throughout the series Skyler repeats "no more secrets." (Of course, Walt probably says, "You're not in this" just as often, keeping her outside "his" world.) She wants to discover what is "real" underneath his "superficial" performances and lies, so she uses a variety of tactics to investigate his activities: asking him directly, using FinderSPYder, and even calling his mother. When she's suspicious about Walt's second cell phone, she continually demands explanations that are not forthcoming. Eventually, Walt tells her "I haven't been a good partner to you, and for that I'm *very* sorry. I love you. And I love this family. And I just want to make sure that we don't lose contact" ("Down"). Skyler listens to his excuse and then asks: "Is that it?" ("Down"). She recognizes that she can always dig deeper into Walt and intends to expose the darkness within him. When he continues lying, Skyler tells him: "Shut up and say something that isn't complete bullshit" ("Down"). This demand to both "shut up" and "say something," however contradictory, is a valid request. She wants him to stop the constructed performance and replace it with authenticity. Of course, this is an uncomfortable demand—not just for Walt but for the audience. Walt does not want to expose himself for what he is. He cannot bring himself to admit the things he has done (even now, I can't think of many instances where he tells Skyler specifics about what he does). Yet, this is what Skyler demands—she wants a full confession.

Now, if we accept the premise that the audience is meant to identify, at least in some ways, with Walt, this is an uncomfortable demand. For those that cheer blindly for Walt throughout the entire series (including his "badass" moments at the expense of others), Skyler's demand is for them to stop providing rationalizations for Walt's behavior. It's a demand that forces the audience to admit that under the guise of empowerment, they're willing to accept deceit, murder, etc. as viable and worthwhile methods of achieving it. If the audience cheers for Walt to empower himself no matter what, they have to pretend as though the collateral damage doesn't exist. It's of course much easier for the audience to accept Skyler as an inconvenience, a nag, or a bitch and target a vitriolic response than to admit that in empowering themselves vicariously through Walt they are willing to accept a great deal of wrongdoing. So, maybe the Skyler-hate derives from her demand for Walt (and consequently the audience) to admit their own fallibility—though of course it remains an open question why Skyler faces so much hatred when Hank serves essentially the same function and receives so little backlash (and even wins support, sometimes!).

Ian Dawe: The level of Skyler dislike, I think, came from those who wanted to see one kind of show being reminded by the creators that they were watching another kind of show. If what the viewer wanted was a crime thriller, where the main characters pull off caper and caper and stay one step ahead of the cops, Skyler was this annoying, bleating nuisance who popped up every now and then and tried to ruin the show by spoiling all the fun. This kind of viewer wants to "escape," to watch a show where he (I'm going with the masculine pronoun) can imagine himself away from the tedium of his life and instead shaking his fist at the system and at authority. The last thing he wants to hear is the voice of reality telling him what credit card he can or can't use or be accused of having an affair when he's just trying to earn enough money to help this ungrateful woman…. These are the germs of "Skyler hate." It is logical, once you accept the logic of the non-feminist viewer looking for genre thrills.

SSG: As Brian says, women are clearly in a second-class position throughout the series, and we're supposed to think about this as a problem I think. They are in no-win situations: Lydia is a control freak who is also a sociopath, Marie has no real emotional support and has to be the rock for Hank through most of the series, Skyler is on her own to try to figure out whether to hold the family together or to just give up and try to live her life. No female here has real agency. But I would argue that no male here has real agency either—just the illusion of choice. The fishbowl is filled with Machiavellian madness, everyone in it out for themselves and looking for power, and we're all just fish swimming in it. Without the tools to think about this water or what might be beyond it (and I don't think any of these characters have those tools except maybe Mike) we just keep swimming around in circles without even wishing someone would change the damned water.

ID: Whether the show itself encourages that or not is an interesting question. I generally take a post-structuralist approach and steer away from any questions or comments on creator intent. Effect is unquestionable, and the fact that *Breaking Bad* brought these Skyler-haters, as well as those who are firmly in the Heisenberg camp of sympathy, simply illustrates to me that there is a repository of untapped anger and resentment towards women in general and conventional professional existence in particular in modern life. Mobilizing and stimulating that anger simply demonstrates how many potential Walter Whites there are in the world, which could be seen as one of *Breaking Bad*'s most important observations. Skyler hate is simply a symptom of that larger disease.

Men of Legacy

Breaking Bad's *Solutions to Mortality*

Ian Dawe

"Have you guess'd you yourself would not continue?
Have you dreaded these earth-beetles?
Have you fear'd the future would be nothing to you?
...
What is called good is perfect, and what is called bad is
    just as perfect,
The vegetables and minerals are all perfect, and the
    imponderable fluids are perfect;
Slowly and surely they have pass'd on to this, and slowly
    and surely they yet pass on."
                                    —Walt Whitman, *Leaves of Grass*

Humans are rare if not unique in being aware of our mortality. It therefore stands to reason that one common concern of our species is what will happen to us afterwards. But another, no less important concern is what will happen to the world afterwards, particularly the parts of the world in which we were personally involved. One word that describes that concern, and that preoccupation is "legacy." The creation of a legacy is one way to overcome the inevitable time when physical and individual presence on the earth no longer exists, no matter what metaphysical or spiritual system is cited. Legacy is the one indisputable way to achieve immortality, in that sense. The desire to overcome death is as natural as the desire to avoid it, and all living things have strong evolutionary adaptations that favor simple survival. But humans, being aware of and to some extent in control of their imminent death, as well as being strongly social animals to whom social reputation is an important aspect of survival, prioritize what will be left after the inevitable event, sometimes even more than the events occurring during their living.

For our purposes, we should arrive at a specific definition. Legacy is the degree to which a single individual person remains active in the world after their death. While the individual themselves may be absent, their legacy makes their own peculiar imperatives manifest in the living world. It is a singular expression of an idiosyncratic ego of a person who is no longer alive. It isn't simply a karmic sense of cause-effect: obviously everything a person does in the world has some consequence, and much of that consequence takes place after their death. But legacy is different in our conception. It is specific, and personal, not general. It deals with individuals, not institutions or cultures or even, necessarily, families. Legacy in our terms requires resources in order to exist, whether those resources be financial or otherwise. But that is ultimately the equation; legacy is where ego meets resources.

Five Forms of Legacy

Legacy takes a number of general forms, and for the purposes of this discussion let us define five of them: biological, cultural, intellectual, financial and physical. Obviously these rough categories will have some interplay between them and cross over, but in general these will serve to frame our discussion.

Biological legacy is the simplest, meaning the leaving of biological, genetically related descendants. In biology this is referred to as "fecundity" or "reproductive success" and is the only meaningful sort of legacy for most living things. Genetic material has a quality of being "semi-conservatively" replicated, meaning that each new double-stranded piece of DNA consists of one of the parental strands and one new strand. So, the persistence of the genetic material of any cell is more or less assured by simple replication. This sort of legacy, simple reproduction, is governed by the rules of natural selection, which selects certain aspects of the past's biological legacy that are useful in the present. But with humans, biology cannot be extracted from culture. For our species, simply reproducing does not guarantee the persistence of the wishes of the departed, or their values. Children can be quite different, philosophically, from their parents, and this would not represent a living legacy as we've described it. Therefore biological legacy is a part of the concept, absolutely, but not an adequate comprehensive descriptor. There is, of course, a part of each individual that lives on physically through their children as genetic material, but even on the simplest possible genetic analytical level we must admit that each person has *two* legacies of this sort, one from each parent. If we define legacy as the will or at least identity of one specific individual living on past the point of physical death, then this biological concept becomes inherently compromised. For example, in the world of *Breaking Bad,* Gretchen and Elliot, Walter's former partners in Grey Matter industries, have no children, so therefore no biological legacy. But Walter's two children, Walter Jr. and Holly, aren't necessarily obliged to carry on their father's will or his values, even though they carry his genes. Walter Jr., in fact, specifically rejects his father's values and his financial legacy (discussed below), since he has his mother's genes and his own individual sense, born out of a seemingly well-developed moral code. Biological legacy, therefore, is not sufficient to encompass all the various implications of legacy, and the degree to which it contributes to the formation of legacy is highly variable.

A *cultural* legacy might be some sort of art piece, whether that be a song or play or film or any other kind of art, that is still seen and appreciated in the world, particularly by subsequent generations of individuals whose lives do no overlap with the originator. The development of mechanical and electronic media has certainly expanded this sort of legacy for those of an artistic inclination. An example might be a ten-year-old in 2014 discovering the Beatles for the first time. That is a form of legacy, as the conversation between their art and this new audience is entirely fresh and thus constitutes the creation of something new in the world, long after the people who made that art have gone. In terms of *Breaking Bad,* as we will discuss below, Walter's approach to chemistry is part art, part science. The scientific and technological legacy is certainly in place when one contemplates a specific scientific procedure. But the nature of science, particularly chemistry, dictates that any procedure developed by Walter is going to be similar to any other chemist's procedure to a large extent. The little touches Walter adds, the specific time for crystallization, for example, or letting a solvent cool or heat up before adding it, or tracking the pH of the solution at a specific time, these are artistic flourishes, not strictly speaking scientific points. Therefore, Walter does have an art and as we shall consider later, it's this art, his unique way of achieving what many others could achieve, that forms the basis of his artistic legacy.

Intellectual legacy applies to individuals whose ideas outlive them, and sometimes ideas become more important after they are gone. To use a scientific reference, Gregor Mendel determined the basics of genetic inheritance in the

19th century but his work was lost until after his death, when it became, in the 20th century, the foundations of modern genetics. Mendel's is therefore an intellectual legacy, but this certainly qualifies, as our understanding of genetics continues to shape the modern world. In *Breaking Bad* terms, as mentioned above, Walter for example, does have an intellectual legacy of scientific knowledge and expertise. As a chemistry teacher, we imagine perhaps that this activity is sufficient to generate a legacy of intellectual and scientific thought from Walter, but he rejects it. Jesse learns the art from Walter, not the science. In fact, even though Walter demonstrates quite a lot of science during the run of *Breaking Bad*, including improvising a car battery from chemicals in the episode "Four Days Out" (209). But Jesse's "take-home" message is always practical, focused on little technical details rather than scientific principles. This artisanal approach differs sharply from the scientific approach. Walter's teaching, formal and informal, and his attempt to transmit a viable, rigorous, science-based legacy come across as half-hearted and ultimately unsuccessful. His interest is in artistic legacy.

Financial legacy is also almost a redundant phrase in the minds of many. An inheritance, consisting of money, property, treasure and the like is probably humanity's oldest conception of the term "legacy." The key distinction here is what sort of use that legacy is employed in the service of in the world. An empty mansion is a rather hollow legacy for example whereas a trust that is managed and put to use building or supporting active endeavors in the world is a bit closer to our conception of the term. To use a *Breaking Bad* metaphor, money buried in the desert is not a legacy. On the other hand, money put to a use other than what the individual who left it intended is also not a legacy. Walter's actions in the final episodes of the series are motivated in no small way by his desire to see his money in the hands of his family rather than the neo–Nazi gang run by "Uncle Jack." Legacy must, in our terms, be an extension of the will of the departed.

Physical legacy is something a bit subtler in terms of its definition, because the common perception is that physical interaction with the world ends after death. Which is, despite the activity of detritovores and the biological forces of decomposition, very much the case. Unless there is some physical object or entity constructed as a direct consequence of an individual's life that continues to play some active role in the life of the community. This can range from something as banal as a school named after a public figure or as monumental as an ancient pyramid. The important distinction is whether the physical object plays a role that is a direct expression of the deceased person's

will. For example, Dr. Charles Best, a Canadian medical pioneer, has a high school named after him in Vancouver but that school was conceived and built long after his death. While the school certainly represents a kind of legacy, it is emphatically not the same as the pyramids of Giza, which were designed and built during the lifetime of a single individual, specifically for that individual. And those pyramids, for example, literally and metaphorically cast a shadow on the Egyptian countryside that represents a very real and active physical presence in the modern world. In terms of *Breaking Bad*, we have to bypass the notion of the RV "the Crystal Ship" as representing some sort of desert tomb, although this is a tempting analogy and certainly, particularly in episodes such as "Ozymandias" (514), the visual imagery of the RV juxtaposed against the backdrop is a powerful evocation of such themes. But the RV, by its very nature, is temporary and mobile, and easily destroyed, as we later see. Whereas the tomb is meant to be exactly the opposite: the most emphatic version of permanent and static. One form of physical legacy is the White house, although Walter's activity leads to its transformation into a symbol of his failures, rather than his successes. The broken, dirty, graffiti'ed building at the end of season five is not the home Walter and Skyler bought. However, it wasn't the home they intended it to become, nor was it just a "starter home" on the way to something bigger. The ruined White home at the end of season five is, in its sad way, Walter's physical legacy, because it continues to upset and influence the neighbors and the surrounding community, acting every day to unsettle them and to remind them of the monster who once lived next door. It doesn't represent the legacy Walter intended, but rather one aspect of the legacy he actually created.

A legacy might take one of these forms (physical, biological, artistic, intellectual or financial) or all of them, or a selection of a few. A legacy need not represent all of these aspects, as for example someone who chooses not to physically reproduce might leave no biological legacy. But the power of the legacy is significant in what it motivates characters, particularly in the world of *Breaking Bad*, to do.

The desire to create legacy, no matter which form it takes (and these categories are rough and fluid) might be driven by fear of death, but no less important is an expression of an ego. And ego is an expression of identity and power, ranging from the simple and timeless scrawl "I was here" to many pathological expressions of ego, particularly when wedded to great political power. In other words, the desire to create a legacy is the same in an individual with no power as an individual with the power to shape nations and history. But it takes some power to actually follow through on that desire, particularly if we define legacy in non-biological terms. Legacy is one possible outcome of the meeting of ego and resources. There must be many individuals in the world whose desire to create legacy is thwarted by their means. They may not even feel as if they desire a legacy until they are granted the means of creating it. Jesse Pinkman, for example, quite probably never gave any thought to the concept of legacy before his path intersected with Walter White's. Examining each of the characters in turn, both in terms of the legacy they intended and the legacy they created, is illuminating.

Jesse

One curious aspect of *Breaking Bad,* and why it might find itself so concerned with the concept of legacy, is that the overwhelming majority of the characters are middle-aged men. All the major characters, with one important exception, are mid to late-career[1] men in their 50s to whom death is an increasingly real proposition, and their thoughts are turning towards legacy. Jesse Pinkman is the exception. Although worldly and streetwise in his own way, Jesse nevertheless finds himself playing the part of the moral, stable voice quite often during the run of the show. Despite his early enthusiasm for cooking along with Walter and the money it brings, Jesse spends most of the five seasons of the show trying to get away from the larger-than-life activities of the middle-aged men. It is he who repeatedly tries to convince Walter to "pull over" and be satisfied with what he has accumulated. It's never quite clear what Jesse plans to do with all the money he's earning, or what his motivation might be for making it in the first place (if any).

Jesse, in fact, demonstrates a resolution to destroy any possibility of his legacy, rather than create it. When, in Season Four, Jesse turns inward and seems determined to waste all his money throwing a party of Roman proportions, it is among other things a violent act *against* legacy. That peculiar rebellion, in so much as he has thought it through, strikes at the heart of what Walter White sees as the central reason for being in the drug business. The sequence in season five in which he literally throws away his money is on the same theme, with even less metaphorical subtlety. When Jesse wastes his money, he is antagonizing Walter, Gus and Mike in part because he demonstrates such ambivalence about legacy, which is so important to all of them. Walter says to Jesse frequently in the latter parts of the series that he is "free" and can "go anywhere," but of course manages to keep him bound to the business and not able to leave. It is doubly ironic that Jesse is a prisoner for most of the latter portion of season five, and so is Walter, in his way. Their money has not brought them freedom, but at least Jesse contemplated what that might mean. In other words, Jesse is the only character who *acts out* being free, throwing the biggest party he can contemplate and literally throwing away his money. This not only disappoints the older men such as Walter and Mike, it is reckless for all of them as it brings them into the crosshairs of authority figures.

In terms of our legacy equation, Jesse demonstrates how important ego is to the equation. He has as much money as his partners and associates, and therefore has equal means with which to build a substantial legacy of his choosing, but Jesse chooses not to do that. Just as his admission that he once carved a wooden box, using a set of skills traditionally associated with artisan men who passed on those skills and those trinkets to future generations, only to sell it for pot money, Jesse's anti-legacy ethos demonstrates his lack of personal ego. Another possibility is that Jesse's ego is very much intact but buried beneath guilt and shame and bad choices that rehab offers him the opportunity to address, an opportunity which he does not exploit. Whether his ego is absent or submerged, this apparent lack of stake in the future sets Jesse apart from the other male characters, concerned as they are with their legacy.

The Feminine Legacies

The female characters on *Breaking Bad,* the four principal women being Skyler, Marie, Lydia and Jane, also demonstrate an ambivalent or non-existent interest in legacy. Not that they have no stake in the legacy the men are creating (it's Jane, for example, who suggests to Jesse many possible uses for the money he's making). It isn't as if these women lacked career ambitions—quite the contrary. Lydia in particular is quite career-focused and businesslike, and even Jane, Jesse's tragic love interest in season two, has a quite well developed sense of her artistic abilities and identity. They have desires for expressing this peculiar individual legacy and express it when they can. The difference between their behavior and that of the men is that, at least as we are shown in the course of the show, they tend to marginalize or at least de-prioritize their ambition and instead cultivate and nurture it in their men. As regressive as that might sound, and it does "read" as anti-feminist, it does seem to be the case for the women in this show. They seem, on the whole, more concerned with preserving what they and their families have rather than constantly thinking about how they will be remembered or what they will pass on. Or, rather, they facilitate the creation of the male ego-driven legacy into which they fold their own.

Skyler's behavior, in the first two seasons, is singularly preoccupied with preserving a stable family environment in the face of Walt's illness. As the show progresses, and she becomes inculcated in Walter's business, her emphasis shifts to preserving whatever funds the business is bringing in. She challenges Walt early and often, and by the end she is simply defeated, cutting Walter out of her life and refusing any of his legacy. It's the refusal of the legacy, or at least the negation of Walter's stated motivation for doing what he does, that constitutes her only power by season five, and she exercises it. For her, Walter's legacy is the desperately poor situation she and her children find themselves in by the end of the series. None of this behavior on her part, though, is designed to establish the singular, idiosyncratic legacy of "Skyler White." Rather, she acts on behalf of a larger familial and societal unit, in opposition to, in tolerance of, and finally by escaping and curtailing the influence of her husband. This appears to be a pattern for Skyler, as she even subsumes her own professional ambitions under those of Ted Beneke as the series goes on, giving up her lucrative eBay business and once again putting her skills, abilities and energy in the service of the creation of a man's legacy.

Marie, too, shows little interest in legacy and much more interest in making sure her husband is safe and home every night, and that her sister and niece and nephew are in no danger. This is not an expression of ego or will, as we've defined legacy, but an articulation of values that, however culturally derived they might be, fall into the home-and-hearth imperatives of traditional western femininity. Marie's way of "acting out" against Hank is visiting open houses and making up elaborate family-oriented fantasies that she spins to the hapless real estate agents (until her ruse is discovered). Through this, she demonstrates some interest in legacy in terms of the creation of a family (fantasized or real) but this is in keeping with the home and hearth imperatives that the female characters in *Breaking Bad* tend to express. Marie might be dreaming of a different sort of life, but it isn't a single life, and this is significant to her motivations.

Lydia is a curious exception to this home-and-hearth pattern, with no obvious ties to family but our background information about her character is so sparse that any number of hypotheses could be fielded. One interpretation is that Lydia is simply an expression of the Madrigal corporate structure and, though ruthless in her professional duties and picky about nutrition, not an ego-driven person. We should take pains to mention at this point that Lydia is not precisely lying when she approaches Walter and inserts the priorities of her company into the story: she does believe in what her company does and honestly represents her work. Just as Gus Fring, in his way, dealt with people honestly to a point. Lydia isn't building "Lydia Industries," however, she is likely positioning herself to take over a position of power and responsibility within the larger corporation and generate some future legacy at some point.

It seems that Lydia, along with Marie and Skyler, are acting out of concern for the here-and-now of their lives, up to and including Skyler taking the job with Ted (and all that that decision brings) and Marie's slightly bizarre coping strategy. They aren't, as the men seem to be, spending the bulk of their time and energy building something that might yield dividends in the future (Lydia, once again, has aspects of this). Rather, they are organizing the lives that face them "today" and trying to keep the imperatives of home and family intact, whereas the men chase some future legacy with wild-eyed ambition.

The Masculine Legacies

But the five core middle-aged men that comprise the central cast of *Breaking Bad* do indeed have more than a passing interest in the notion of legacy. For Hank Schrader, Gustavo Fring, Hector Salamanca, Mike Ehrmentraut and Walter White, and in contrast to their younger associate Jesse Pinkman, legacy is the reason to have means, even if their commitment to its creation wavers at times. Each has their own way of gauging their success and of distributing their legacy to the world after their end, but they are united in their preoccupation with asserting their influence over the world in the present and the future. No matter what form their intended legacy takes, all of these men can be provoked into extreme acts when it is threatened. The energy of their reaction demonstrates the importance of the concept.

Hector Salamanca, the Mexican gangster played in the series by Mark Margoils, is concerned with family with the characteristically aggressive and commanding fashion of Latin culture. Thought paralyzed by a stroke in the show's present, flashbacks show him exhibiting much the same behavior in the past, most notably in his brutal treatment of his nephews. In one sequence he holds the head of one nephew in a bucket of water, nearly drowning him, in response to an act of disrespect (307, "One Minute"). When he finally lets the boy up, he growls (sitting in that phallocentric, legs-apart fashion of masculine authority), "Family is everything." Family, to Hector, is literally an extension of his will, controlling the activity of the cartel even from the supposedly helpless state of being confined to a wheelchair and communicating only with a bell.

Hector is never shown taking much of an interest in financial or business affairs, as such. His concern is that the rules of the subculture are enforced, and that the appropriate people are treated with the appropriate amount of respect. Sensitive to any perceived slight, Hector returns the obedience shown to him with loyalty, giving the DEA only his bodily functions in response to their attempts to use him against his family. The importance of family might lead one to think that Salamanca's primary sense of legacy is biological, and that certainly is important to him. It is, in fact, important enough that Gus Fring knows how much it will hurt him to know that his sons are gone and that "the line will die with you" (411, "Crawl Space"). It is that final piece of disrespect, along with the assertion that Gus has spoiled Hector's legacy as well as his grip on immediate power that leads Gus to his death. Hector's stroke took everything from him except his legacy, and the thought of losing that galvanizes him into action. Hector's death, triggering the explosion that killed Gus Fring, is an active, assertive expression of revenge, saying to Gus, "You take my legacy? I take yours." This is, of course, referring to Hector's biological legacy, but Gus's Financial and perhaps Intellectual and Artistic legacies as well. Hector has an artistic legacy, if one wants to consider how his actions influence Jesse's attitude towards crime and generally how to be a "bad man" even when severely physically disabled.

The thing that keeps Mike Ehrmentraut in the drug business is his granddaughter. As with our other male characters, it's only through threatening his legacy that anyone can get Mike to do anything that wasn't his idea. Unlike Gus, who appears successfully mid-career, and Walt, for whom the finish line always seems to be a moving target, Mike is admittedly close to retirement, ready to settle down and watch TV. This makes him just a little more realistic about what the business will be like, and what his family will be like, after he is gone.

Mike's biological legacy is his family, and in this case his close involvement with his granddaughter makes this a meaningful extension of his personality and values into the future. His intellectual legacy is a way of working, a no-nonsense and realistic approach to conducting business in a dangerous and sometimes cutthroat world. We see Mike attempting, somewhat reluctantly, to take Jesse under his wing in this manner on Gus's orders, and when Jesse takes the Mexican cartel's chemists to task for the way they keep their lab and choose their surroundings, the look on Mike's face is one of pride and respect. Jesse learned the mechanics from Walter, but the calm, commanding masculinity he brings to that situation is pure Mike, and part of Mike's legacy. Mike's pride in that moment is partially an authentic sense that "the kid" is going to work out and partially a satisfaction in seeing his legacy in action.

By our definition, Mike's approach to business with his grim rationalism is also part of his cultural legacy. Prior to his introduction into the show, Mike has accumulated a number of "guys," most of whom are now in prison and being supported financially to keep quiet for the authorities. We never see these "guys" in action, nor do we get a substantial opportunity to see how Mike relates to them outside of the strict prison environment. But if his reaction to Jesse's performance in Mexico is any indication, Mike hasn't had a promising young disciple like him very often. Mike seems genuinely impressed, but it is entirely possible that he was equally impressed by every one of his "guys" before they were sent to prison. They are part of his cultural and intellectual legacy, which is probably what Mike would consider to be his "professional" legacy. They are all-important to him, even Mr. Chow who becomes the focus of some intrigue in season five.

Mike's use of the term "legacy" when referring to the support he must pay these former associates is one of the few times a character uses the term in *Breaking Bad* and it isn't in the same sense as in our discussion here. The word is used in the context of Mike arguing with Walter, and at this point, early in Season Five, Walter is fully committed to his post–Gus ego. He will not be told by anyone, even Mike, how to use the financial resources his business is acquiring. When Mike says "legacy," he is using it as a term that might appeal to Walter's more white-collar instincts, evoking trust funds and employment standards. It appears to be a deliberate attempt to frame the obligation in Walter's peculiar language. But those men in prison have a different relationship with Mike, and it's possible that Mike uses the term with many meanings. To him, legacy is a word that carries with it a responsibility, a duty to other men that Mike expresses in his traditional masculine terms.

For Mike, looking after the men in prison, both in terms of buying their silence and ensuring their safety, is as much of a "man's duty" as being loyal to a wife and family, being punctual, respecting authority or other sorts of traditional "masculine" obligations in western society. It irritates him that he even has to explain this to Walter in any way, because in his moral system, supporting your fellows is a given. This value system is part of Mike's cultural legacy, and he ultimately dies for it. And with it: his last words, "Shut up and let me die in peace" (507, "Say My Name"), are one last expression of his frustration with this arrogant fool who refuses to understand that legacy is important, and that it is part of a man's complete duty.

Mike has a biological legacy (his granddaughter), a cultural legacy (his style of doing business) and a financial legacy, and he fights to keep all three sorts of legacies intact. There is evidence that he succeeds on at least one count, as Jesse may well carry his professional values forward (cultural legacy), but the DEA investigation makes the prospect of his granddaughter inheriting his "drug money" somewhat remote. As for a physical legacy, Mike simply falls off a log: this sort of legacy isn't important to him. And Mike is, for all his intelligence and wisdom, not an intellectual and thus lacks that form of legacy. He fights to protect the legacies he's capable of creating, even if Walt's arrogance and bluster essentially destroys most of it. Mike dies bitter and angry at Walter, not simply for what he's done to the business in the here-and-now, but for the damage he has done to the future.

Hank Schrader shares some of Mike's masculine sense of duty, obligation and responsibility. He might be less explicit about it, preferring to demonstrate his devotion to his family through loving actions rather than rhetoric or the cold comfort of providing large amounts of money, but his sense of male duty is no less developed. Hank's legacy, both in terms of how he sees it and what form it actually takes, is less obvious.

Hank and Marie don't have children of their own, so in the strictest terms the biological legacy is out of the picture for them. And while the Schraders are well-off and comfortable, even sporting a four-bedroom family home even though they do not have children themselves, they are certainly not a wealthy family on a government agent's salary. Financial legacy does not seem to be a high priority for Hank and Marie. Neither does Hank make any claim to an intellectual legacy such as a novel approach to crime solving or a novel notion concerning justice. Hank's interest in mineralogy may lead him to contemplate a physical legacy, but the Schraders don't seem interested in producing some sort of permanent monument to their relationship. Hank's professional work is well done and his tenacity, combined with his excellent skills as an investigator, leads him to unravel the truth about Madrigal, Gus Fring and Heisenberg when his colleagues at the DEA are in the dark. But this is simply an example of a person who is professionally competent.

Aside from Hank's professional acumen, his motivation, unlike Gus, Hector and Walter, is not legacy, but immediacy. Hank is preoccupied with maintaining peace, scoring points in the ongoing "war on drugs" and enjoying a BBQ with his family. His one traditional expression of legacy is his home-brewed beer, "Schraderbrau." Having a family label beverage is certainly an effective way of ensuring the survival of a name (Samuel Adams is remembered to this day, possibly more so than his cousin John, who was only president). And the dialogue suggests that Hank has made this before, possibly several times, and perfected his own recipe. It would be tempting to equate Schrader-brau with Heisenberg's "blue meth" as Hank's legacy product, but in the context of the show it seems more appropriate to categorize it as a narrative echo, an ironic bit of character resonance. Hank isn't concerned with his brew to the exclusion of anything else, nor is his so protective of its secret that he has to teach someone else how to make it. Some of his personality might be invested in Schraderbrau, particularly in the sense that it conjures up images of hoisted Steins full of beer and good social times. But Hank isn't defined by Schrader-brau and, if that is all that survives him, it would be a hollow legacy.

Hank's professional work is also curiously devoid of legacy connotations. As was mentioned above, he does not innovate some sort of hitherto unknown investigation strategy or new legal concept. He simply performs his job well. *Breaking Bad* rarely explicitly comments on the politics and ethics of the "drug war," but this absence is, in and of itself, very telling. Hank, like his colleagues at the DEA, is under no illusions about how effective their work is. Addicts will still get high, even if they bring down the entire Mexican meth cartel. Drugs will still make it across the border into the U.S. even if all the DEA resources are marshaled towards capturing a drug kingpin. But government agents, particularly those working in law enforcement, seem to survive at least in part by personalizing their work and breaking their challenges into manageable portions. The FBI agent who captured famous Columbian drug queen Griselda Blanco (Palumbo, *Cocaine Cowboys*) remembers today how much he wanted to "give her a big kiss" as he was taking her into custody. It's the sort of behavior one might see from a man catching a trophy fish or hunting a prized deer. The notion that the cocaine trade, in that case, would be essentially unaffected by taking the woman into custody didn't register. Like a photograph of a fisherman next to a prized catch, he was only interested in his portion of the overall struggle, and satisfied when he had achieved success in those terms. Hank is that kind of agent, and while we can be certain that Marie was told all sorts of stories about how Hank died a "hero" and was fighting to make American "safer," in the end, his professional efforts don't amount to much "on the street." His sacrifice was in pursuit of a personal enemy, with a private vendetta, mixed with some unquestionably legitimate legal motivations. But it would be miscasting Agent Schrader to characterize his work as his intellectual or cultural legacy.

Hank's interest in legacy shows itself only when he is at his most vulnerable, after his attack and injury. It's then that he finds his interest in geology ("Not rocks: *minerals*!" as he reminds Marie). Geology is an odd choice of hobby for Hank, who had previously only shown interest in work and family dinners. But wounded as he is, and "living from bowel movement to bowel movement," in his words (402, "Thirty-Eight Snub"), he takes up the study of rare minerals possibly as a way to pass the time. Marie is confused by this and interprets it as another way of Hank further isolating himself in his hospital bed. Hank himself never explicitly states the fascination, but there are poetic reasons why this behavior highlights Hank's interest in legacy.

Hank's injury is so difficult for him, in part, because of shame. He dislikes being physically limited and dislikes even more the false positivity offered by Marie and others in the medical establishment. A vigorous and virile sort of man, to be confined and disabled in this way reminds Hank that he is in a dangerous profession and also takes him "out of the game" in terms of the hunt for the source of the "blue meth," at least temporarily. It also makes him appear vulnerable in front of his wife, which seems to be a serious blow to his sense of masculinity and power. It surely isn't a coincidence that Marie uses her demonstration of his sexual potency as a motivation for him to take his physical therapy seriously: she knows her man. But even Marie can't seem to figure out Hank's interest in geology.

One possible interpretation of this hobby, which is germane to this discussion, is that Hank is expressing a subconscious need to consider his legacy. It is a scientific truism that the minerals that make up this planet will outlast any organism currently living. They will still be here even after the oldest tree has fallen over. Touching "rocks" is as close as a living thing can get to touching eternity, and the image of Hank turning over minerals, contemplating their history and their future, while lying relatively helpless in his bed speaks of a character who is considering the passage of time. Time is the one thing that Hank seems to feel he's losing in his struggle with his injury. When he eventually does make physical progress, he returns to the casework as soon as he's minimally able, and essentially tosses the rocks aside (other than using them as a cover story when he and Walt team up to perform surveillance on Gus). Therefore, while it is a passing interest, it is a significant one. The one moment when Hank considers legacy, and possibly his relative lack of it, spurs him to act in the only way he knows how. Hank's work is a big part of what gives his life meaning, just as with all of the other male characters on the show, and Hank's long contemplation of rocks during his convalescence becomes a useful and transformative meditation for him, rather than a serious scientific study.

As soon as Hank has internalized the lessons of the minerals and quite possibly made an unconscious connection between them and his own stubbornness, it galvanizes him into action.

Another motivation for Hank might not be his own legacy, but his interest in the legacy of Heisenberg. "Heisenberg," up until the mid-season climax of Season Five, represented a combination of personalities and forces for Hank. He knew that this was the name the infamous meth cook was using, and suspected that Gus Fring had something to do with it, but he also knew that capturing Heisenberg himself would not stop the drug trade. What it would do is curtail or eliminate Heisenberg's legacy, a criminal empire and a singular drug product. In the end, it seems to be the thought of Heisenberg having a legacy, and moreover one that supersedes anything that Hank himself was creating, that motivates Hank to take action. This is a case of dueling legacies, an attempt to control how the future would perceive the men and their actions. In his way, Hank's attempts to destroy Heisenberg's legacy without creating one of his own is as much an expression of ego and means as any other legacy. Justice factors into it, but much more immediately important is a male pride that, despite in this case being put into the service of law enforcement, is almost equal to that of Walt.

The difficulty in applying these principles to Gustavo Fring is that as viewers we are told so little about his background, but so much is suggested. We do know that Fring was from Chile, that he had groomed at least one other apprentice in Mexico, that the Mexican drug cartel considers him "untouchable" and protected against attack and that he appears to be fairly independently wealthy. The actor Giancarlo Esposito, who played Gus, ventured a theory that the character was from a very well-connected Chilean family, aristocratic and connected in politics and crime, similar to the Kennedys (personal communication). But we are given very little solid information. As Hank and his DEA colleagues put it when investigating him, "Everything before 1986 is a blank." It is worth noting that 1986 was an important year for Chile. The rising tide of opposition to the dictatorship of Augusto Pinochet[2] had reached a critical mass by the end of that year, culminating in an unsuccessful assassination attempt on Pinochet in September of 1986 and his subsequent declaration of a "state of siege" (Loveman, "Military Dictatorship"). This state of emergency remained in effect until January 1987, but Pinochet's increasing repression drew a vigorous response, ultimately leading to his defeat the following year (Loveman, "Military Dictatorship"). This appears to be the sort of political climate from which a wealthy young aristocrat might wish to escape, even if Hector Salamanca questioned his credentials in the past, and also accept that without a home country, criminal activity could be a viable long-term source of income. Gustavo's political connections may have also continued to haunt him as an ally to a dictator whose power was rapidly slipping away, and he may have taken advantage of a version of the "cleaning" service offered by Saul Goodman and assumed a new identity, which is an explanation for why there are no records of his existence in Chile.

Gus, over dinner with Walter, does mention that he has a family (311, "Abiquiu"), but this is never confirmed and the character's motivation at this point for giving any information to Walter is a professional seduction attempt, so this might be a fabrication. It is equally likely that Gus had a family in Chile and was forced to leave them behind when he fled. Either way, the wealth that he is accumulating through his large criminal empire does not seem to be going back to Chile. His financial and biological legacy, therefore, is either something he keeps hidden or he fabricates. He must be a very wealthy man by this point in his career, but Gustavo appears to have no intimates, therefore his money is simply gathering dust. The question of Gus's family is an interesting one: when Gus has Walter over for dinner, there are toys lying around on the floor of the handsomely appointed middle class home. Walter certainly seems to accept the idea that Gus is a family man, based on what he says and the visual evidence, which is entirely circumstantial. Gus's family is never seen on film, and when he has Jesse over for dinner in a later episode (409, "Bug"), there are no toys visible and the subject of family is not addressed. Therefore the question of whether Gus has a family, or is using that ruse strategically to attract support from certain quarters, is an open one.

Gus and Walter are alike in that they are both creating two legacies: one private and one public. And one of those legacies is a deception, perhaps even a self-deception. Gus claims, when speaking with Walter, that he, too, has a family and their values are comparable. This is his public legacy: a family man doing what he must. Walter shares the same public legacy, and while it's arguable whether that is a meaningful goal for Walt, it seems a complete falsehood for Gus. Gus's private legacy, his true lasting influence on the world, is his criminal organization. Gus isn't a cook, nor is he a chemist. But he is an excellent businessman, managing with calm competence and accepting the often brutal side of the business that stretches all over the southwest U.S. That organization is an instrument of his will, but it has many legitimate and quasi-legal cells (the laundry is a functioning business, although staffed with illegal immigrants) and is kept together by a coherent and professional command structure. Mike's contribution is important, but it is Gus who sets the tone. He is, in fact, so good that this, his intellectual legacy, really does function after his death in a very clear example of our definition. As Hank puts it in the Season Five episode "51," "Six feet under and half a face and he's *still* screwing with us!"

Gus is not a perfect businessman, however, despite his very effective talents. A truly great business leader would never have allied himself with Walter in the first place, and it is that relationship which ultimately brings him down. Walter's skills present Gus with a business opportunity, which appeals to his preoccupation with his legacy. The opportunity is quite significant: with a skilled cook and an equipped lab and his own well-established distribution network he can achieve what appears to be his goal: independence from the Mexican cartel. He isn't satisfied being a major, high-ranking member of a larger organization: Gus wants control, and the freedom that it confers. This appears to be much more important to him than money or family or any other consideration. Unfortunately, Walt's arrogance and incompetence isn't taken into account early enough by Gus, and Walt's dangerous engagements with the cartel and insistence in handling (or mishandling) those issues drag Fring's organization down. It isn't simply Walt's influence, however. As with the other major male characters in *Breaking Bad*, Gus Fring is prompted to act most aggressively when his legacy is threatened.

Gus's business, his true legacy, is built around his need for control. That control is exercised through his absolute authority over every aspect of the business. He plays the role of a South American benefactor, and in keeping with the underlying history and traditions of that culture, he expects the people he pays to be absolutely obedient, more of a master-slave relationship than an employer-employee. Mike and other "Generals" are given more freedom to exercise their independence, but Gus is "God" and has to be. The episode "Box Cutter" (401) is an excellent example of this, as Gus brutally murders one of his loyal henchmen in front of Walt and Jesse in a vulgar but effective display of power and authority. This is a salient point worth repeating: Gus isn't motivated by revenge or score settling (at least not in the box cutter case) but rather by the need for control and the power and freedom to shape his own business. His violence against the cartel leaders themselves in Mexico in the episode "Salud" is partially revenge for their killing of his former partner and cook, but more immediately born out of his desire to go it alone in the U.S., and he knows by this point that this is something the cartel would never knowingly, freely give him. Gus's legacy might be a bit more difficult to isolate and identify than some other characters, but his preoccupation with it is betrayed by the ease with which he is brought to violence when it is threatened.

Gus represents, at least in our proposed character history, a consequence of political instability and injustice in Latin America. His reasons for leaving Chile, and the peculiar timing, cannot be a coincidence. He is driven from his home country by its own actions and the actions of the U.S., whose involvement in the deposition of Allende and the installation of Pinochet in 1973 is now well-known. It is revealed in the show that he came through Mexico to the U.S., slipping into the country at a time when background checks were far less rigorous than they are today. And in the U.S., he operates a large and successful illegal business, supplying a product to a market that happily buys his product, a wonderful example of pure capitalism. What perhaps Hank and the other intelligent DEA agents realize is that Gus Fring would not be a problem were it not for the political actions of the United States, the drug policies of the United States and the immigration policies of the United States. Gus is a criminal who chose that life, about this there is no question. But he was nourished professionally and guided into a very logical path to New Mexico by U.S. action and U.S. policy. In other words, Gus doesn't create legacy as much as he *is* a legacy. He carries with him a genetic and cultural legacy of his powerful family in Chile, but his presence and his current activities in the U.S. make him a very clear legacy of American policy and action in Latin America. As the DEA is a federal organization, in some ways Hank and his colleagues are chasing their own legacy. And moreover, Gustavo's final defeat doesn't come at their hands: it comes from a random element (Walter), whose financial situation is, in part, also a result of U.S. government policy. Governments and policies leave legacies, just as logically as actions have consequences, and while this is different in many ways from our notion of personal legacy, it still remains a living, active extension of attitudes and idiosyncratic decisions. But that definition, Gus is living embodiment of legacy.

Finally, we turn to Walter White. Walter, like Gus, has a private and a public legacy, but unlike Gus he often confuses the two. The question of Walter's motivation in *Breaking Bad* is thorny because he himself is ambivalent and contradictory in his words and actions. One thing is always clear: the ferocious masculinity that drives Walter to act out and hold his ideas about legacy in an iron fist, to the point where he essentially strangles the life out of it like some sort of tragic Greek God. Walter destroys his own legacy in the process of creating it, but forgets the many ways in which his legacy is already in place prior to his entering the drug trade. He does leave a legacy, but not the one he intended, and therefore this is a hollow and meaningless outcome in our terms.

In the pilot episode of the series, Walter takes an explicit interest in legacy, in several forms. His financial legacy is in question from the start, as we see him teaching at a mid-level high school and working a part-time job at a car wash and still the financial situation in the White house is bad enough that Skyler has restricted their credit card use. Walter considers what part of himself will be left after he has gone and decides that without him, his family will live in poverty. The knowledge that he has cancer and that Skyler is pregnant with their second child makes the situation even grimmer, and makes legacy and even larger part of his motivational equation. Walter sits down and carefully calculates how much money his family will need in order to maintain their lifestyle after he has died. From that behavior, we might deduce that Walter's primary motivation is to create a financial legacy that will play at least part of his living role as breadwinner in the family. This sum becomes larger and more out of reach as the series progresses, but in his initial estimation, Walter seems to be driven by financial considerations.

Walter, to put it mildly, is a complex character. Though leaving his family with a very clear and visible means of financial support is a noble notion, but Walter is a rank amateur in the drug business, not even taking into account legal fees or money laundering scenarios. When challenged on these issues, he reacts much the same early on as he would later in season five when Mike reminds him that there are expenses and procedures associated with this business, that is, with hostility and childishness. A truly wise and intelligent person would investigate all these possibilities well in advance, or at least respect the expertise of the individuals in the business and accept their educated advice. But this is Walter's greatest flaw: his titanic ego which stops him from accepting even the mildest forms of advice, particularly when the subject turns to money. In terms of our discussion the salient point here is that while Walter states repeatedly and emphatically that his motivation is to leave a financial legacy, his actions contradict this time and time again. If leaving money to his family were his primary goal, he would be wiser and more modest from the very start. This is the problem with discussing Walter in an attempt to unlock his motivation: he lies about it to others and to himself.

Walter's intellectual legacy is something that is much closer to the heart of his approach to his life and business. We can make that statement based, among other things, on the notion that threatening that legacy is what spurs him into action. Yes, sometimes threatening to take Walter's money motivates him, as it does in "To'hajiilee" (513), but the final deadly act from Walter White comes about not because his son has rejected him, or because his money has been stolen, or because his partner is trapped and enslaved. What prompts him into action is seeing Elliot and Gretchen, his old business associates, claiming on *The Charlie Rose Show* that Walter had nothing substantial to do with the intellectual development of their startup company. He breaks into their home and leaves cash with them with the explicit purpose of giving it to his family when he is gone, but his pleasure in the situation derives from scaring, dominating and ultimately striding about like a Bond villain and demonstrating to his former partners that it is he who controls this situation. This humiliation of Elliot and Gretchen is a pointed gesture, a deliberate revenge for their rewriting of their shared intellectual history. Their company, Grey Matter, is something that Walter considers part of his intellectual legacy, although if he had acquired a larger share of the financial rewards (he was bought out for $5,000 and the company is now worth billions), the conflict motivating the show would not exist.

Aside from Gray Matter, Walter's other intellectual legacy is his "blue meth," synthesized in a series of chemical reactions that Walter knows and he imparts this method to Jesse Pinkman. A chemical synthetic pathway is something every upper level undergraduate course in Organic Chemistry teaches. The skills necessary to synthesize essentially any molecule, starting from any other molecule, are widely available to anyone with this education. Chemical companies that specialize is proprietary products patent their pathways, or at least claim limited exclusivity before, in the case of drugs, being obliged to release the method publicly and compete with generic manufacturers. Therefore it is unlikely that Walter White's formula for methamphetamine is a unique and original process. Walter, it seems, would like to think that he invented a way of synthesizing this drug that was unknown to the world but this is not the case. Hank himself calls it "seventies biker meth," clearly indicating that the formula and steps are known and could easily be researched. This begs the question, if "blue meth" does not represent a unique intellectual legacy, then why is Walter so protective of it? The answer is in something closer to a cultural legacy.

Intellectual ideas such as a formula for "blue meth" belong in the world of science, but while a talented chemist such as Gale Boetticher can synthesize the product to a high degree of purity (over 90 percent), and even an untalented chemist such as Todd Alquist can synthesize the product at 74 percent purity, only Walter, and later Jesse, can get the purity above 95 percent and that characteristic blue color. Therefore it isn't the formula itself that is Walter's legacy, but his technique, his methodology and his lab practices. This is much closer to an art than a science, and thus falls into the category of a great artistic innovation, a cultural legacy. Walter, for example, is highly insulted that an inferior version of his product is circulating and attempts to convince Jack's group to simply hire him and Jesse to make, as he puts it, "Classic Coke" (507, "Say My Name"). When Jesse is taken by Gus and Mike to Mexico to cook for the cartel (410, "Salud"), his first act is not to explain the stereochemistry or some other technical aspect of the process to the laboratory workers, but instead to go into areas of technique, cleanliness and methodology: the artistic part of the process that is Walter's true legacy.

Walter attempts at legacy are thwarted by the forces surrounding the world of *Breaking Bad* from the very first scene of him running for his life in the "Crystal Ship" RV to the very last scene of Jesse escaping the compound where Walter lies dying in the lab where his cultural progeny worked. The last thoughts on Walter White's mind in "Felina" (516) seem to be about his particular way of cooking meth. He smiles as he caresses the perfectly clean reaction vessels and other lab equipment, possibly remembering how much he taught Jesse, who had been working with this equipment for months. He may regard this as his legacy in action, and he lives just long enough to see it take shape in the world before dying among it. But Walter is mistaken if he thinks that his meth, his technique or his money is going to represent his legacy the way he intended. Jesse's jubilant escape and experiences as a prisoner on the compound make any further "cooking" on his part an open question. After having been forced to cook meth for several different parties over the course of the series (starting with Walter, and including Gus, Uncle Jack and the Mexican cartel), as well as his obvious rejection of the profits from such activity by tossing away his money and having to be held prisoner in order to carry out the task of cooking, it seems evident that Jesse's cooking days are done—at least for some time. We can only speculate as to Jesse Pinkman's future activities, and while circumstances may arise that oblige him to make use of this skill (and thus perpetuate part of Walter's cultural legacy), it seems fair to hypothesize that cooking is not positioned as his number one career choice, at least in the short term. And it is far from certain that Elliot and Gretchen will honor Walter's wishes that whatever money he left for them will go to his children. Walter's own family has rejected his offers of help even though they are struggling, and, in a note that must strike at the heart of Walter's masculine pride, his son Walter Jr. even stops using that name, preferring to distance himself from his father. Walter therefore dies in a state of deep delusion about his place in the world and his own influence on it.

Throughout this discussion we have focused on legacy as it applies to the male characters in *Breaking Bad* and their preoccupation with it. But what is the significance of their peculiar fascination with leaving behind a living extension of an individual will? What makes this, at least in *Breaking Bad*, a singular male interest?

Much of this must come from culturally embedded gender normative behavior, which in American society rewards men who dream big and accomplish "great things" while telling women that their greatest triumphs should be domestic or at least revolve around young children. This is evident in, as previously discussed, the attitude of the female characters on the show with regards to legacy. Skyler and Marie are committed to preserving the family unit and making sure that the next generation, Walt Jr. and Holly, have as stable and as "normal" an environment as possible. Walter also states that he shares this goal, but as we have seen, Walter often deludes himself while deluding others about his true intentions. Skyler and Marie don't talk: they act and they work, not on behalf of themselves, but on behalf of the family unit in the here and now. Walter and Hank, though they both profess a commitment to family, nevertheless express that commitment by seeking out career success, not by being present or attentive or have an interest in creating stability in the present.

It should be noted that this gender normative behavior is not particularly empowering for the women, as it obliges them to subsume whatever personal ego they may have in order to commit to the preservation of the family. By contrast, Walter is free to let his ego run wild and still be able to profess a deep commitment to family. Skyler, in fact, feels obliged to send the children to live with Hank and Marie after Walter's actions, motivated though they may be by a desire to provide in the future, have destroyed his family life in the present. Once again, Skyler acts on behalf of the family, and Walter acts on behalf of himself, justified by rhetoric about family. The gender normative values contribute to, or even encourage, the development of a raging personal ego on Walter's part, as he can pursue personal glory, ignore his family, destroy their day-to-day lives and then claim in the end that it was all for them.

There is legacy and there are consequences. Perhaps that is the best way to describe the difference between what characters such as Walter and Gus intend (their legacy) and what they actually create in the world (consequences). Because in our conception, legacy is driving by the desire to defeat death and make one's self immortal by setting in motion forces (whether they be biological, physical, intellectual, cultural or financial) that will continue to act in one's stead. The future, however, cannot be fooled and cannot be controlled. The all-consuming male ego, driven by visions of a glorious future in which women thank them and children gather at their feet as in some sort of familial tableaux, acts in the service of this legacy without ever really considering what is happening in the here and now. These are the consequences of their actions, as unlike some hoped-for legacy far in the future, the characters can see the consequences right before their eyes. Gus's business lies in ruins. Walter's family is destroyed and he is ruined. Hank's body lies in the desert and his police work remains unfinished, the drug "war" rages on. These are the facts "on the ground," but they were all trying in the end to use their legacy to somehow defeat death. The consequences of their actions, which they could have controlled by making different choices, ultimately defeated their legacy. As Shelley puts it, "Nothing beside remains. Round the decay of that colossal wreck, boundless and bare."

Notes

1. *Breaking Bad* creator Vince Gilligan is himself a middle-aged man, which partially explains the show's perspective.
2. Creator Vince Gilligan has made it explicitly clear that he intended Gus to be an associate of Pinchoet's, either through family or personally.

Works Cited

Loveman, Brian. "Military Dictatorship and Political Opposition in Chile, 1973–1986." *Journal of Interamerican Studies and World Affairs* 28, no. 4 (1987): 1–38.
Palumbo, Agt. Robert *Cocaine Cowboys*. Dir. Billy Corben. Los Angeles: Magnolia Pictures, 2006.

Men in Control

Panopticism and Performance

Jeffrey Reid Pettis

His name is Walter Hartwell White. He lives at 308 Negra Arroyo Lane, Albuquerque, New Mexico, 87104. And, being forever subject to surveillance, everybody knows it.

One of the dominant tensions pervading *Breaking Bad* is that the "truth" of Walt's identity will be discovered, that he will be "found out" by the DEA, or worse, his family. Walt perpetually faces the challenges of concealing himself from others, disguising his criminality, and reconciling his multiple existences. Being subject to the surveillance of so many, Walt must increasingly concern himself with how he acts, negotiating the expectations that others have of him, particularly of him as a man. He alternately acts as violent aggressor and familyman, both loving husband and hardened criminal, both mad man and man of business. It is through these performances of typified masculinity that he enters closed-off spaces and escapes the scrutiny of his observers.

Panopticism

In *Discipline and Punish*, Michel Foucault describes how the Panopticon, a prison designed by Jeremy Bentham, reconstituted power relations in the modern age. The prison is circular and contains a central tower from which guards look down onto inmates, who are all in cells along the periphery. The inmates' cells, then, become "so many small theaters, in which each actor is alone, perfectly individualized and constantly visible" (*Discipline* 200). The inmates, though, cannot see the guards in the tower and hence never know when they are being watched. In this structure, power maintains an "omnipresent surveillance," while it itself "remain[s] invisible" (*Discipline* 214). The objective of surveillance here is to "induce in the inmate a state of conscious and permanent visibility that assures the automatic functioning of power" (*Discipline* 201). The convict is trained to regulate his own behavior "automatically," because, as far as he knows, he is being watched at any moment. He must behave himself *just in case* the guard happens to be watching.

This model, Foucault argues, has defined modern society, in which discipline is exercised through a distinctly visual mode. Discipline "coerces by means of observation" (*Discipline* 171), and placing people under constant scrutiny prompts them to constantly behave. If a guard notices misbehavior, punishment, of course, follows. Consequently, whoever is most observed, or at least potentially observed, is most disempowered. In a panoptic society, power is decentralized: those subjected to it cannot locate it in a specific space or with a specific agent. Again, this serves to restrict the subjectivity of those who are hypothetically observed—one must confine oneself to the identities permitted by power unless one wants to be punished.

That said, Walter White, and indeed *Breaking Bad* as a whole, poses a significant challenge to the alleged inescapable reach and influence of panoptic structures. Walt is increasingly limited by observation, but rather than causing him to regulate his behavior, surveillance instead prompts Walt to dismantle the networks of observation in which he is ensnared. Walt traces what theorists Gilles Deleuze and Félix Guattari might call lines of escape from the surveillance network that defines and classifies individuals, that trains and codes their behaviors (*Reader* 214). Through a series of evasions, Walt's actions and reactions allow us to reread panopticism, suggesting that, even when faced with the threat of surveillance, disruption is still possible.

Of particular interest is that Walt's evasions often take the shape of calculated performances—performances, I will suggest, of masculinities that grant him access to spaces that are otherwise inaccessible in a panoptic framework. These performances provide him mobility in an increasingly rigid network of behavioral norms; by rendering himself intelligible through the performance of various familiar, gender-conforming roles, Walt is in fact able to render himself unpredictable and unintelligible. In so doing, he disguises himself from the ever-penetrating gaze of panopticism.

Gus Fring as Panoptic Guard

While panopticism pervades throughout all of *Breaking Bad*, the Gus Fring story arc gives it its most explicit iteration. Notably, Foucault writes that "the Panopticon functions as a [...] *laboratory* of power" that could "be used as a machine to carry out experiments, [and] to alter behavior" (*Discipline* 204, emphasis mine). At the risk of an all-too-literal reading, we see Walt transposed into the super-lab in conjunction with his subjection to Gus Fring's immense panoptic network. The super-lab becomes his new workplace; it also increasingly becomes his prison.

Gus embodies the ultimate panoptic observer, putting increasing pressure on Walt to control himself—to normalize his behavior and render himself predictable. Consider the following guidelines for a panoptic guard developed by John Haslam, a nineteenth-century medical writer quoted in Foucault's *Madness and Civilization*:

> It is a very important object [...] to arouse in [deviants] feelings of respect and obedience [...] superior discernment, distinguished education, and dignity of tone and manner [...] [the guard] must be endowed with a firm character, and on occasion display an imposing strength. He must threaten little but carry out his threats, and if he is disobeyed, punishment must immediately ensue [*Reader* 160].

Gus behaves as nothing less than a professional, simultaneously panoptic guard and "businessman." The first time Walt meets Gus, he says, "I was told that the man I would be meeting with is very careful. A cautious man. I believe we're alike in that way." Gus responds, "I don't think we're alike at all, Mr. White. You are not a cautious man [...] you have poor judgment" (211, "Mandala"). Gus positions himself as the eye of superior discernment; he can calculate and evaluate rationally, whereas Walter cannot. After Gus coordinates the shootout between Hank and the Salamanca twins in the episode "One Minute" (307), Walt meets Gus to discuss the "deeper game." "We're both adults," Walt says, "I want there to be no confusion [...] I respect the strategy" (309, "Kafkaesque"). Further, Gus "threatens little" in a direct fashion, claiming that he doesn't "consider fear to be an effective motivator" (304, "Green Light"), at least no more than the amount inherent in the panoptic system. Gus comes to occupy the position of panoptic guard, with Walt as his prisoner. Gus commands respect, not only in his role as an observer, but also as a "rational" man, which is increasingly aligned with his power. Even more significant, though, is that Gus evokes the trope of a "businessman" and is referred to as such several times throughout the series. Gus' hiding in plain sight is deeply connected to the conception of an ordered, rational masculinity—precisely the opposite of the disordered and unpredictable behaviors Walt comes to inhabit in his performances of masculinities later on.

Gus' professionalism as an observer is largely dependent on his network of surveillance, including Mike, Victor, Tyrus, and a variety of technology. Foucault discusses the development of ocular technologies as coextensive to the deployment of panopticism (*Reader* 189), and indeed video cameras have an integral role in supervising Walt. Most notably, of course, is the camera in the lab. Viewing from the camera's perspective, we see the label CAM001, implying the possible existence of any number of others (403, "Open House"). Walt recognizes that Gus has cameras at the lab, the laundry, and "who knows where else" (501, "Live Free or Die"), pointing again to Gus' unlimited potential for observing. Hence, Walt recognizes of his criminality, "It's all on tape somewhere, or a hard drive" (501). Walt's deviant behaviors have been rendered permanent, fixed in place. Further, when Walt is trying to kill Gus, he says, "[Gus] can *see* me coming like he's some kind of—" (408, "Hermanos," emphasis mine). We can reasonably conclude that he would finish his sentence with "God"—the bird's-eye-view of a Panopticon.

Indeed, Gus seems to see everything, and the audience becomes aligned with him through the inventive camerawork in *Breaking Bad*. Early in the series there are shots from inside the drain of a bathtub (102, "The Cat's in the Bag... "), from the bullet holes in the RV (106, "Crazy Handful of Nothin'"), and so forth. However, the unique angles multiply as Gus' observation of Walt escalates. In the episode "Fly" (310), we see Jesse cleaning from the perspective of a machine, we look down from the ceiling of the lab—incidentally from the same angle Gus' video camera later watches them—and we see them from the fly's perspective. The audience becomes the fly's compound eye, penetrating Walt and Jesse with its many lenses. We see Jesse from inside a vat (312, "Half-Measures"), Gale from inside a box (401, "Box Cutter"); we see shots from inside mixers (404, "Bullet Points"), and from behind shelves of acid (401). Our observation even extends to domestic space as we watch Skyler from behind a basketball net (401) and Jesse from his Roomba (402, "Thirty-Eight Snub"). We watch from anywhere, which is to say everywhere, even at the molecular level when watching a cook in "Hazard Pay" (324).

Walt as Inmate

The continuous scrutiny over Walt incites his behavior to change. Alberto Brodesco, in his essay, "Heisenberg: The Epistemological Implications of a Criminal Pseudonym," cites Colin Bruce's 2004 book *Schrödinger's Rabbits*: "the acquisition of knowledge about a system by an observer [...] can somehow change the behavior of that system" (61). Brodesco continues, "Walter White tries to act like an 'external' experimenter in the world of drug dealing but his entrance into the field changes the entire domain, making it impossible for him to stand outside" (61). With a slight shift in thinking, I suggest that it is indeed impossible for Walt to stand outside the field. In fact, it is impossible because he is not the experimenter, but the experiment. Gus' supervision in the lab-prison acts upon Walt; as an object of study, Walt changes—is forced to change—as a response to the panoptic gaze that focuses on him.

Throughout season four, surveillance both in and out of the lab increases, making Walt's behavior more erratic. Citing Bigot Préameneu's discussion of prisoners' attitudes, Foucault writes:

> The feeling of injustice a prisoner has is one of the causes that *may make his character untamable.* [...] *he becomes habitually angry* against everything around him; he *sees every agent of authority as an executioner; he no longer thinks that he was guilty*; he accuses justice itself [*Discipline* 266, emphasis mine].

This prototypical prisoner is a perfect description of Walt and is indicative of the "untamable" masculine roles he comes to occupy as surveillance acts upon him. First, he is referred to as "mad man," a man incapable of rational thought (412, "End Times"). This is bound up in the notion that he is "untamable," continually defying the expectations of others, particularly authority figures— Gus, Skyler, Hank, and even Bogdan or the police officer who pepper sprays him in "Caballo sin Nombre"; Walt refuses to be controlled. He is "habitually angry" and operates as aggressor, violently lashing out at being observed, whether by Gus or Jesse or Skyler or Hank. Ultimately, he is convinced that Gus intends to murder him, and rather than see himself as guilty he instead justifies his "extreme measures" (401, "Box Cutter")—killing Gale through Jesse and murdering Gus—under the pretense of "good reasons" (502, "Madrigal")—the well-being of his partner and especially his family. His justifications for his "untamable" behaviors are continually rooted in protecting and providing for his family, which allows him to re-present himself as a familyman whenever he has done something reprehensible. He "no longer thinks he is guilty."

Evading the Eye[1]

To deflect the gaze of the Panopticon, Walt engages in a number of evasions, disruptions, and performances, strategically shifting between the position of madman and man of reason, provider and aggressor, and any number of other performances. Despite the apparently limitless reach of both Gus and the audience (via the camera angles), panoptic power still fails. For one, the use of montage during moments of criminality (i.e., during cook scenes) fragments our vision and limits our ability to probe into his delinquency. Further, when Brock is poisoned, we are struck by epistemological doubt. Jesse tells Walt, "Only you and I knew about the ricin" to which Walt responds, "No! You don't even believe that! Gus' cameras everywhere—please! [...] He has known everything all along" (412). Because they are always being watched, Gus *has* to have known, and Walt's limited mobility proves his innocence. The final shot of "Face Off," the lily of the valley, forces us to recognize our own ignorance as panoptic figures, our inability to probe into Walt's deviancy.

Walt, rather than regulating himself, gambles on the potential for anonymity. He is able to evade the panoptic gaze precisely by abandoning the conception of the "rational" man projected by Gus—by becoming "madman." Rather than being ordered, rational, and, in sum a "cautious man," Walt becomes a "disordered" man, using poor judgment and gambling on a number of factors to escape Gus' gaze. By occupying an alternative conception of masculinity, one that appeals to risk, not reason, Walt achieves his freedom.

Thus, under the threat of observation, Walt develops two main lines of escape. The first is his capacity to evade directly, that is, to hide from his observers. For example, when the video camera is installed in the lab, Walt maintains a pretense of normality whilst finding spaces outside of the camera's limited view (407, "Problem Dog"). The second tactic, however, is his ability to construct what is observed—to *perform* a role for his own pragmatic purposes. Indeed, because a panoptic system depends so heavily on the visuality of its subjects as the criterion by which their deviancy is measured, Walt's main strategy is to outwardly perform according to his guards' expectations, while effectively undermining their surveillance.

Recall that when Walt is trying to murder Gus, he requires a place from where he himself cannot be seen, but where Gus remains "in view." He lists the common places that Gus goes, and notes that they are all wired with cameras (413, "Face Off"). The proliferation of cameras limits his capacity to evade directly, and he resorts to his other tactic: controlling what is "in view." Walt and Jesse know that they *could* be watched, so they *demand* to be watched and bring themselves into view more strategically. They create a theater of calculated disruption, drawing the eye to what is most beneficial for them. After Brock is poisoned, Jesse waits in the hospital for him to recover, refusing to cook. His failure to cooperate stages a scene that then forces Gus to divert his gaze. Simultaneously, Walt draws attention to Hector Salamanca under the pretense of a false DEA confession (413). This act distracts Gus by using a figure of "deviant" masculinity. Hector is in poor health, and now, apparently, a coward—traits that go against normative conceptions of masculinity. When Gus arrives to kill Hector, he asks, "What kind of man goes to the DEA, Hector? No man at all" (413). Thus, Walt's line of escape is contingent on staging a performance of deviant masculinity; Hector is not only disordered, but subversive. In this instance, Walt is the lesser of two deviants and, by exploiting Hector, he is granted freer movement in the panoptic network. It is noteworthy that the diversion also disrupts Gus' performance of rational "businessman," which he abandons for the less rational, vengeance-seeking impulse that leads to his demise. The panoptic gaze is unable to focus on two deviants simultaneously, and Walt's plan to kill Gus comes to fruition.[2]

From Inmate to Warden

Walt's theater of disruption is part of a more elaborate inversion of the panoptic gaze that allows him to move about freely and fashion himself as the new prison warden. Under Gus' penetrating gaze, Walt trains himself to occupy the same role. Walt inspects minute details in the super-lab and watches over Jesse as he steals meth (309, "Kafkaesque"). In the episode "Fly" (310), Jesse bends over in an attempt to continue the cook. When he stands up again, Walt is standing behind him, watching. Subsequently, Jesse breaks up the product, and Walt again stands behind him, and though Walt remains out of sight, Jesse is aware of being watched (311, "Abiquiu"). Jesse, consequently regulates his behavior and tells Badger and Skinny Pete that Walt is "watching his every move" and that it is becoming harder to move product (311).

Since his employment with Gus has been ridden with surveillance, Walt becomes increasingly adept at carving out his own network of observation. When paralyzed by surveillance, Walt uses Jesse to expand his own ocular network, getting Jesse to find Gale's address—to become his auxiliary eyes (313, "Full Measure"). Later, paranoid that anyone could be a guard, Walt reverses the gaze on Jesse by planting a bug on Jesse's car. He checks Jesse's phone and recognizes that there were meetings between he and Gus (408, "Hermanos"). Following from the theater of disruption Walt enacts, the symbols of observation become increasingly aligned with Walt; he shifts toward monitoring

Gus through binoculars, his glasses (an ocular symbol), propped up on his head (412, "End Times").

Walt's training as a panoptic figure has effectively ended by season five and he becomes the panoptic guard. Following Gus' death, he, Mike, and Jesse execute the plan to destroy Gus' laptop—the final symbol of Gus' ocular power. As they drive away, Mike challenges Walt and asks how he knows if their plan even worked. Walt, notably out of view in the backseat, replies: "Because I say so." In this scene, Walt commands his "equal partners" from behind, leaving Mike and Jesse unable to see him while he sees them. Walt becomes the out-of-view figure—the Panopticon— that exercises arbitrary power over his inmates (501, "Live Free or Die"). Walt expands his network by infiltrating the DEA and, after faking emotional instability, plants surveillance bugs throughout Hank's office (505, "Dead Freight"). Note that Walt enacts an emotional, distraught performance—a deviant, "unmanly" masculinity in front of, arguably, the most "macho" character in the show. In so doing, he strategically diverts attention away from himself, much in the same way that Hector's deviant masculinity was exploited to distract Gus. In both instances, Walt forces the panoptic gaze to a deviant masculinity in order to pass by undetected and reverse the observed-observer dynamic.

The narrative of Walt as a panoptic figure culminates in the episode "Gliding Over All" 508), where Walt literally fashions himself as a prison warden. Walt expands his network, hiring Jack and the Neo-Nazis, and takes control over a series of prisons, with the goal of killing those prisoners who are a threat to his power for having *seen too much*. Not only that, but the prisons exist in different locations: Walt's network of observation is no longer limited, even by geography. In this scene, Walt simultaneously adopts the rational conception of masculinity set forth by Gus—his plan is calculated and precise—and the trope of a violent aggressor. In addition, the music during the prison montage is "Pick Yourself Up" by Nat King Cole. The lyrics of the song code the prison murders as a masculine pursuit. A notable refrain in the song promises Walt manhood, particularly through violence. The lyrics in the chorus align Walt with great masculine figures. Further, the chorus implies that Walt (to reverse his phraseology from season one) will decay and grow and then transform. The last words Nat King Cole sings point to the idea that Walt's masculinity is not fixed. At any moment, he is able to escape, to reconfigure himself ad infinitum in any number of masculine guises, including deviant ones—in this case both man of reason and violent aggressor.

In *Breaking Bad*, then, we see evasions and disruptive performances as tools for drawing new lines of escape from panoptic tyrannies. In short, Walt behaves "irrationally" and takes risks to find holes in the fabric of the ocular. Walt demonstrates that the threat of observation is not enough. Forcing the eye elsewhere and carving out new networks of observation: these are Walt's tactics. Most significantly, Walt's disruptions are performed in a specifically gendered fashion. Indeed, he enacts a number of masculine tropes to subvert the ever-present eye and better navigate through the over-coded network of observation.

"Get that sweet ass out of here": Overcoding Gender and Space

Recall that we began with Foucault's comment that the cells in the Panopticon can be considered "so many small theaters, in which each actor is alone, perfectly individualized and constantly visible" (*Discipline* 200). Further, he states that panoptic prisoners are both inmates and guards, that is, they "play both roles" (*Discipline* 202). The very language that Foucault uses to describe a surveillance society—theaters, actors, roles—contains intimations of performance.

As such, surveillance society tends to codify behaviors in rigid terms; each actor is prescribed a stage and is expected to perform his or her role accordingly. Social spaces become the stages for performance. In "Breaking Bad and Blending Boundaries: Myths of Masculinity and the Superhero," Lisa Weckerle writes that "femininity has been traditionally associated with the private sphere and domestic work, [and] masculinity has been traditionally associated with the public sphere and wage-earning work" (Weckerle 10). Because panopticism demands "normal" behavior, surveillance society tends to reify gender roles and attribute them to fixed spaces. Here we may utilize the term "overcoding" as defined by Deleuze and Guattari. In *Capitalism and Schizophrenia*, they suggest that

> life is spatially and socially segmented. The house is segmented according to its rooms' assigned purposes; streets, according to the order of the city; the factory, according to the nature of the work and operations performed in it. We are segmented in a *binary* fashion, following the great major dualist oppositions: social classes, but also men-women, adults-children, and so on [...] We are segmented in a *linear* fashion, along a straight line or a number of straight lines, of which each segment represents an episode or "proceeding": as soon as we finish one proceeding we begin another [*A Thousand Plateaus* 209].

As it applies to our discussion here, Deleuze and Guattari note that each place is divided from others and spaces like domestic homes have sub-divisions within them. Similarly, people are divided—most relevant to our discussion is the men-women binary that is established as part of the process of overcoding society. Finally, Deleuze and Guattari note that each person is divided into parts (identities) that lead into one another in a specifically linear way, unable to deviate. Space and identity are bound up in this same process of overcoding. In a society that demands visuality, and hence demands the performance of identity, the scripts that govern interactions become "exceptionally rigid" (*A Thousand Plateaus* 210) in both where and by whom they can be performed.

Hank and Marie arguably represent the most reified separate spheres, relying on scripts of overcoded gender. After Hank kills Tuco, he is unwilling to show weakness (his PTSD) directly, and overcodes his masculine behaviors even more dramatically, engaging in the stereotypically masculine pursuit of making Schraderbrau in his garage, which Marie refers to as his "man cave" (205, "Breakage"). When she enters his masculinized space, she asks him what he's doing and he responds, "What does it look like I'm doing? Beating off?" and later tells her, "Get that sweet ass out of here so I can concentrate" (205), using sexual deflections to deny her access to his "man cave." This persists throughout the series, where Hank's career and other pursuits are at the forefront and Marie is consistently excluded. For example, when Hank becomes increasingly obsessed with finding Heisenberg, he spends all night on a stakeout trying to find the RV. When he comes home, he and Marie have a conversation where Hank stands on one side of the shower curtain and Marie on the other, a division that further sub-divides their domestic space. Marie asks how Hank "feels" about Stephen going to El Paso in his stead. Hank says that he "turned it down. End of story." He continues, "I needed some time here. I'm deep into this investigation and I couldn't do both. I made a judgment call." The husband and wife are set up in rigid binaries. Hank refers to his decision as a "judgment call," establishing himself as a "reasonable" man as opposed to Marie's emotional focus. Marie then offers him the opportunity to talk about things and tells him he doesn't have to go through the situation alone, offering emotional support. The two continue:

HANK: Do you ask me which lead bib to put on someone before you nuke 'em? Jesus Marie. I made a decision. I'm not going through anything. I'm doing my job.
MARIE: I would like —
HANK: I know. A condo in Georgetown. I know.

MARIE: If you would let me finish, I was going to say, I'd like to be included. That's all [305, "Más"].

Marie tries to "be included" in Hank's sphere through emotion, but Hank's identity is comprised of a conception of masculinity focused on strength, providing, and work. When she continues to use the language of an overcoded femininity, encouraging him to talk about his feelings, he responds by arguing that he doesn't tell her "which lead bib to put on someone before [she] nuke[s] them," redirecting to her career as a nurse, and then justifies his actions under the guise of his own job. He assumes her wants are centered on the domestic —a condo, in particular—and he continually deflects her using the masculinized space of his career. He ultimately asks her if she's late for work, yet another appeal to wage-earning as the dominant discourse, in order to get her to leave; he even tells her not to worry about his career, though her concerns are clearly directed towards his own emotional well-being.

Clinging to conceptions of masculinity-as-strength, when Hank is injured he becomes overly aggressive toward Marie, overcoding his position in the family unit. After a successful walk around the house, during which Hank literally navigates space, his personal trainer says "That's what I call kickin' some ass," pairing violence with his mobility, and Hank gives him an enthusiastic high-five; Marie receives one only reluctantly. Immediately after an enthused discussion with his personal trainer, Hank kicks Marie out of his room, not allowing Marie to see him in a weakened state (242, "Thirty-Eight Snub").[3] Even when Hank and Marie start acting as a team to catch Walt, Marie is relegated to a separate space. For example, Hank brings Jesse to their home, packs a bag for Marie and books her a spa package, setting aside a feminized space away from his pursuits (512, "Rabid Dog"). Hank, Steve, and Jesse are in the Schrader household preparing to film Jesse's account of events. Marie brings them coffee, and then says she'll go run some errands, literally removing herself from the space and figuratively withdrawing from their masculinized pursuit (512).

Overcoding Overhauled

Unlike Hank and Marie, Walt refuses to consistently commit to a set performance of gender, which allows him greater freedom. In season three, when Walt and Skyler are experiencing tensions in their marriage, Junior reproaches Walt. Walt apologizes to him in the following way: "I am the man that I am, son, and there's plenty I would change about that, but here we are. And this is just what it is" (306, "Sunset"). At first glance, Walt seems to be positing an unchangeable notion of masculinity; he "would change," implying that it is not actually possible. However, more subversively, Walt equivocates on what defines his masculinity. The tautology of "I am the man that I am" offers no real definition and allows Walt the freedom to change the parameters of masculinity as suited to his interests at the time.

In her book *Gender Trouble*, Judith Butler describes how gender is not an inherent quality, but rather constructed through performance. She reflects on alternatives to rigid gender norms and discusses "identities that are alternately instituted and relinquished according to the purposes at hand" that permit "divergences" and avoid "definitional closure" (Butler 22). Walt adopts and rejects, at various times, various conceptions of masculinity in order to achieve his goals. His avoidance of "definitional closure" is precisely what allows him to disrupt surveillance.

In a system that segments individuals and fixes them in place, Walt, then, is the exception to the rule. Walt is able to pass at will between segments, occupying different spaces on the spectrum of masculinity as he pleases. Moreover, his movement is not unidirectional; he is able to jump between segments without a smooth progression. As Weckerle states, "Walt evolves in his performance of significant ideals of masculinity: man as provider, property owner, active subject, sexual dominator, competitor, and inflictor of violence" (Weckerle 13). I argue that this is not a linear progression, but rather Walt uses each of these alternately for pragmatic purposes.

In order for this to be possible, though, he codes himself in terms that are intelligible and coherent to the normalizing judgment of panopticism and the people around him. His performances must be perceived as realistic to be acknowledged, and must be acknowledged in order for him to subvert surveillance. Yet, Walt's masculine identities are "discontinuous" (Butler 23) in that he refuses to limit himself to a uniform conception and instead uses a range of typified masculinities. Weckerle writes that Walt is "unable to inhabit all areas of masculinity simultaneously" (Weckerle 19). This is true, but he does not need to occupy all spaces at once; his very strength lies in his ability to abandon one performance for another when it is no longer efficacious for him.

I've established that ocular culture reifies separate spaces and posited the fact that, through the performances of masculinities, Walt is able to evade suspicion and enter new spaces. To make this discussion more specific, it will be helpful to examine what, exactly, are the performances Walt adopts and what effects they produce under the surveillance he is exposed to.

The Rational Businessman and the Madman

One performance is best reflected in Gus: man-as-businessman. Having discovered that Gus' dealers used Tomas to kill Combo, Jesse develops the plan to murder them using the ricin. He is brought to the chicken farm to discuss his actions and Gus tells him, "Listen to me. You have one friend in this room. This man [referring to Walt]—if it wasn't for this man, and the respect I have for him, I would be dealing with this in a much different manner" (312, "Half-Measures"). Gus posits Walt as a respectable, rational man at this point in the arc. Walt has used reason as a means for saving his partner, but shortly after he comes to Jesse's aid and murders the two rival dealers (312). Ostensibly, this is not a "rational" business decision, in terms of a cost-benefit analysis, and Gus challenges him on his choices. Gus asks if Walt's medical condition has worsened[4] and Walt responds that he's "quite well." Gus responds: "No, clearly you are not. No rational person would do as you have done. Explain yourself" (313, "Full Measure"). Walt, having temporarily deviated from the man-as-businessman trope and adopting the man-as-aggressor trope in order to save his partner, returns to the performance of masculinity that will most appease Gus. He says, "You've always struck me as a very pragmatic man so if I may I'd like to review options with you" (313); he then does a cost-benefit analysis of killing Jesse, listing the resources that would be expended in order to follow through. He states that they could simply forget about Pinkman and have a "long and fruitful business arrangement" (313). Essentially, Walt evokes the performance of a businessman as a strategy for evading Gus' discipline. Walt pleads for his life in economic terms when he is about to be punished for arranging Gale's murder. He explains why it isn't financially viable to kill him and/or Jesse. His appeal ends: "Don't do this. You're too smart. You can't afford to do this ... let us just go back to work. We're here. Let us work. We're ready to go to work" (401, "Box Cutter"). He evokes the economic terms once more, telling Gus that he "can't afford" to kill him and positing himself again as a rational businessman.

In Season Five, when Walt has been established as the most significant panoptic figure, he tries to get Mike to join him and Jesse in their new business operation. He tells Mike to "leave emotion out of this decision" (402, "Thirty-Eight Snub"), positing reason above emotion. When Mike establishes the division of labor for the new venture, he says, "I handle the business.... You do not tell me how to take care of business" (402). Saul is surprised that Walt is "okay with that" and Walt responds: "He handles the business and I handle him" (402). Walt fashions himself as a business manager, establishing himself at the top of a hierarchy and thereby allowing him free reign over the space of business.[5] He handles both the cooking and the economic decisions, dismantling the notion of separate spaces through a masculinized role—a rational, controlling businessman.

It should be noted that Walt's performance of control extends beyond business and into the realm of health, which becomes aligned with masculinity. Consider the scene when Walt is waiting for a scan and another cancer patient discusses his challenges. The man tells Walt, "the biggest wake up call [was] letting go. Giving up control. It's like they say. Make plans and God laughs." Walt responds:

> That is such bullshit. Never give up control. Live life on your own terms [...] to hell with your cancer [...] every life comes with a death sentence. So every few months I come in here for my regular scan knowing full well that one of these times, hell maybe even today, I'm going to hear some bad news. But until then who's in charge? Me. That's how I live my life [408, "Hermanos"].

Walt enacts courage, physical strength, and health—all of which are part of traditional notions of masculinity. He enacts control, but this scene occurs while is totally subservient to Gus, totally disempowered when at work in the lab, which points to the fact that his control is a performance, as at this point he is most assuredly not "in charge."

The Unfaithful Spouse, the Estranged Husband and the Familyman

Weckerle discusses the "traditional masculine role as 'breadwinner, nine to fiver, and father, at the helm of both the economic and the social order of the family" (Weckerle 10). Hence, when Walt is trying to launder his money he refuses to let it be acquired by "a mystery benefactor or blind luck" (212, "Phoenix"), hesitant of using Junior's website for laundering. He wants the credit as businessman and provider for his family—performances that occasionally overlap. Consider, for example, the convergence of businessman and provider when he and Skyler opt to buy the carwash; his world of business blends with his domestic space.[6] While Walt's performance as a rational, in-control businessman allows him to enter new realms of criminality and save his life several times, his performance of man-as-provider is a much more ubiquitous evasion throughout the series.

Skyler is one of Walt's most active panoptic guards for most of the series, constantly trying to probe into his criminal activities and indeed into the very core of his being, which he resists through his "familyman" performances. Throughout the series Skyler attempts to define Walt and his acceptable spaces. In season one, she frequently asks Walt where he was. When she becomes suspicious of Walt's second cell phone, she continually attempts to bring definition to their relationship. A pattern emerges in which the cell phone is tied to the notion of the unfaithful husband, a ready-made trope Walt tries to use to his advantage. When Skyler first finds out about the second cell phone, she says: "Okay, then, let's assume there's a second cell phone. So what, is he having an affair?" (203, "Bit by a Dead Bee"). Walt first lies about its existence (203) and later tries to explain the call she heard him receive the night he disappeared. He goes through the following performance:

> I was thinking about what you asked me the other night. You know, you were wondering if I had a second cell phone and I've been thinking about that a lot and I think what you heard was my cell phone alarm going off. Yes, I've been using it a lot as a medication reminder to uh—well remind me to take my medication. And uh, well, the weird thing is that the alarm sound is almost exactly the same as the regular phone ring, which is really a poor design if you ask me but I think that was probably it. I tried to go in to change it to a different sound other than the phone ring but they so overcomplicate these things. Anyway, it was probably just as well that I lost it [204, "Down"].

By this point, Skyler has stormed out of the house. While Walt's "ers" and "uhs" are enough to render his explanation suspect, his performances of masculinities are unrealistic because they are radically out of sync with performances he has enacted before. He plays the role of a bumbling husband, unable to use his technology properly. Moreover, he references his ill health. Both of these are disconnected from the rational, healthy man he has projected thus far. Skyler sees through it. Walt, then, adopts another tactic—that of an unfaithful spouse—which we saw Skyler ready to accept previously. Walt prompts her to talk about their issues and says, "I feel like you're upset with me because you think that I'm up to something." When Skyler asks what he could mean, Walt says, "I have no idea, Skyler. What, that I'm having an affair? Is that it? Is that what you think? Is that why you asked me about the—some other phone, because you think I'm being unfaithful?" and demands that she ask him outright, claiming that he would tell her. He concludes by saying, "And no, I'm not. I'm not having an affair, okay? Now what do I do to prove that to you? Swear an oath? Okay, my right hand to God I am not having an affair" (204).

His earlier performances—that of a bumbling husband unable to operate a cell phone and the "deviant" performance of the unhealthy man—are here replaced with the ready-made trope Skyler was ready to accept: that of an unfaithful husband. However, this serves to provoke Skyler's annoyance: "I heard you, Walt. You're not having an affair. Congratulations" (204). By the end of the conversation, Skyler has stormed out and Walt chases after her, immediately changing the tactic of his performance. He stands at the car window and demands, "Do you know what I've done for this family?" (204), beginning to evoke the man-as-provider performance as one last gambit.

The authenticity of Walt's performances, whether because they are unrealistic (in terms of the bumbling husband) or laid on too thick (in terms of the unfaithful spouse) fail to prevent Skyler's panoptic scrutiny. After Skyler asks Walt if he brought his cell phone and he responds, "Which one," she tells him that she wants him out of the house. In so doing, she tries to subdivide the domestic home and overcode their relationship with rigid divisions. He tries to claim that the issue of the second cell phone was "asked and answered." Walt demands, "You tell me exactly what it is you think I'm lying about. What? An affair? I'm having an affair? Is that what you think?" and asks, "With whom? Who am I having an affair with?" (213, "ABQ"); he repeats a similar refrain to his earlier performance: "Jesus, Skyler, get me a Bible to swear on if that's what it takes. I am not having an affair with Gretchen" (213). At this point, Skyler catalogues the extent of her surveillance of Walt, saying that she called Gretchen, checked with the doctor, and called his mother. Clearly, Walt's repetition of the unfaithful spouse trope has not allowed him to escape surveillance.

Subsequently, Skyler deduces that Walt is a drug dealer (301, "No Más") and threatens him with divorce, a "punitive" disciplinary action for his criminality that would rigidly overcode their relationship. Consistently throughout seasons three, four, and five there is much discussion about who is allowed in their domestic space, with a particular emphasis on creating divisions and subdivisions for their family unit. Consider their discussions about separating the children from Walt, whether by sending them to Hank and Marie's or boarding school (504, "Fifty-One"; 505, "Dead Freight"). Interestingly, Skyler takes on the role of subdividing their household and refers to Hank and Marie as a resource, who have themselves defined the boundaries of their own home quite rigidly.

Exposed as a meth manufacturer, Walt abandons his unfaithful spouse performance and successfully adopts his familyman performance to evade Skyler's disciplinary measures. He acts as a provider to Skyler and the family, despite the fact that his earnings are from an illicit business. He brings Skyler his money and lists all the things that his money can pay for: college tuition for both children, health insurance for Skyler and the kids, Junior's physical therapy and SAT tutor, groceries, gas, birthdays, graduation parties, and the mortgage on the house (306, "Sunset"). All of the expenses he lists are family-oriented. In redirecting his criminality through the performance of man-as-provider, he is able to reopen discussions Skyler had closed off.

Walt enacts overcoded masculine performances pragmatically; first, to evade scrutiny and then re-enter closed-off spaces. Walt successfully deflects attention away from his second cell phone, however temporarily, by fixing the garage door and water heater (210, "Over"). When threatened with estrangement, he brings pizza over to the house. Skyler subverts his performance by telling him she's making dinner and Walt asks, "What kind of example do we want to set here?" He appeals to her sense of *performing* as a functional family for Junior's benefit.

Skyler later threatens to segment their respective spaces with a restraining order,[7] but ultimately, Walt is able to physically re-enter the restricted domestic setting through the crawl space beneath the house (302, "Caballo sin Nombre"). Notably, he is able to enter through the very crawl space that he cleared of rot when he adopted the familyman performance earlier. His earlier performance cleared the space, both literally and figuratively, for him to transcend overcoded boundaries.

Moreover, once Walt has entered the home he spontaneously shifts his performances between tropes of aggressor to familyman. After re-entering the house, Skyler returns and threatens call the police, that is, to utilize the institutions of justice to recode the situation. Walt begins his defense by adopting the role of familyman, stating, "Do what you have to do, Skyler. This family is everything to me. Without it, I have nothing to lose" (303, "I.F.T."). Skyler continues with her rival performance of estranged spouse and tells the 911 operator that her "soon-to-be-ex-husband" broke in. Walt, adopting the role of familyman, refuses to respond to her enacted script. Instead, he plays the fatherly role and makes grilled cheese when Junior comes home. When the police arrive, Walt's familyman persona is familiar; the police are able to recognize him as someone who belongs in the given space.

Skyler, refusing to say that the situation involves violence, does not go far enough in her performance of abused spouse to have him removed. Notably, the police say, that they "can't arrest a man for breaking into his own house" (303). The cultural scripts of a nuclear family that Walt adopts in his performance, for example picking up his crying infant daughter and telling Skyler that he's "got it," have allowed him to regain entry to the space from which he had been divided. His performance culminates with him telling the police that he hasn't "been the most attentive husband lately," with Junior chiming in "my dad is a great guy" (303). By playing up his role as familyman (and moreover head of the household, proprietor of the house, etc.), he is able to avoid scrutiny by his son and the police, and is finally granted re-entry, which Skyler bitterly acknowledges when she says, "Welcome home, Walt" (303).

As they continue to experience marital tensions throughout season three, the two try to negotiate their separate spaces. Skyler becomes more invested in having a plausible "story"—that is, performance—that will help them avoid scrutiny from the police. Skyler ultimately recognizes the need for Walt to perform the familyman role for the story to be plausible. When Walt gains this ground through the familyman trope, he continues to bargain for more privileges, for greater entry, into the space. He says the story would be better "if the husband were no longer estranged" and tells Skyler that he wants his own key for "emergencies and *appearances,*" again focusing on the visuality of their lives. Walt continues: "I am going to babysit my own daughter. I am going to help my son with his homework. I am going to be part of this family. And that is how we'll sell your little fiction" (312, "Half-Measures"). He defines the terms of a family man performance, citing each act in the future tense. He decides on the behaviors he will perform in a fixed and definitive fashion and gains that much more ground, simultaneously evading scrutiny from the police and allowing him to re-enter his home.[8]

In season five, Walt performs as the ultimate familyman. He starts cooking the meals, doing the dishes, etc. As Skyler mourns in bed her actions and the consequences for Ted, Walt comes in and states, "You missed a good meal. The lasagna came out very well if I do say so myself. I wrapped some up for you if you'd like some later" (502, "Madrigal"). Skyler is rendered docile, and Walt continues to perform the acts of a good husband, dismantling any "objective" reason Skyler could provide in order to keep him out. In the following episode, Walt decides to officially move back in. Skyler notices him unpacking and ask if he's moving back in and asks him if he thinks it's a good idea. He replies, "Yes" (503, "Hazard Pay"). Their discussion ends there. Walt is able to assert his control over their shared domestic space. Discussion is no longer possible as he performs his role as provider and family man so flawlessly that any objection to his performance would be seen as unintelligible.

The Aggressor

Of course, all of these performances run concurrent to Walt's perform-ance as aggressor. Acting as a family man, Walt goes to the hardware store to buy supplies for the crawl space. He meets a rival meth manufacturer and gives him helpful advice, almost like a father figure. Immediately thereafter he enters the parking lot and adopts his hyper-aggressive masculinity. With a menacing sneer he tells his rivals: "Stay out of my territory" (210, "Over"). Immediately after serving as familyman, he makes the aggressive demand at the heart of the matter: Walt wants to control the space—to control the territory, and does so through an ever-shifting conception of masculinity.

Of course, one of the reasons Walt's performances are effective is because he shifts between them and allows them to bleed into one another. Consider, for example, when Skyler attempts to redefine their domestic space by having the children move out (504, "Fifty-One"). Skyler tells Walt that "a new envi-ronment might be good for them," and he asks "What's wrong with their envi-ronment?" (504). Skyler is posing a challenge to the domestic(ated) space that Walt has established.

To control the discussion, Walt first makes light of the situation and then plays the role of supportive husband. He reassures Skyler that there is "absolutely nothing to be afraid of any more" and then goes on to talk about his birthday party, re-establishing him as the head of the household. Skyler re-opens the discussion later in the episode. Walt says that it has never been safer for them and they have the following exchange:

> SKYLER: Never been? A couple weeks ago a man was coming to this house to kill us. To murder your entire family. You were in the crawl space screaming.
> WALT: And I dealt with him. It's over.
> SKYLER: It is not. You're right back in the meth business again.
> WALT: This is different. Now I'm running things.
> SKYLER: So wait now that you're in charge, it's what? It's going to be smooth sailing from here on out?
> WALT: I don't see why not. I keep the work at work, Skyler. And nothing will ever impact you or the kids [504].

Walt simultaneously portrays a variety of performances. He asserts himself as a familyman, ostensibly putting his family's safety above all else. He also asserts his role as businessman, moreover a businessman in control. He assumes that due to his control there will be no more problems and that in enacting that role, "nothing will ever impact" his family, allowing him to deflect Skyler's concerns. He says that he keeps "the work at work," reinforcing the fact that there is a separate space for his criminality and that he alone is able to transcend the boundaries between work and home. Skyler continues to protest, claiming that his work has affected her as well, alluding to Ted Beneke. Walt tries to over-code her performance by appealing to family once more, stating, "You made a mistake and things got out of control. But you did what you had to do to protect your family and I'm sorry, that doesn't make you a bad person. It makes you a human being." Skyler challenges Walt's rationale (note that she disrupts his performance of man of reason) and the two engage in a sort of strategizing to redefine the space. Skyler claims to have gotten the kids out of the house and they continue from there:

> **WALT:** To a sleepover at their aunt and uncle's? They spend a day or two. Junior stays up late watching movies and then what happens?
> **SKYLER:** We'll see.
> **WALT:** No, I'll tell you what happens. They come home. To this house. To their parents that love them.
> **SKYLER:** No. I will not let our business endanger them [504].

At first, Walt enacts the role of family man, stating definitively that the kids come home to "their parents that love them," using his role as father figure to persuade Skyler. When this tactic doesn't work, Walt starts to advance in a very similar way to his performance of aggression in "Over" when he advances on the rival dealers and sneers, "Stay out of my territory." He adopts a new guise of masculinity as a way to gain ground in the discussion and dominate the home. The conversation continues with Walt asking, "What are you going to do to stop it?" calling for her next move and demanding a rational, mathematical performance from her. Skyler claims that she'll hurt herself so that Hank and Marie can see that they're struggling and make it clear that they need more time. Walt's next move is to suggest that her performance would only indicate her own struggle and that he would put her in an in-patient facility while he cares for the children. Skyler ups the ante by suggesting she'll "show up with bruises" to suggest that Walt beat her after finding out about Ted (504). Walt criticizes her as follows:

> I see. So you want to involve Ted. Oh well that'll be fun bringing the police up to speed on all that. But not as much fun as telling your sixteen-year-old son that his father is a wife beater. Also not a very good plan, what else you got?

After some more discussion Walt continues:

What are you going to do? What, are you going to run off to France? You
gonna close the curtains? Change the locks? This is a joke. Come on, Skyler.
You wanna take me on? You wanna take away my children? What's the plan?
[504].

In this discussion, there are several details worth mentioning. Skyler's plan,
first of all, is to let Hank and Marie *see* that they're struggling. Both actors in
this domestic scene recognize that they must present a visual display in order
to evade scrutiny from Hank and Marie, arguably the largest panoptic figures
at this point in the series. Walt, abandoning his family man role, first shifts
into his performance of rational man, and demands a step-by-step account of
Skyler's plan. Then, he reinforces the performance of a familyman, knowing
Skyler would not want Junior to see his father as a wife-beater. As the discussion escalates, Walt enacts his man-as-aggressor role. Thus, throughout the
discussion, Walt continually shifts between his performances of masculinities.
Skyler, however, continually enacts the same performance of feminine weakness, whether in regard to her suicide attempt or being an abused spouse. She
is limited to one performance, while Walt freely navigates performances and
continues to dominate the domestic space, forcing Skyler to recognize that
she "can't go to the police. [She] can't stop laundering [Walt's] money. [She]
can't keep [him] out of this house. [She] can't even keep [him] out of [her]
bed" (504). At this point, she recognizes that Walt can transcend any barriers
he wants. Walt is an actor, playing a number of roles in a theater that he increasingly controls.

A Convergence of Performances

The most explicitly iterated script is the literal one enacted by Walt and
Skyler in "Bullet Points" (404). The two develop the gambling story to explain
their decision to purchase a car wash and escape scrutiny into their finances.
Skyler focuses on the authenticity of the "story." She tells Walt: "We have to
get our stories straight. We've got to be on the same page," pointing to the fact
that the two must enact a performance together. Using her fiction writing
background, she prepares a script to perform for Hank and Marie, stating, "we
need this story to be solid and sympathetic and most of all completely believ-
able." Skyler tells Walt that Hank thinks insurance is paying for everything
and that Marie has not mentioned their contribution. Skyler specifically
accommodates for Hank's masculinized space; the script allows him to maintain both male provider and healthy man. She continues, "Coming clean with

Hank and Junior—*appearing* to come clean will be the best thing for everyone." Skyler is privy to the difference between performance and authenticity. She corrects herself when speaking to Walt, drawing his attention to the fact that in "appearing" one way, the reality of the situation can pass by unnoticed. She runs through the script, but Walt is clearly disengaged, perhaps because he is already an expert in performing roles. Skyler continues:

> Okay. So I really think we should tag team the narrative, okay? We'll each be responsible for certain portions of the story, and then we can, uh, we can hand off so we don't leave anything out, and it'll seem the most natural.

Skyler points to the fact that the two must act together. They must abandon their estranged spouse performances for the story to be effective. By acting in conjunction, Walt is able to resume his family man role to deflect surveillance. Also noteworthy is the fact that Skyler wants it to "seem" natural. The reality is irrelevant. Walt is reluctant to use the line "It's a doozy, so hold on to your hats." Skyler responds, "It accomplishes two things. It keeps it light while letting them know to expect something big." She looks at what the narrative *accomplishes*, pointing to the specifically pragmatic function of the performance. Significantly, the conversation continues as follows:

> Okay. Anyway, that's where you will take over, starting with your diagnosis, pages 1 and 2. Okay, and it's—it's pretty much going to run parallel to the truth, which makes it easier, but, um, just make sure to really hit the cancer, really touch on the fear and despair. It's good to remind them and to get their sympathy right off the bat. We want them to understand why you could do something so stupid [...] after you say "gambling became an addiction, and I just couldn't control it" [...] I'll chime in about how it affected our marriage, uh, starting with the confusion, uh, the deceit, why we couldn't tell anyone.

Skyler constructs a role for Walt that runs counter to his other performances. It entails playing up his cancer treatment and the "fear and despair," unmanly qualities. She tries to arouse sympathy from her audience, despite Walt's prideful nature, in order to have them understand why he "could do something so stupid," which runs counter to his rational businessman performance. He is no longer "in control," but subject to his gambling addiction. Skyler then plays up their marital difficulties and the estranged spouse performance. It is written that Walt will say he is "terribly, terribly sorry" and expresses dissatisfaction with the two "terribly"s? "I just wouldn't use that word. I would never say the word 'terribly' [...] And why—why am I so ashamed? [...] I was and am providing for our family [...] I'm weak, and I'm out of control. I mean, this whole thing makes me look like crap." Walt does not want to show weakness or shame, hoping to retain his masculine identity. He asserts that he is a provider and wants credit for it. Moreover, he wants to be seen as a worthy father-figure, stating "I don't want Junior thinking less of me." For her own part, Skyler plays up her emotions as a feminine appeal to Marie, in particular. She suggests to Walt that he "look down on the floor with remorse," emphasizing that he doesn't have to mean it. For her part, she says, "I was thinking thinking of taking Marie's hand and saying something emotional like, 'It's such a relief to tell you. We're just so glad we have a strong family to help us through this. That we can all support each other.' And then maybe I'll tear up a little." Skyler emphasizes a performance of distress, trying to bond with Marie through feeling, echoing Marie's concern when Marie probes into Hank's experiences. Skyler encourages Walt to express remorse, deflecting attention with a "deviant" masculinity; Hank does not engage well with emotion and will not by likely to ask follow up questions about how Walt feels. Each move, in turn, deflects the suspicions of their audience.

Perhaps the most impeccable performance of masculinities is the one Walt makes in "Ozymandias" (514) when he calls home to Skyler for the last time. Junior and Skyler are aware that Hank has arrested Walt. Walt returns home and tells them to pack their bags, and they get into an argument following the miscommunication that Walt has killed Hank. Walt kidnaps Holly and leaves Skyler screaming in the street. Later, he makes a phone call home in which all of his performances of masculinities converge, utilizing over-coded tropes once more, though discontinuous with one another, to escape scrutiny for both himself and Skyler, and carve out a new space for himself. There is much to discuss in that final phone call, so I will quote portions of it at length:

> **WALT:** Skyler, it's me. Pick up.
> **SKYLER:** (to police) That's him. That's my husband.
> **WALT:** Skyler. I know you're there. So pick it up. Skyler. You hear me? Answer the phone.
> **SKYLER:** Walt. Where's Holly?
> **WALT:** Are you alone? No police?
> **SKYLER:** No. No police. Where are you? Where's Holly? Walt! [514].

The discussion begins with Walt cast in the role of husband and father. When Skyler states that there are no police, Walt infers otherwise and immediately shifts into his role as aggressor, demanding, "What the hell is wrong with you? Why can't you do one thing I say? [...] This is your fault. This is what comes of your disrespect. I told you, Skyler. I warned you for a solid year. You cross me—there will be consequences. What part of that didn't you understand?"

Walt here codes the discussion as being between an aggressor and his abused spouse, creating a situation wherein Skyler is absolved of guilt. She is coded in the readily intelligible role of victim as a means of escape. Skyler demands that Walt bring her child back. Walt continues:

> Maybe now you'll listen. Maybe now you'll use your damn head. You know you never believed in me. You were never grateful for anything I did for this family. 'Oh no! Walt! Walt you have to stop! You have to stop this. It's immoral. It's illegal. Someone might get hurt.' You're always whining and complaining about how I make my money—just dragging me down while I do everything. And now, now you tell my son what I do after I told you and told you to keep your damn mouth shut. You stupid bitch. How dare you? [514].

As Walt continues the conversation, he enacts his provider role, insinuating that he always provided for his family, without Skyler ever being grateful. Moreover, he starts to place all agency within himself and Skyler now recognizes that this is a performance to grant her plausible deniability. Towards the end of his line, Walt tells Skyler to keep her "damn mouth shut" and calls her a "stupid bitch," ready-made language for the trope of an abusive spouse. Skyler adopts her own role in this performance and follows the script of a victim. She replies: "I'm sorry." The discussion continues with Walt over-coding his role of man-as-businessman, demanding recognition for his efforts and stating his control over his criminal business. Meanwhile, Walt tears up on his end of the line. Thus, when presenting himself to the police, he does so in the various intelligible roles of masculinity. On his end of the line, however, out of sight, Walt tears up—pointing to the fact that his performances are solely for the benefit of escaping the scrutiny of others. For him, emotion starts to pour forth.

> **WALT:** You have no right to discuss anything about what I do. What the hell do you know about it anyway? Nothing. I built this. Me. Me alone. Nobody else.
> **SKYLER:** You're right. You're right.
> **WALT:** You mark my words, Skyler. Toe the line. Or you will wind up just like Hank.
> **SKYLER:** Walt. Tell me what happened. Where is Hank? Please. We need to know.
> **WALT:** You're never going to see Hank again. He crossed me. You think about that. Family or no. You let that sink in [514].

Walt performs as aggressor to strategically divert attention away from Skyler. He dismantles his familyman performance, saying that not even his family is safe from his aggression. In subverting that performance, he strengthens that of himself as aggressor and takes control over what the police are able to observe, which, incidentally, allows Skyler to avoid scrutiny. Meanwhile, he begins crying on the other end of the line—his "authentic" identity breaking through. After Skyler asks Walt to please just bring Holly home, he replies: "I've still got things left to do" (514). Walt ends his performance by acting as a man of action, hangs up the phone and sobs.[9] The alternating performances of masculinity that Walt uses deflect attention away from Skyler and allow her to avoid the gaze of the law. Meanwhile, Walt is able to escape using the vacuum cleaner repairman. He relegates himself to a new, separate space in near-total isolation, carefully hidden from the gaze of society (514).

Intelligible Femininity

It is worth noting here the difference between Walt's performances of masculinities and the gendered performances of Skyler and Marie. Consider, for example, when Skyler is accused of shoplifting. She feigns going into labor, performing in a specifically feminized mode (107, "A No-Rough-Stuff-Type Deal"). When Walt does not come home the night of Gale's murder, Skyler tries to follow up with Saul, who is evasive regarding Walt's safety. Much in the way that Walt is able to transcend boundaries, Skyler is able to enter his condo. Again, her performance relies on stereotypical representations of women. She holds her crying baby as a prop, feigns panic that they "could've been stabbed" when a man stole her purse, and that she does not have her medication (401, "Box Cutter"). As a result of this performance of frailty, she is granted access into Walt's private space.[10] Not only is she able to enter new spaces, but her over-coded performance of femininity allows her to escape scrutiny. For example, consider when Ted is under investigation for tax fraud. Not wanting her own criminality to be discovered, Skyler comes to the meeting dressed and behaving as a stereotypical "bimbo." She talks about how the building is "so confusing [because] there are doors everywhere." She feigns ignorance, having the following exchange with the IRS agent that centers around her not being able to follow what he says. When he tells her that what she has done is wrong, she protests and ultimately says, "Well you know what they say about opinions, right? Everyone's got one. [*laughs*]" (409, "Bug"), imitating ignorance. She says that "[because] nothing flashed red" it means that everything is okay, she refers to Quicken as "like having a calculator on your computer," and when the agent asks how Skyler got the job, she responds: "Oh, Ted hired me" (409). By enacting the tropes of a wealthy businessman and a ditzy secretary, she is able to spin her "little fiction" as a way to deflect attention. Their roles are recognized, established through the pattern of our cultural imagery and consequently her performance of gender allows her to escape (409).

In her book *Unbearable Weight: Feminism, Western Culture, and the Body*, Susan Bordo examines how mental illness among women is bound up with societal expectations. For example, when discussing anorexia she argues that:

> loss of mobility, loss of voice, inability to leave the home, feeding others while starving oneself, taking up space, and whittling down the space one's body takes up—all have symbolic meaning, all have *political* meaning under the varying rules governing the historical construction of gender [2365].

Walt is discussing getting through chemotherapy and performing vulnerability on his birthday when Skyler interrupts his performance by attempting suicide. She demonstrates her loss of voice and inability to leave the home by willingly subjecting herself to drowning—submerged and subdued, just as Walt would prefer (504, "Fifty-One"). It is noteworthy that through this act, Skyler gains a partial victory in controlling the space. Marie offers to take the kids and acts as a marriage counselor; Skyler subverts herself, but in so doing is able to re-establish the parameters of her children's homes (504).

Bordo writes that "the ideological construction of femininity [...] is always homogenizing and normalizing [...] the construction of femininity is written in disturbingly concrete, hyperbolic terms: exaggerated, extremely literal, at times virtually caricatured representations of the ruling feminine mystique" (2365). Skyler renders herself a caricature particularly in her scenes of feigned weakness and as a "bimbo" secretary. Bordo writes that "ideological moorings for a rigorously dualistic sexual division of labor [cast] woman as chief emotional and physical nurturer [here we should be considering Marie]. The rules for this construction of femininity [...] require that women learn to feed others, not the self, and to construe any desires for self-nurturance and self-feeding as greedy and excessive" (2367). Bordo continues: "women must develop a totally other-oriented emotional economy" (2367–2368). This speaks very directly to Skyler's subservience to Walt. She is totally other-oriented in her interests, primarily focused on caring for her children. "Muteness," Bordo writes, "is the condition of the silent, uncomplaining woman—an ideal of patriarchal culture" (2371). Skyler adopts this stance. In the fall-out after Gus' murder, Skyler outlines her position to Walt:

> I'm not your wife. I'm your hostage. But, since you insist on keeping me imprisoned I will make you a deal. I will launder your money. I'll keep your secrets. But the kids will stay at Hank and Marie's and have a chance of being

safe. [...] There's nothing you can say that'll convince me there won't come a day that somebody will knock on the door looking to harm you or me or all of us. And when that day comes, the children cannot be here. You agree to that and I will be whatever kind of partner you want me to be" [505, "Dead Freight"].

Skyler adopts an other-oriented economy. She will agree to whatever Walt wants without protest. She will engage in criminality provided that she can define the space for her children. In subverting herself, in taking on the role of mute woman, she's given some degree of control over the situation. Incidentally, it is this very performance of woman-as-hostage that allows the plausible deniability to be effective. Hank, for example, when confronting Skyler about her involvement says that Walt is "a monster [...] I don't know what he did to you to force you to keep his secrets, if he threatened you or what—the mind games he played. I don't know if there was abuse [...] you're done being his victim (510, "Buried"). Hank immediately casts Skyler into the role of victimized woman. Thus, by taking on a stereotypical or self-subverting performance, Skyler is ultimately freed from scrutiny.

Marie, too, enters new spaces through a hyperbolic gender performance. Consider Marie's behavior in "Open House" (403); each time she enters a new home, she enacts similar roles, with minor variations that allow her to occupy different marital, economic, and feminine positions. She acts as a middle-upper class woman, enacting domesticity, rambling on about her children. She adopts these fictitious identities in order to explore other spaces, both figurative and literal, for living. When she returns home to Hank with a variety of purchases for him, he immediately corrects her and criticizes her ability to shop, undermining her performance as caregiver. She returns to the open houses and acts as a hand model married to a NASA employee; in this performance she enacts control over her life and fictitious husband, telling him to quit his job and having him listen (403), notably dismantling his role as provider. Marie's entry into other states of being is intimately bound up with her notions of femininity as a domestic force. Marie is consistently branded as having mental health issues. When she finds out that Walt is Heisenberg, she goes to her much-alluded-to therapist, Dave, and he tells her to "focus on [her] feelings." She tells Dave that she spent hours online looking for undetectable poisons. Dave tells her that no matter how difficult a situation is, violence will make it worse and Marie responds: "I know, don't worry. I won't hurt anybody. It just feels good to think about it" (512, "Rabid Dog"). Marie, still refuses to act violently. Much in the same way that Skyler is reprimanded for encouraging Walt to kill Jesse (512), and that Lydia covers her eyes after having Declan's crew murdered (510, "Buried"), Marie is not allowed to enter the violent space of masculinity and must adopt hyper-feminized performances to meet her interests.

Implications

Where, then, does this leave us with regard to the performances of masculinity and femininity within a panoptic network of surveillance? Susan Bordo writes that "through seemingly trivial routines, rules, and practices, culture is '*made* body,' [...]—converted into automatic, habitual activity. As such it is put "beyond the grasp of consciousness [...] [untouchable] by voluntary, deliberate transformations" (2362). *Breaking Bad*, though, challenges this idea, particularly through Walt, who can enact voluntary, deliberate transformations for his pragmatic purposes. We have seen that discipline and visuality go hand-in-hand and that Walt is able to evade and disrupt the observation placed upon him by his panoptic wardens (Gus, Hank, Skyler, etc.), primarily in the form of gendered performances in which he uses masculine tropes instrumentally to subvert his guards. The aim is twofold: first, to escape discipline and, second, to transcend the boundaries of the reified spaces in a panoptic society. These performances—as well as the feminine ones adopted by Skyler and Marie—rely on over-coded conceptions of gender that are immediately comprehensible by the observers. Essentially, by enacting stereotypical tropes and gender norms, the characters in the show do not draw attention to themselves as deviant, thereby opening for themselves new, unsupervised vistas. Walt, in particular, is an expert in this regard, able to jump between multiple conceptions of masculinity in a pragmatic way, specifically to meet his own interests. While Skyler adopts a similar method, she acts on behalf of her children, adopting an other-oriented economy with her performance. *Breaking Bad*, as a whole, then, suggests the unavoidable failings of panoptic structures; when so much emphasis is placed on the visuality of deviancy, panopticism cannot help but miss the subversive acts concealed by over-coded gender performances.

Notes

1. Related to the issues discussed in this paper is the pattern of ocular imagery that ought to be discussed in greater detail elsewhere. Consider the multiple instances of Jesse getting a black or swollen eye, Walt's broken glasses, Walt getting a black eye in his "bar fight" with Mike, Hank punching Walt in the eye when he discovers that Walt is Heisenberg, Gus losing his right eye in the explosion—damaged vision coincides with moments of disempowerment for these characters. The teddy bear eye, however, survives intact after the Wayfarer accident, it's eye an ominous symbol that continues to watch a number of characters throughout the series.

2. There are two aspects of Gus' death that warrant further attention. First, when Gus exits Hector's room, he stands erect and his last act is to adjust his tie. Even to his death, he enacts the performance of his businessman persona. Further, in the grotesque destruction of Gus' face, his right eye has been replaced by a gaping hole, the symbolism of which points to the connection between his fallibility as an observer and his death.

3. Also worth noting is that Marie tries to provide for Hank in his home and act as the "caretaker," a stereotypically feminine role that is also reflected in her career as a nurse. When Hank is in the hospital, Marie tells him that he can go home and that they have made the home more accessible. Hank snaps at her and says "A hospital bed? In my bedroom? [...] You get that out of my house" (311, "Abiquiu"). Hank refuses to let the hospital permeate into his home, flat-out refusing to co-operate and thereby overcoding the boundaries of his home.

4. Note that this also places emphasis on the connection between health and masculinity.

5. Note also that Walt's stance toward Mike, one of domination and control, echoes his justification for having Jesse as a partner. Initially, Gus refuses to do business with Walt on the grounds that Jesse came to the meeting late and high. Probing into Walt's choices, Gus says, "I have to ask [...] why? Why him?" Walt responds: "Because he does what I say" (211, "Mandala"), again pointing to his performance as a rational, in-control businessman.

6. Note the contrast with the reified spaces of Hank and Marie.

7. It is worth noting that moments before this, Walt finds the dismembered eye from the pink teddy bear staring out at him from under his bed, a reminder that he is being watched.

8. Part way through the Gus Fring story arc, Skyler offers Walt the opportunity to move back in "Just so that it's easier to explain to everyone" ("Shotgun"), pointing to the fact that these are indeed performances for the benefit of others—for the benefit of avoiding their scrutiny.

9. The scene is immediately juxtaposed with Walt leaving Holly at the fire station, where firefighters play chess, the imagery a clear statement that Walt's phone call is "a move" in a series—a stratagem.

10. Worthy of mention is that as Skyler enters Walt's home as an observer, and she finds the dismembered teddy bear eye; she inspects Walt as she herself is inspected by this ominous, ever-present eye.

Works Cited

"Abiquiu." *Breaking Bad: The Complete Third Season*. Writ. Vince Gilligan, John Shiban, and Thomas Schnauz. Dir. Michelle MacLaren. Sony Pictures Home Entertainment, 2011. DVD.

"ABQ." *Breaking Bad: The Complete Second Season*. Writ. Vince Gilligan. Dir. Adam Bernstein. Sony Pictures Home Entertainment, 2010. DVD.

"A No-Rough-Stuff-Type Deal." *Breaking Bad: The Complete First Season*. Writ. Vince Gilligan and Peter Gould. Dir. Tim Hunter. Sony Pictures Home Entertainment, 2009. DVD.

Bordo, Susan. "From *Unbearable Weight: Feminism, Western Culture, and The Body*. Chapter 5. The Body and the Reproduction of Femininity." *The Norton Anthology of Theory and Criticism*. Ed. Vincent B. Leitch, William E. Cain, et al. New York: Norton, 2001. 2360–2376. Print.

"Box Cutter." *Breaking Bad: The Complete Fourth Season*. Writ. Vince Gilligan. Dir. Adam Bernstein. Sony Pictures Home Entertainment, 2012. DVD.

"Breakage." Breaking Bad: The Complete Second Season. Writ. Vince Gilligan and Moira Walley-Beckett. Dir. Johan Renck. Sony Pictures Home Entertainment, 2010. DVD.

Brodesco, Alberto. "Heisenberg: Epistemological Implications of a Criminal Pseudonym." *Breaking Bad: Critical Essays on the Contexts, Politics, Style, and Reception of the Television Series*. Ed. David P. Pierson. Lanham, MD: Lexington, 2014. Print.

"Bug." *Breaking Bad: The Complete Fourth Season*. Writ. Vince Gilligan, Moira Walley-Beckett, and Thomas Schnauz. Dir. Terry McDonough. Sony Pictures Home Entertainment, 2012. DVD.

"Bullet Points." *Breaking Bad: The Complete Fourth Season*. Writ. Vince Gilligan and Moira Walley-Beckett. Dir. Colin Bucksey. Sony Pictures Home Entertainment, 2012. DVD.

"Buried." *Breaking Bad*. Writ. Vince Gilligan and Thomas Schnauz. Dir. Michelle MacLaren. AMC. 18 Aug 2013. Television.

Butler, Judith. *Gender Trouble*. New York: Routledge Classics, 2008. Print.

"Caballo sin Nombre." *Breaking Bad: The Complete Third Season*. Writ. Vince Gilligan and Peter Gould. Dir. Adam Bernstein. Sony Pictures Home Entertainment, 2011. DVD.

"Crazy Handful of Nothin.'" *Breaking Bad: The Complete First Season*. Writ. Vince Gilligan and George Mastras. Dir. Bronwen Hughes. Sony Pictures Home Entertainment, 2009. DVD.

"Dead Freight." *Breaking Bad: The Fifth Season*. Writ. Vince Gilligan and George Mastras. Dir. George Mastras. Sony Pictures Home Entertainment, 2013. DVD. Deleuze, Gilles, and Félix Guattari. *Capitalism and Schizophrenia: Anti-Oedipus*. Trans. Brian Massumi. Minneapolis: University of Minnesota Press, 1987. Print.

Deleuze, Gilles, and Félix Guattari. *Capitalism and Schizophrenia: A Thousand Plateaus*. *Trans. Brian Massumi. Minneapolis: University of Minnesota Press, 2008.*

Foucault, Michel. *Discipline and Punish: The Birth of the Prison*. Trans. Alan Sheridan. New York: Random House, 1995. Print.

_____. *The Foucault Reader*. Ed. Paul Rabinow. New York: Pantheon. 1984. Print.

"End Times." *Breaking Bad: The Complete Fourth Season*. Writ. Vince Gilligan, Thomas Schnauz and Moira Walley-Beckett. Dir. Vince Gilligan. Sony Pictures Home Entertainment, 2012. DVD.

"Face Off." *Breaking Bad: The Complete Fourth Season*. Writ. Vince Gilligan. Dir. Vince Gilligan. Sony Pictures Home Entertainment, 2012. DVD.

"Fifty-One." *Breaking Bad: The Fifth Season*. Writ. Vince Gilligan and Sam Catlin. Dir. Rian Johnson. Sony Pictures Home Entertainment, 2013. DVD.

"Fly." *Breaking Bad: The Complete Third Season*. Writ. Vince Gilligan, Sam Catlin and Moira Walley-Beckett. Dir. Rian Johnson. Sony Pictures Home Entertainment, 2011. DVD.

"Full Measure." *Breaking Bad: The Complete Third Season*. Writ. Vince Gilligan. Dir. Vince Gilligan. Sony Pictures Home Entertainment, 2011. DVD.

"Gliding Over All." *Breaking Bad: The Fifth Season*. Writ. Vince Gilligan and Moira Walley-Beckett. Dir. Michelle MacLaren. Sony Pictures Home Entertainment, 2013. DVD.

"Green Light." *Breaking Bad: The Complete Third Season*. Writ. Vince Gilligan and Sam Catlin. Dir. Scott Winant. Sony Pictures Home Entertainment, 2011. DVD.

"Half Measures." *Breaking Bad: The Complete Third Season*. Writ. Vince Gilligan, Sam Catlin, and Peter Gould. Dir. Adam Bernstein. Sony Pictures Home Entertainment, 2011. DVD.

"Hazard Pay." *Breaking Bad: The Fifth Season*. Writ. Vince Gilligan and Peter Gould. Dir. Adam Bernstein. Sony Pictures Home Entertainment, 2013. DVD.

"Hermanos." *Breaking Bad: The Complete Fourth Season*. Writ. Vince Gilligan, Sam Catlin, and George Mastras. Dir. Johan Renck. Sony Pictures Home Entertainment, 2012. DVD.

"I.F.T." *Breaking Bad: The Complete Third Season*. Writ. Vince Gilligan and George Mastras. Dir. Michelle MacLaren. Sony Pictures Home Entertainment, 2011. DVD.

"Kafkaesque." *Breaking Bad: The Complete Third Season*. Writ. Vince Gilligan, Peter Gould and George Mastras. Dir. Michael Slovis. Sony Pictures Home Entertainment, 2011. DVD.

"Live Free or Die." *Breaking Bad: The Fifth Season*. Writ. Vince Gilligan. Dir. Michael Slovis. Sony Pictures Home Entertainment, 2013. DVD.

"Madrigal." *Breaking Bad: The Fifth Season*. By Vince Gilligan. Dir. Michelle MacLaren. Sony Pictures Home Entertainment, 2013. DVD.

"Mandala." *Breaking Bad: The Complete Second Season*. Writ. Vince Gilligan and George Mastras. Dir. Adam Bernstein. Sony Pictures Home Entertainment, 2010. DVD.

"Más." *Breaking Bad: The Complete Third Season*. Writ. Vince Gilligan and Moira Walley-Beckett. Dir. John Renck. Sony Pictures Home Entertainment, 2011. DVD.

"No Más." *Breaking Bad: The Complete Third Season*. Writ. Vince Gilligan. Dir. Bryan Cranston. Sony Pictures Home Entertainment, 2011. DVD.

"Open House." *Breaking Bad: The Complete Fourth Season*. Writ. Vince Gilligan and Sam Catlin. Dir. David Slade. Sony Pictures Home Entertainment, 2012. DVD.

"Over." *Breaking Bad: The Complete Second Season*. Writ. Vince Gilligan and Moira Walley-Beckett. Dir. Phil Abraham. Sony Pictures Home Entertainment, 2010. DVD.

"Ozymandias." *Breaking Bad*. Writ. Vince Gilligan and Moira Walley-Beckett. Dir. Rian Johnson. AMC. 15 Sep 2013. Television.

"Phoenix." *Breaking Bad: The Complete Second Season*. Writ. Vince Gilligan and John Shiban. Dir. Colin Bucksey. Sony Pictures Home Entertainment, 2010. DVD.

"Problem Dog." *Breaking Bad: The Complete Fourth Season*. Writ. Vince Gilligan and Peter Gould. Dir. Peter Gould. Sony Pictures Home Entertainment, 2012. DVD.

"Rabid Dog." *Breaking Bad*. Writ. Vince Gilligan and Sam Catlin. Dir. Sam Catlin. AMC. 1 Sep 2013. Television.

"Shotgun." *Breaking Bad: The Complete Fourth Season*. Writ. Vince Gilligan and Thomas Schnauz. Dir. Michelle MacLaren. Sony Pictures Home Entertainment, 2012. DVD.

"Sunset." *Breaking Bad: The Complete Third Season*. Writ. Vince Gilligan and John Shiban. Dir. John Shiban. Sony Pictures Home Entertainment, 2011. DVD.

"Cat's in the Bag...." *Breaking Bad: The Complete First Season*. Writ. Vince Gilligan. Dir. Adam Bernstein. Sony Pictures Home Entertainment, 2009. DVD.

"Thirty-Eight Snub." *Breaking Bad: The Complete Fourth Season*. Writ. Vince Gilligan and George Mastras. Dir. Michelle MacLaren. Sony Pictures Home Entertainment, 2012. DVD.

Weckerle, Lisa. "Breaking Bad and Blending Boundaries: Myths of Masculinity and the Superhero." *Myth in the Modern World: Essays on Intersections with Ideology and Culture*. Ed. David Whitt and John Perlich. Jefferson, NC: McFarland, 2014.

• ROUND TABLE DISCUSSION •

Is *Breaking Bad* a Feminist Text?

Participants:

—Bridget Roussell Cowlishaw (BRC)

—Robert G. Weiner (RGW)

—Ian Dawe (ID)

—Stephanie Stringer Gross (SSG)

—Susan Johnston (SJ)

BRIDGET ROUSSELL COWLISHAW: Because this book pointedly reads *Breaking Bad* as a text about contemporary understandings of masculinity—with a moral / ethical critique—I wanted to address a question that has arisen among some reviewers of the show: its portrayal of women. Certain writers have taken exception to what they consider to be weak female characters. For example, Slipa Kovvali blasts the series' writers by accusing them of an "inability to create a single non-infuriating female character." Rebecca Nicholson finds the women of *Breaking Bad* to be poorly written and suggests that the Bechdal Test be applied to TV drama serials. Mind you, she doesn't actually apply the test to *Breaking Bad*. I don't think every episode would pass the test but the series in general does because of the relationship between Skyler and Marie. Kate Werner exemplifies another feminist response when she expresses her anti-hero fatigue: "I have consumed enough stories about how hard it is to be a man. I don't care anymore." Maureen Ryan found Skyler a shrew until season three. On the other hand, Alyssa Rosenberg, who is also weary of the macho masculinity, argues that the character of Skyler White is strong enough to change the landscape of anti-hero dramas with weak female roles.

So, the question I want to throw out is whether *Breaking Bad* is, or is not, a feminist text. Or, could it be even considered an anti-feminist text?

Sarah Burke suggests as much by concluding her review with the question: "Does *Breaking Bad* shine a negative light on feminism by positing it in direct confrontation with escapism?"

ROBERT G. WEINER: Ultimately it is in the mind of the viewer as to whether the show is feminist or anti-feminist. There are certain aspects of Anna Gunn's character that are strong and forward-thinking, but she never gets rid of the chain around her neck until the very end. So in that way one could say she steps up to the plate as it were and exercises feminist qualities in a positive way. She runs the car wash business and does a good job with it overall. But she also gets drawn into various aspects of White's dysfunctional and dangerous world.

IAN DAWE: As I've said in the previous Round Table discussions, I try to stay post-structuralist, so what the intention of the creators were in terms of feminism isn't that important to me. It can certainly be *read* as feminist, given particularly its neo–Gothic portrayal of family abuse and the way men wield power in the home. Feminist doesn't have to mean "portrayal of strong women with iron breastplates and swords" after all. It's feminist to demonstrate to a larger audience some of the struggles that women face personally and professionally. In that sense, this is a quite feminist show.

BRC: Absolutely, Ian. To be clear, we're only talking about *reading* the text of the show as feminist, not whether it was intentionally written as such. Those who have accused the writers of not being able to present complete women characters are *reviewing* the series rather than *interpreting* it. That's the basic difference between what a bunch of Humanities professors like ourselves do and what online TV critics do.

STEPHANIE STRINGER GROSS: And, for that reason, Bridget, I think it's neither. I think it is a series that shows that the culture we live in is misogynist but that men face incredible odds if what they want to be is a kind, generous, thoughtful human being. The culture rewards a lack of consciousness in pretty much all areas: gender relations, power seeking, ego-centrism, and violence. I think it is pretty accurate in showing the choices or lack thereof for both men and women. I think the straight men and women shown are representative of the power base still at work (we don't see any transgendered or even gay men or women except perhaps Gus, whose sexuality is still unclear) with any real presence. This suggests to me that *Breaking Bad* is after a critique of what is, in the best possible tradition of good realist fiction, and sees no way out, nor does it offer some facile, fabricated solution. It's a hard look at the requirements for men to be "men" in this culture, and for women to be "women" in it. It's certainly not anti-feminist. What it does show is that feminism, as it has become mainstreamed and channeled off into the domestic sphere where couples partner to raise children and change diapers, is not the complete answer. In fact, it's been watered down so much that it's hard to think of it as "feminism." To the point that such things do happen, and are expected (Walt will change diapers, he will cook, he will clean) feminism (such as it is) is at work. Skyler can work or not. Marie works. But the fundamental relationships and roles of men and women have *not* changed. The asymmetry of sheer numbers of men in the series as opposed to the few female characters also speaks to the reality of most workplaces, I think. Even with larger numbers of women present, often the power rests with he who has the right equipment. But showing this imbalance does not make the show "anti-feminist": in fact by calling attention to the realities, it makes it if anything more of a feminist statement.

SUSAN JOHNSTON: Yes. I agree with Stephanie that it is surely closer to feminist critique than to anti-feminist, and I want to add that part of the challenge here—and it's one I've encountered before, as a pro-life feminist, which for many people is an oxymoron—is that the discussion of feminism and anti-feminism at the level of the culture has really become every bit as static and binaristic as the so-called traditional gender roles it seeks to deconstruct, so that if something doesn't flaunt its feminist credentials sufficiently then it must be anti-feminist. I love that Stephanie is talking about the real challenges men face if they want to be kind, generous, thoughtful—and I want to talk about how those challenges for men and women ramify when they are being confronted within a context we read, and often dismiss, as one of traditional gender roles or domesticity.

RGW: Other female characters (like Lydia and Skyler's sister Marie) are emotional cripples who, in this scholar's view, do not seem like strong female characters. They have all kinds of psychological problems despite both highly entertaining and contributing to the narrative. However, none of the female characters seem like the damsel in distress type of woman which is at least refreshing. The women do at times take charge of certain aspects of business or do things that require a type of leadership despite whatever other flaws they may have.

SJ: And yet, analysis of masculinity is also a feminist project. In my essay I talk about the idea of custodial masculinity, that self-sacrificing and protective masculinity that acts in and out of a love, oriented to the dignity and ends of the other. I think this version of masculinity is actually incredibly important, and it's one we aren't spending enough time talking about or publicly valuing.

For that matter I think our feminist / anti-feminist binary makes it hard for us to value self-sacrificing femininity because we see it as passive, dominated, coerced—and because if something is not obviously feminist it seems to fall into anti-feminism. But surely we can say that care of and for the other is something that matters, and that we want to matter to us. Surely we can say that it is possible for human persons to be what George Eliot calls "equivalent centers of self." We need not turn ourselves into mere instruments of the ends of others in serving them; we *can*, of course, just as we can be treated as tools—Walt does this to everybody all the time—but I think care ethics shows us that the question of care is not one that can be easily engaged by asking if it is feminist or anti-feminist. Sometimes that's not the most important or interesting question. And sometimes asking it actually deforms the way we look at the thing we are asking questions about.

SSG: Right. Codes of masculinity dictate what is valued in a culture. This is not just an issue for men. In my essay, I mention that, while we hate the KEN-WINS guy, we also resent that we "should" be like him. Something in the culture drives us to BE him. To *win*. There are codes for men and codes for women which guide us in this direction (though it's still a war of all against all). This applies whether we are male or female, but the men seem to still have it worse (though perhaps their payoffs are generally better if and when they do "win"). When a woman competes at that level there are still other problems she will face. Walt's seething resentment against the guy is not just because he's a douchebag (note the feminine element of that slur) but because he represents the expectations he himself can't meet. *Breaking Bad* asks us to think about those expectations, where they lead, why they seem so coercive, what the alternative might be, and why stalking those alternatives lead to dead ends. I won't say the series is "post-feminist." It's way too focused on the still extant problems that traditional gender roles, however inflected by more recent feminism they are, present for us. The series is, for me, really about how culture shapes us, and how little real choice we have. We can go much further back than Machiavelli to see this, but he is a great example of how codified "being a man" expectations can be. And his arch-enemy is a woman: Fortune—everything a man cannot control, but boy does she need a good smack down (Yo! Bitch!). She remains feminine, even if she doesn't always manifest as an actual female. Great realist fiction can call attention to these things and articulate a "feminist" statement just in the act of doing so, without proselytizing a solution, and that's exactly what I think *Breaking Bad* does. In that sense, I guess it's closer to "feminist" critique. Surely it is *not* anti-feminist.

Annotated Bibliography

Bridget Roussell Cowlishaw

At the time of this writing (September 2014), the scholarship on *Breaking Bad* is only just beginning to be published. Obviously, all such scholarship is included below, however, there is no shortage of *Breaking Bad* analysis in the form of online essays and episode recaps. Because many of these address ideas that scholars will no doubt address in the future, I have chosen to include the most substantive of these extra-academic texts in this bibliography and my notes on these will emphasize whatever point(s) led me to regard the piece as significant enough for inclusion. I will acknowledge that my criteria for "substantive" is heavily influenced by my interest in the series' unique moral tone and its critique of gender norms.

I have omitted the many interviews with the creators of *Breaking Bad* because this book is interested in how the text can be read within its social/political context, not with the intentions of its makers. The only texts omitted for reasons other than content are texts self-published as e-books and personal blogs—with the exception of Jason Read's and Leonard DeLorenzo's blogs as they function as part of the writers' professional academic work. Admittedly, this involves judgment calls that reflect my own bias for the reasonably well thought-out as when I decided to omit all articles from websites self-identifying as last bastions of justice for the disenfranchised white male.

Books

Bruzzi, Stella. *Bringing Up Daddy: Fatherhood and Masculinity in Post-War Hollywood*. London: British Film Institute, 2005. Print.
    This book "examines narrative treatments of the father figure, not only in relation to other films but also in reaction to social, cultural, and political history" (ix). The author's analyses employ Freud and consider the father in each decade through various genres and selected films. She concludes that 1990–2000 saw fathers as renouncing machismo and in need of turning to the home. In *Mad Men*, *Masters of Sex*, and *Breaking Bad*, the new millennium father returns to his position as breadwinner:

"The breadwinner's public face is a masquerade, a performance put on to deflect attention from suppressed ambitions and emotions, his conformist appearance obliquely resonant of lost sexuality and what he has renounced" (45–46).

Guffey, Ensley F., and K. Dale Koontz. *Wanna Cook? The Complete Unofficial Companion to Breaking Bad*. Toronto: ECW, 2014. Print.

Designed for fans of the show preferring all the minutia within the pages of a book rather than spend hours surfing the internet, each episode is summarized, each chapter covering a season. At the end of each episode summary are "Lab Notes." These notes are lists of "Highlights" (favorite bits of dialogue from the episode), "Did You Notice" (observations about symbolic uses of set, costume, or dialogue), "Miscalculations" (aspects of the episode that were less than completely realistic), "Shooting Up" (camerawork and cinematography in the episode), "Music," and "Interesting Facts." Within the book's 433 pages, the editors also include brief observational writings of specific repeated phenomenon: "Marie and the Color Purple," "The Cars of *Breaking Bad*," "Veggie Trays," "Walt & the Backyard Pool," "Hank & Marie & Kids," and "An Interview with Michael Slovis." At the end of each chapter is a short analytical essay. It is those that I summarize below.

- "Walter White and the Antihero" (pp. 53–57). The editors provide the reader with a definition of "antihero" with examples from classic literature and contemporary fiction. They then go on to explain how *Breaking Bad* is unique in television because it shows how an ordinary person transforms into an antihero thereby differentiating itself from other television shows which employ stable antiheroes. They compare Walter White's initial conflict to Lawrence Kohlberg's "Heinz Dilemma."
- "'Better Call Saul': Lawyers and Advertising" (pp. 141–44). This piece is an overview of attorney ethics in regard to advertising in the U.S. from the time of Lincoln to the present.
- "'This Ho Has Got to Go!!!!!!' Fan Hatred of Skyler White" (pp. 231–34). Focusing on the Facebook page "Kill Off Skyler White," the editors recount the hateful posts to that page and offer a reasoned response in which they attribute the posts to misogyny of varying frankness. Anna Gunn's article in the *New York Times* is addressed.
- "Buying the House: Place in *Breaking Bad*" (pp. 302–08). This piece is a truncated version of Ensley F. Guffey's essay in the *Breaking Bad* anthology edited by David P. Pierson (2014).
- "The Ones Who Knock: Violentization in *Breaking Bad*." Using the model and terminology of sociologist Lonnie Athens, the editors map the stages of *Breaking Bad* characters—but particularly Walter White's —descent into a violent mentality.

Koepsell, David R., and Robert Arp. *Breaking Bad and Philosophy: Badder Living Through Chemistry*. Chicago: Open Court, 2012. Print.

As Volume 67 in the series Popular Culture and Philosophy (edited by George A. Reisch), this edition is pitched toward the reader with interest in (but no education in) philosophical concepts. The text is probably best used to explain select theories to high-school level readers using *Breaking Bad* as the object of analysis. The tone of many of the essays in this volume, however, moves from quippish to crass. For example, the two men killed by Walter in "Half Measures" are referred to as "Aztek Speed Bumps 1 and 2" (9). On page 18, we read, "Abelard was an infamous playa until his lover's father and brother castrated and dishonored him (cutoff [*sic*] his junk and sent him packin')" Another jarring example is from page 28: "I try to make sure I'm addressing real gaps in understanding; or at the very least not sounding like a pompous dick. To eliminate the already dangerously high risk of sounding dickish for this discussion." And while a later essay considers whether *Breaking Bad* is a feminist program, the reader is expected to be unoffended by speculation as to whether Walter White could realistically "bag the Skyler level of hotness" with a winking "right?" tagged to the sentence (Murphy, 18).

The essays in this volume fall into four categories. (These categories are of my own making in order to efficiently summarize the book's contents. The actual arrangement of the essays in the book seems to have little logic except to put the more complete ones toward the front.)

The first category is the most clearly relevant to the book's purpose: *Breaking Bad* Viewed through the Lens of a Specific Philosophical Theory/Concept:

- "Meth, Liberty, and the Pursuit of Happiness" by Aaron C. Anderson asserts that Walter White constitutes a John Stuart Mill–style hero who embodies "individual spontaneity" and "the sovereignty of the individual over himself."
- "Finding Happiness in a Black Hat" by Kimberly Baltzer-Jaray explains existentialism to the reader through Camus' retelling of the myth of Sisyphus and a South Park movie, then goes on to describe Walter White as a well-adjusted individual when he transforms into Heisenberg because in doing so he has "become authentic" and is finally living "in good faith."
- "If Walt's Breaking Bad, Maybe We Are Too" by J. C. Donhauser claims that Walter White is an "Agent-centered Consequentionalist" à la Bentham and Mill. Hank is explained as a potential "Act Consequentialist" or "Rule Consequentionalist," and all manner of consequentionalist titles are tried on Tuco.
- "Better than Human" by Stephen Glass includes analysis of *Mad Men*'s Dan Draper alongside Walter White and uses the comparison to establish that Walt is a more compelling character because he more completely exemplifies Nietsche's "Will to Power." It is observed that flashbacks reveal Walt has always had the Will to Power within him and the author asserts that Walt reaches Übermensch status in "Faceoff."
- "Been through the Desert on a Horse with No Name" by Oli Mould employs Lacan to assert that the catalyst for narrative changes in *Breaking Bad* always comes when Walt's "constructed reality" is breached by "the real."

• "Hurtling Towards Death" by Craig Simpson claims that the significance of flashbacks in *Breaking Bad* is an illustration of Heidegger's "Dasein." Reading Walter White through Heidegger also explains that Walt's unhappiness at the beginning of the series is a consequence of his scientific worldview being necessarily reductionist. In this reading, Walt reaches "authentic being toward death" only when he is in the "meditative state" induced by Jesse's sleeping pills in "Fly."

• "Walter White's Will to Power" by Megan Wright focuses primarily on the series pilot and reads Walt's mounting humiliations as his persistent "failure to use the Will to Power." When Walt makes the decision to cook meth, he becomes the Übermensch.

The second category is Walter White read through various philosophers:

• "Walter White's American Vice" by Jeffrey Stephenson examines how Walt can be analyzed through Kantian "deontologism," the utilitarianism of Mill, and the Aristotelian concept of virtue. The conclusion is that Walt was never a virtuous person and his fall is due to his acceptance of modern American materialist culture.

• "I Appreciate the Strategy" by Sara Waller compares a Utilitarian view of Walter and Skyler compare to Existentialist views of them. Hank is analyzed as a Utilitarian-Existentialist and Maries as an Existentialist.

The largest of the categories of chapters is that of Evaluative Essays/Social Issues Essays:

• "It's Arbitrary?" by Adam Barkman is essentially a piece arguing that addictive drugs should not be legalized.

• "What's So Bad about Meth?" by Patricia Brace and Robert Arp uses Kant and Mill to conclude that "lots" is bad about methamphetamine.

• "Breaking Bonds" by Denise DuVernay examines whether the series is feminist or not. The author concludes that the first two seasons are not but that Skyler's strength in the later episodes redeems the show as feminist.

• "The Riddle of Godfather Gus" by Jeffrey A. Hinzmann employs Adorno and Habermas to consider Gus a case of "instrumental rationality." Machiavelli and Hobbes are also considered. Gus is evaluated as a CEO type and a sociopath. The writer is not convinced that the character is actually a Chilian.

• "You're Supposed to Be a Scientist" by Lisa Kadonaga explains popular notions of "the scientist" and misconceptions about Ph.D.s. The scientific method is explained alongside the "Traditional Knowledge Movement."

• Walt's Rap Sheet" by David R. Koepsell and Vanessa Gonzales is what it sounds like: an inventory of all deaths directly or indirectly due to Walter White's action or inaction. Utilitarianism is employed along with a consideration of "special obligations," along with Aristotelian elements of moral responsibility. The conclusion is that Walt has reached the level of actual evil in Season Four.

• "Does Cooking Meth Make Walt a Bad Guy?" by Greg Littmann examine whether cooking methamphetamine is more egregious than other business ventures.

• "Was Skyler's Intervention Ethical? Hell, It Shouldn't Even Be Legal!" is by

Dam Miori who self-identifies as a bioethicist. It is as such that he examines the "talking pillow" scene in "Grey Matter" concluding that Skyler unethically coerces Walt into treatment. The writer also presents the results of his own survey of colleagues on the question and the majority agree with his conclusion.

Two of the essays are of a more literary bent:

• "*Macbeth* on Ice" by Ray Bossert employs *Macbeth* to "help us understand Walter White" (65). It is noted that Lady Macbeth uses taunts against her husband's manhood to prod him into action—a theme at the heart of Walter's demise: "We can more easily understand a 'good guy' becoming a 'bad guy' if we focus on what it means to be a guy" (68). It is concluded that Walt is like Macbeth in that he seeks power through shameful means; that he is like Macduff in that he abandons his family in pursuit of his goal; and that he is like Lady Macbeth in his strategy of goading others into action. It is also noted that Walt is also like King Duncan, Banquo, and "for a while, Walter has been almost every character in *Macbeth*" (68).

• "Heisenberg's Uncertain Confession" by Darryl J. Murphy employs St. Augustine's Confessions as a lens through which to view what the writer sees as Walter White's basic longing for redemption—though, like Augustine, he prefers to have it "not yet." Focusing on the episode "Over," it is noted that Walt's dismissal of the existence of the soul and his materialistic outlook would make him likely to understand all human behavior and thought as mere chemical reactions. There is significance then in his choosing the street name he does: "Heisenberg's uncertainty principle makes room for free will in the otherwise-deterministic materialist paradigm by turning rigid laws of particle behavior into *tendencies*" (22).

Logan, Elliot. "Unacceptability and Prosaic Life in *Breaking Bad*." *The Unacceptable*. Ed. John Potts. Houndmills, Hampshire, United Kingdom: Palgrave Macmillan, 2012.
    Acknowledging *Breaking Bad*'s ethos as a western, this chapter employs theory by film scholars Rita Felski, John Frow, James Walters, V.I. Perkins, Deborah Thomas, Gilberto Perez, Robert Warshow, and Robert B. Pippin. The author focuses on the series' constant movement between the incompatible world of drug dealing and the domestic sphere with a close reading of the episode "Over."

Lotz, Amanda D. *Cable Guys: Television and Masculinities in the 21st Century*. New York: New York University Press, 2014. Print.
    Surveying American television series of all eras and genres, the author examines the patriarchal and feminist masculinities offered throughout the decades. In her conclusion, the author provides a list of "dictums of good manhood" gleaned from her survey.

Martin, Brett. *Difficult Men: From* The Sopranos *and* The Wire *to* Mad Men *and* Breaking Bad. New York: Penguin, 2013. Print.

While the rest of the book deals with the much-discussed prevalence of the anti-hero in contemporary television, chapter 13 is an account of the author's spending a day in the *Breaking Bad* writers' room ("The Happiest Room in Hollywood") on a day when they were breaking episode 405, "Shotgun." The author explains the series are writer-focused and devoted to visual storytelling, giving us an insight into the series of drafts each script goes through and the writer's obsessive interests in minute details. The author acknowledges that it's difficult to know who to root for in *Breaking Bad* which he calls "the most visually stylized show of the third Golden Age" of television.

Pierson, David. *Breaking Bad: Critical Essays on the Contexts, Politics, Style, and Reception of the Television Series*. Lanham, MD: Lexington, 2014. Print.

This book is the first scholarly anthology devoted exclusively to analysis of *Breaking Bad*. As such, it has the expected weaknesses of anthologies (inconsistent quality of essays) and first-to-press analyses (the final season had not yet aired when the volume went to print). Nonetheless, as it comes before all others—and the editor of this anthology is confident that there will be many others—observations and connections made by these researchers must be consulted by all of us who come after.

- "A Life Not Worth Living" by Jami Anderson is no doubt the first of what will become many analyses dealing with impairment and disability in *Breaking Bad* and focuses on the "undisciplined" or "unruly" bodies of Walt (cancer patient), Jesse (drug addict), Skyler (cigarette addict), Marie (kleptomaniac), Hank (PTSD sufferer and later paraplegic), and Walt Jr. (cerebral palsy patient)—all of whom manage to come to terms with their impairments except for Walt. Anderson examines how three myths of contemporary culture obstruct acceptance of body (dis)functions: the myth of bodily control, the myth of normalcy, and the myth of bodily realism. Anderson concludes: "In effect, Walter's fear that cancer would make his life not worth living propelled him to make terrible choices such that much of what makes life worth living is gone or so thoroughly damaged, that his life *is* not worth living" (115–114).
- "Breaking the Waves" by Pierre Barrette and Yves Picard focuses mostly on Season Two's "737" and "ABQ" and examines the cinematography of *Breaking Bad*. Employing comparisons of Barthes' "zero-degree style," Genette's "second-degree style," and their own description of "maximum-degree style," the writers do close readings of specific scenes to demonstrate the complexity of visual story-telling. The authors observe that until very recently, self-referential visuals had been confined to comedy in network television—a medium now dominated by reality TV programs. But cinema-quality camera work and editing are becoming a norm on cable TV where most fiction is being created. The writers account for the divide between those who admire *Breaking Bad*'s artistry and those who denounce it as a negative cultural influence: TV Studies scholars are interested in reading form, while culture critics focus exclusively on themes.

- "Heisenberg: Epistemological Implications of a Criminal Pseudonym" by Alberto Brodesco provides a close reading of scenes from the second season surrounding the use of the name "Heisenberg" and the recurring theme of observing/being observed. The writer concludes, "Walter White tries to act like an 'external' experimenter in the world of drug dealing but his entrance into the field changes its entire domain.... Walt is part of the field. He has produced a change in the international drug business" (61). Brodesco also makes note of "Heisenberg: Uses and Misuses in Contemporary TV Series" (64–6) and the importance of the Coen brothers' work exploring "uncertainty" to show runner Vince Gilligan.

- "Taking Control: Male Angst and Re-Emergence of Hegemonic Masculinity in *Breaking Bad*" by Brian Faucette employs R. W. Connel's model of masculinity, addresses Kimmel's "crisis of masculinity," and references the work of Stella Bruzzi, Amanda Marcotte, and Sally Robinson. The author asserts that money is manhood to Walt, that Walt adopts Jesse as a surrogate son, and that Walt uses a perceived crisis in masculinity (connected to emergence of women's, minorities', and LGBT's rights movements) as an excuse to revert to older forms of masculine performance.

- "The Economy of Time and Multiple Existences in *Breaking Bad*" by Dustin Freeley cites Leong, Gallagher, Heidegger, Bergson, and Deleuze for alternative conceptions of time to defy what we have constructed as "clock time"—a major theme of *Breaking Bad*. The author notes that Walt's intelligence is perceived as a social detriment and no real advantage in a capitalist market place. Freeley employs gaming analyses to examine how "Heisenberg functions like a gaming avatar." Notions of time specific to twelve-step programs are examined alongside some fairly poetical musing on the episode "Fly," and consideration of the series' use of non-linear time sequencing.

- "Buying the House: Place in *Breaking Bad*" by Ensley F. Guffey focuses on the place and space of the White and Pinkman residences via human geography. The writer also employs Gaston Bachelard's theory of the home as a mirror of the psyche to read Jesse's homes. The episode "Over" is given a close reading to understand the meaning of Walt's attempts to impose order on chaos. Guffey analyzes the meaning of "crawlspace" and asserts that the White home is Skyler's domain while only laboratories are really "home" for Walt. By turns, Gus' superlab becomes for Walt his fantasy, ambition, prison, and Hell.

- "Not Your Average Mexican: *Breaking Bad* and the Destruction of Latino Stereotypes" by Andrew Howe concludes that the series disrupts Latino stereotypes at every turn: the character of Steve Gomez is less macho than his white partner, Combo is assumed to be white until we find out by learning his real name that he is Latino, and the extreme polar opposite personalities given Gus and Tuco. Even Don Eladio's pool party (which ends in an unexpected way) and the Salamanca cousins (who are "intelligent, dedicated, contemplative, and logical" [93]) are read as violations of stereotype. Howe observes that boarder culture itself is complicated in the series by demonstrating that there is more than one boarder to cross in New Mexico where Native American nations have sovereignty on their own land.

- "Mediating Fictional Crimes: Music, Morality, and Liquid Identification in *Breaking Bad*" by Carlo Nardi employs Zygmunt Bauman's concept of "liquid modernity" ("an individualized, privatized worldview where ... responsibility is on the individual's shoulders" [173]) and the strategies by which viewers are led to identify with Walter White via the music chosen for various scenes. Possibly offering a reason some viewers don't register the ways in which the lead protagonist's behavior is intended to be called into question, Nardi explains that depending on viewers' tolerance for cognitive dissonance, s/he will experience either critical evaluative thought or dissociation when music contradicts the action on screen. The essay examines the distinctions between music written for the show and soundtracks chosen for it as well as between diegetic music and "metadiegetic music" (e.g., the narcocorridos song). An interesting speculation is made that the use of the song "Crapapelada" played a part in many viewers mistaking a change in camera angle for Jesse having moved his gun away from Gale before firing.

- "Breaking Neoliberal? Contemporary Neoliberal Discourses and Policies in AMC's *Breaking Bad*" by David P. Pierson cites media studies social science and government sources to assert that neoliberal penal codes treat crime as a business rather than aberrant behavior and that "*Breaking Bad*'s criminal market with its constantly changing market territories and wealth, its winner-take-all ethos, and unwanted government intrusion ... into its operations represents the brutalities best associated with the global, neoliberal marketplace" (23–4). The author outlines ways in which the drug trade is styled as hyper-macho in the series while making note that "methamphetamine has been called a neoliberal drug because it provides low-wage workers with more energy to work longer hours" (25).

- "Feeling Bad: Emotions and Narrativity in *Breaking Bad*" by E. Deidre Pribramm invokes Foucault's concepts of power relations and then goes on to conduct a rhetorical analysis of strategies characters employ to gain leverage over one another. The writer concludes that emotional coercion is used at least as much as physical coercion in the series as Walt manipulates Jesse, Walt Jr., and Skyler by appealing to their feelings—mostly negative feelings. Though Walt and Skyler may seem to have fluid gender roles at home, they can be shown to be completely traditional in terms of their differing definitions of "love" and "marriage."

- "Uncertain Beginnings: *Breaking Bad*'s Episodic Openings" by Rossend Sanchez-Baro provides readers with a history of the "teaser" or "cold opening" which the writer likes to follow David Lavery in calling "minisodes" as they establish the parameters of what Umberto Eco called the "possible world" of the fiction. Sanchez-Baro reads various Breaking Bad teasers for the ways in which they establish viewer expectations and relies on original scripts from the series to demonstrate authorial intention for these meanings (rather than seeing them as aesthetic choices of the cinematographer or director). This is put in the context of sequential artists' current interest in the concept of beginnings and the vogue for viewer disorientation in twenty-first century TV (via decontextualized shots, temporal disorder, and genre hybridity).

Weckerle, Lisa. "*Breaking Bad* and Blending Boundaries: Revisioning the Myths of Masculinity and the Superhero." *Myth in the Modern World: Essays on Intersections with Ideology and Culture.* Ed. David Whitt and John Perlich. Jefferson, NC: McFarland, 2014.

Employing Joseph Campbell on myth and R.W. Connell on masculinity, the author argues that Walter White fits two contemporary myths: the myth of masculinity (in his transformation from emasculated to sexual man) and the myth of the superhero (in his alter-ego, Heisenberg—including an analysis of masks and costumes in *Breaking Bad*). "While the show may reify gender norms by celebrating Walt as a fantasy of hyper-masculinity, Walt's performance of masculinity actually deconstructs these norms by revealing them as unreachable, mythic ideals" [19]. Interesting observations about the use of mirroring in the series—right down to the many palindromes of letters and numbers.

Print Scholarly Articles

Chambers, Samuel. "Walter White Is a Bad Teacher: Pedagogy, Partage and Politics in Season 4 of *Breaking Bad*." *Theory & Event* 17.1 (2014). Print.

In reading the relationship between Walt, Jesse, and Gus as a triangle of two potential sets of teacher-student relationships (Walt-Jesse and Gus-Jesse), the author employs theory from Jacques Rancière to conclude that Gus is a better teacher than Walt. Preventing this from being a facile argument, the author's analysis includes *Breaking Bad*'s formal aspects in addition to its thematic ones in, for example, comparing Vince Gilligan's "visual storytelling" to *Rancière's le partage du sensible*. The *objects du partage senible* that the author examines specifically are the box cutter, eyeglasses, tequila, and Lily of the Valley. Asserting that a reading of Walt as Machiavellian man is facile compared to a pedagogical reading which sees Gus as a liberating teacher who permits the possibility of equality, the author concludes that *Breaking Bad* demonstrates a "radical pedagogy [that] is also a radical (democratic) politics."

Lewis, Mark. "From Victim to Victor: *Breaking Bad* and the Dark Potential of the Terminally Empowered." *Culture, Medicine and Psychiatry* 37.4 (2013): 656–669. Print.

The author traces the use of militaristic language and the rationalization of extreme measure in the treatment of cancer patients, focusing on the LiveStrong movement and its emphasis on choice and control. After considering the plot of the series, the author goes on to relate Walt's varying responses to his diagnoses to actual cancer patients' experiences and then concludes with a comparison between Walt's cancer and moral descent to that of LiveStrong's founder Lance Armstrong.

Lewkowich, David. "Love, Hate, and Crystal Meth: Abjection and Teacher Narcissism in *Breaking Bad*." *Journal of Curriculum and Pedagogy* 9: 141–157, 2012. Print.

The relationship between Walter and Jesse is examined for its pedagogical structure employing the theory of Julia Kristeva. From the abstract: "In this article the author looks at ... the television show, *Breaking Bad*, as a means to explore the pedagogical implications of the Kristevan notion of abjection, and its relationship to the emotions of love and hate, and the emergence of teacher narcissism as an inevitable offshoot of the antagonisms in learning."

Logan, Elliot. "Flashforwards in *Breaking Bad*: Openness, Closure and Possibility." *Television Aesthetics and Style* (2013): 219–226. Print.
  In response to Lisa Coulthard's *Flow TV* piece, the author employs Jason Mittell in a close reading of the episode "Crazy Handful of Nothin'" (106) to argue that considering the series' cold openings/teasers puzzle pieces underestimates their complexity by assuming they direct the reader to a single interpretation.

Online Scholarly Articles

Coulthard, Lisa. "The Hotness of Cold Opens: *Breaking Bad* and the Serial Narrative as Puzzle." FlowTV. Flow, 12 November 2010. Web. April 2014.
  The author employs Thomas Elsaesser to argue that cold openings function as puzzles to encourage multiple viewings (with focused attention on details) and a common memory among viewers (promoting a devoted fan base)—a point Jason Mittell will develop further and the author acknowledges the "complex narrative" theory Mittell applied to *The Wire* is also applicable to *Breaking Bad*. Reading the cold openings from "Negro y Azul," "Seven Thirty-seven," "Down," "Over," and "ABQ"; Coulthard traces the origin of cold openings to their popularity in the 1950s and 1960s TV. Interesting observation: "White ... embarks on a life of crime that does not change him so much as enables him to express the person he has always been."

García-Martínez, Alberto Nahum, and Pablo Echart. "Crime and Punishment: Greed, Pride and Guilt in Breaking Bad." academia.edu. 2 December 2013. Web. August 2014.
  This text was originally presented as a conference paper at "Apocalypse: Imagining the End" at Oxford University in July 2013 at which time the authors could write: "Although *Breaking Bad* ... is one of the most critically acclaimed TV Series of the last decade, it has been the subject of little academic research." The authors suggest that contemporary American culture's obsession with material success allows Walter's response to learning of his impending death to be the reverse of what we have come to expect from literary examples who almost always respond by trying to make amends for their sins. The authors focus on the psychological significance of Walter White's pride in overcoming his shame and guilt.

Greven, David. "Strike through the Mask: Male Faces, Masculinity and Allegorical Queerness in *Breaking Bad*." FlowTV. Flow, 5 March 2013. Web. April 2014.

The author gives hints of a more fully developed analysis in his forthcoming book, only outlining here his argument that 20th-century television and film make use of the male face as a "shifting symbol of masculinities." Particular attention is paid to Gus though it seems to this editor that Walt and Jesse are even better examples.

Kemsley, Jyllian. "*Breaking Bad*: Novel TV Show Features Chemist Making Crystal Meth." *Chemical & Engineering News* 86.93 (32–33). March 2008.

The writer provides a description of the series emphasizing plot points that deal with actual chemistry an includes statements by Vince Gilligan and Bryan Cranston as to their fascination with science and commitment to keeping the series faithful to the real thing. (For descriptions of the readers' letters this brief article provoked see this bibliography's section "Farther Afield" below.)

Kuo, Michelle, and Albert Wu. "In Hell, 'We Shall Be Free': On *Breaking Bad*." *Los Angeles Review of Books*. 13 July 2012. Web. September 2014.

The authors assert that *Breaking Bad* is "a human-centered vision of the origin of evil. It is Old Testament to its core." They then go on to perform a close reading of the episode "Fly" alongside Milton's *Paradise Lost* with Walt in the role of *Breaking Bad*'s Satan and the super-lab as his Hell. The social context of Milton's work and that of the series are compared. The authors make the case that the world of *Breaking Bad* is highly moral and make a larger claim for the repeated observation that *Breaking Bad* is visual, not dialogue-driven: "For Walt to say 'I'm sorry' is not quite right.... *Breaking Bad* suggests that there is nothing intrinsically good about language, language does not elevate us. Walt cannot find his magic sequence of words, not because he is a poor writer, but because no such combination exists. Language, however finely ordered, is ill-used. It merely justifies the poor choices we make.... Indeed what is affecting about Walt is what he cannot bring himself to say." The authors poetically come to the correct conclusion as to what the series end will be.

Lavery, David. "Bad Quality: *Breaking Bad* as Basic Cable Quality TV." *CST Online. Critical Studies in Television*, 22 November 2012. Web. April 2014.

Written the day after the 2012 Emmys broadcast, the author asserts that in addition to Aaron Paul and Bryan Cranston, *Breaking Bad* deserved the Emmy (given that year to *Mad Men*) before going on to pinpoint the qualities that make the new wave of exceptional cable television programs what they are: local color, the claustrophobic, tour de force set-pieces, the titles, cold opens, and a burst of color.

Mittell, Jason. "The Qualities of Complexity: Aesthetic Evaluation in Contemporary Television." Just TV. 15 December 2011. Web. September 2014.

Wishing to elide Pierre Bourdieu's terms of critique and the notion of "Quality Television," the author analyzes the "complexity" of television programming. Focusing on *Breaking Bad* and *The Wire*, the author describes "complex TV" as "violating storytelling conventions in a spectacular fashion" (paragraph 44). Asserting that Walter White is "the richest character in all of fiction," Mittell marks him as unusual among TV's current collection of antiheroes in that Walter is not a charismatic leader who is sexually desired. Theorizing about the mechanics that make viewers bond with Walter (particularly in Seasons One and Two), the author notes that the use of silence during which the viewer is encouraged to be wordlessly thinking along with Walt, the shared tension as the audience witnesses Walt continually "wriggling" out of tight situations, and the fact that all plot developments result from Walt's decisions, not larger social/political forces. By season three, the viewer is on Jesse's side. Mittell asserts that *Breaking Bad* is a moral tale about masculinity: "...Overtly patriarchal rhetoric contrasted with the hideous actions Walt does toward others ... articulates the hollow, rotten core of traditional masculinity as portrayed in the series." (paragraph 34) He explains Skyler-hating as the result of the series viewing Skyler from Walt's point of view rather than providing the viewer with a sense of her interior thought/feeling. In contrast to others who theorize how binge-watching effects viewers' perceptions, Mittell considers the role of time between episodes as significant to developing complex TV's relationship with the audience particularly as *Breaking Bad* intentionally plays with the audience in the second season's use of cold openings—and that this leads to experiences of "shared memory" among viewers. (The author makes interesting observations about how "unintentional ambiguity" had to be dealt with by the show's creators.) Mittell considers how Walter White's being portrayed by the same actor who played the father on *Malcolm in the Middle* might affect viewers' reading of the character.

Van Dorp, L. J. *The Dramatization and Criticism of the Ideal of Success in American Society on American Television: A Case Study of the Representation of Success in Mad Men, Breaking Bad and Boardwalk Empire.* Faculty of Humanities Theses, University of Utrecht. 17 August 2011. Web. September 2014.

Abstract: "This paper will look at the reasons why work and success are such integral parts of American society, and specifically in which way the success-related themes of the self-made man, ambition and crime are dramatized and criticized in American television series. This paper proposes that the dramatization and the prevalence of the ideal of success in the American television series *Mad Men, Breaking Bad* and *Boardwalk Empire* suggests an ingrained fascination and a recent disillusionment with the narrative of the American Dream within American culture." The chapter titles are telling: "The Self-Made Man: Reinvention and Transformation," "Being the Best: Ambition and Competition," and "By Any Means Necessary: Immorality and Consequences." American obsession with material success is attributed to American Exceptionalism, the protestant work ethic, and the "American Dream."

Werner, Kate. "Why Don't I Like *Breaking Bad?*" FlowTV. Flow, 11 February 2014. Web. April 2014.

A Ph.D. in television studies acknowledges the technical brilliance of the series but outlines her "issues of taste" that prevent her from *liking Breaking Bad*: gender issues ("I have consumed enough stories about how hard it is to be a man. I don't care anymore."), character ("Walt isn't an unlikable character because he is bad. He is unlikable because it is disheartening to watch someone make the same mistake over and over."), and community—or lack thereof ("Even when the show represents the community's hurt ... it then mocks this grief by presenting its most facile aspects and by using it to embarrass Walt.").

Wetherbee, Ben, and Stephanie Weaver. "You Know the Business and I Know the Chemistry: The Scientific Ethos of *Breaking Bad*." *Excursions* 4. 1 (June 2013). Web. September 2014.

Employing Aritotle's definition of ethos, the authors focus on the "dialectic between business and science" within the storyline as well as "*Breaking Bad* marketing and reception as a commercial and cultural product in the real world." The analysis of the series' ethos as that of an implied author (á la Wayne Booth and Seymour Chatman) who is neither Vince Gilligan nor Bryan Cranston but a complex construction of many individuals is particularly interesting and merits further consideration. (Perhaps because *Breaking Bad*'s science advisor is at my alma mater, the error of identifying Donna Nelson with the University of Nebraska instead of her actual affiliation, the University of Oklahoma, stood out to this editor.) The authors make note of Walter Whites' presentation as the socially awkward intellectual and examine how that positions him to take the narrative lead. They read the third and fourth seasons as Walt's struggle to regain his Heisenberg identity that has been overpowered by the hyper-science of Gus' super-lab. This rhetorical analysis further asserts that *Breaking Bad* has excellent kairos as it rides a sudden public interest in science.

Yang, Fan. "Science and Intellectual Property in *Breaking Bad*." *FlowTV. Flow*, 22 November 2012. Web. April 2014.

Noting that science is Walt's most powerful weapon, the author interprets this as "a symptom of America's attempt to cope with its perceived 'decline'" and "an ambivalent attitude toward intellectual property (IP)" which plays out in the relationship between Walt (concerned with "the ownership and control over the exclusivity of the brand—much like the IP rights holders of the Global North who constantly fuss over the developing world's tendency to 'steal' their tangible assets") and Jesse (increasingly interested in appropriating IP and redistributing it in a "Pink(o-commie)" socialist disruption.

Extra-Academic Texts

Alter, Charlotte. "*Breaking Bad*: I Want Walter White to Survive the Finale." *Time.* 27 September 2013. Web. September 2014.

Insisting that rooting for the bad guy (Walt) is not a bad thing, the author refutes Nussbaum, Seitz, Poniewozik, and even Vince Gilligan himself by insisting, "If Walter ... escapes with any shred of dignity or happiness, then he lives in a world without consequences.... Don't we all secretly wish that such a place existed?"

Burke, Sarah. "*Breaking Bad*'s Biggest Mystery." Feminista. 1 September 2013. Web. September 2014.

The writer asserts that Skyler is unlikable because "her strong female character refuses to be a submissive archetype and thus refuses to allow us, and Walter, to completely indulge in our renegade fantasies." She concludes by posing (but not answering) the question: "Does *Breaking Bad* shine a negative light on feminism by positing it in direct confrontation with escapism?"

Dodds, Eric. "*Breaking Bad* Watch: Confessions of a Middle-Aged Drug Kingpin." *Time*. 26 August 2013. Web. July 2014.

The author recaps the episode "Confessions" (511) and articulates the "'Jesse Conversation Procedure,' which nearly always involves the following two steps: 1. Immediately request the essential information.... 2. Dispense the requisite fatherly advise in an attempt to gain the desired result." The writer gives a close reading of Mike Slovis' camera angles during the Walt-Jesse scene.

Duane, Anna Mae. "Why Flynn Is the Real Hero of *Breaking Bad*." Salon.com. 29 September 2013. Web. July 2014.

Looking at the series from a Disability Studies perspective, the writer examines Walter White (in stark contrast to his son) as the ultimate example of someone taken in by the myth of entitlement to a perfect, behaving body: "Skyler's surprise pregnancy, Flynn's cerebral palsy, Hank's life-altering injury, and Jane's misbehaving gag reflex all render them vulnerable to the man whose control over his environment is so complete that stage 3 non-operable lung cancer is no match for his badassery." The author then goes on to compare this with Walt Whitman's embrace of the imperfectly embodied in "Song of Myself" and its attendant love for humanity.

Foley, Brendan. "*Breaking Bad*: Why We Follow Philanderers and Murderers But Hate Their Wives: We'll Call It—The Skyler Syndrome." What Culture. 19 August 2012. Web. September 2014.

The author attributes fan hatred of Skyler to the natural urge of viewers to see a storyline progress and "the wife" often stands in the way of the protagonist's forward movement while acknowledging that the writers made her character unpleasant in the first seasons. The writer concludes by pleading with viewers who have not been able to see the Skyler's development into a character more sympathetic than her husband to carefully consider the terms in which they express themselves online.

Goldberg, Jonah. "*Breaking Bad* Breaks Through." *National Review Online*. 23 September 2013. Web. June 2014.

    Citing Nietzsche and Chesterton, the author recognizes that *Breaking Bad* is ultimately a conservative, ethical series. "Great novels are, by nature, conservative.... *Breaking Bad* is one of the great novels of our age."

Hinksman, Jake. "*Breaking Bad* 21st Century *Scarface*." *Mystery Scene*. 132 (2013). Web. May 2014.

    The writer observes that Walter's priority has always been to build a legacy and compares the series to several 1930s gangster films, *The Godfather*, and *Scarface*. Noting that gangster films flourished during economic crisis, he concludes, "*Breaking Bad* is the classic gangster narrative updated to the modern world. The national disgust at the Great Recession may have had no better expression."

Hudson, Laura. "Don't Cry for Walter White. He's Already Dead." *Wired*. 12 August 2013. Web. August 2014.

    In this rather poetic recap of the episode "Blood Money" (509), the writer notes the significance of oranges, "Chekov's machine gun," and all the evidence that Walter will die at the end of the series.

Klosterman, Chuck. "Bad Decisions: Why AMC's *Breaking Bad* Beats *Mad Men, The Sopranos,* and *The Wire*." Grantland.com. 2 August 2011. Web. April 2014.

    The author justifies the conclusion stated in the title: "*Breaking Bad* is the only one [of the four series] built on the uncomfortable premise that there's an irrefutable difference between what's right and what's wrong, and it's the only one where the characters have real control over how they choose to live.... It's not just that watching White's transformation is interesting; what's interesting is that this transformation involves the fundamental core of who he supposedly is, and that this (wholly constructed) core is an extension of his own free will."

Kolb, Leigh. "'Yo Bitch': The Complicated Feminism of *Breaking Bad*." Bitch Flicks. 15 August 2012. Web. September 2014.

    Calling Mike, Walter, and Jesse "the holy trinity," the writer argues that *Breaking Bad* can be read as a feminist text by explicating the series' images of entrapment and suffocation. "The negative reactions to the female characters reveal misogyny in the audience, not in the series."

Kovvali, Silpa. "*Breaking Bad*'s Big Critique of the Macho (and Its Problem with Women)." *The Atlantic*. 1 October 2013. Web. June 2014.

    The author notes that *Breaking Bad*'s initial appeal was as a revenge fantasy. She charges the writers with the "inability to create a single non-infuriating female character" but admits that the show was harder on men than women as it demonstrated that contemporary codes of masculinity are "standards to die by, not to live by."

Lanham, Andrew. "Walter White's Heart of Darkness: Does Any Space Remain for Moral Judgment?" *Los Angeles Review of Books*. 11 August 2013. Web. June 2014.
Writing at the beginning of the final season, the author notes that Bryan Cranston's previous role in *Malcolm in the Middle* set the stage for viewers' understanding of Walter White. Invoking Neitzsche as Kuo and Wu did in their article a year previous, Lanham refutes their conclusions as well as Klosterman's, questioning whether morality is relevant in *Breaking Bad* for the very reason Kuo, Wu, and Klosterman argue the reverse: the centrality of human agency in the series.

Lindelof, Damon. "*Breaking Bad*: How Heisenberg Is Like Batman." Vulture. 23 September 2013. Web. September 2014.
The co-creator of *Lost* poetically explains that Walter always had the germ of Heisenberg within him by doing a close reading the flashback sequences of the series with special attention to "Full Measure" (313).

Marcotte, Amanda. "*Breaking Bad* TV Expectations." *The American Prospect*. 17 August 2012. Web. September 2014.
Tracing fan hatred of anti-hero's wives back to *The Sopranos* in 2002, the author attributes the phenomenon to audiences' sexism as well as their inability to adjust the rooting-for-the-protagonist tradition when confronted with the anti-hero.

Marcotte, Amanda. "How to Make a Critically Acclaimed TV Show about Masculinity." Jezebel. 7 September 2011. Web. April 2014.
The author notes that difficult men struggling with concepts of masculinity have become a "formula" for successful TV (*Mad Men, Breaking Bad, Friday Night Lights*) but interesting women characters seem to flourish only in comedy on TV (*30 Rock, Parks and Recreation, The Sarah Silverman Show*). She asserts that the series reached its best-show-on-TV status when Skyler "wised up to what was going on in her life" in season three. *Mad Men*'s Don Draper is compared to Hamlet, Walter White to Macbeth.

Matthews, Dylan. "Here's What *Breaking Bad* Gets Right, and Wrong, about the Meth Business." *The Washington Post*. 15 August 2013. Web. July 2014.
Among the interesting facts: super-labs are real, methylamine is not difficult to get/make, there are two meth markets (DIY small-batch operations where purity can be an issue and the cartel market where purity doesn't matter), many meth customers use it to stay awake while working multiple jobs.

McNamara, Mary. "On *Breaking Bad*, Walter White Comes Clean." *Los Angeles Times*. 29 September 2013. Web. June 2014.

In this review of the series' final episode, the writer approves of the (perhaps too tidy) wrap up of unfinished business and interprets the end poetically: "But the only things [Walt] was allowed to touch in farewell were his infant daughter and the equipment in his lab. And as he finally surrendered to his choices and himself, it was easy to tell which he loved more. And he died knowing it."

Nicholson, Rebecca. "*Breaking Bad* Is Great TV, but with No Real Women, It Can Never Be 'My' Show." *The Guardian*. 13 August 2013. Web. September 2014.

Comparing *Breaking Bad, The Sopranos, The Wire*, and *Mad Men*, the writer finds *Breaking Bad* to be the only one without well-written females. She argues that *Breaking Bad*'s weak women cannot be dismissed due to the show's focus on masculinity because the other three shows were also about masculinity and had remarkably well-developed female roles. She suggests that long-form TV drama should employ the Bechdal Test.

Nussbaum, Emily. "Child's Play: *Breaking Bad*'s Bad Dad." *The New Yorker*. 24 July 2011. nymag.com. Web. June 2014.

Nussbaum examines the risk the series took when it allowed the murder of a child in "Dead Freight" (505) and goes on to discuss child endangerment as a feature of *Breaking Bad*. She is also watchful of fan responses (most particularly, "Bad Fans" as she will name them in her September 16, 2013, piece. Nussbaum reports that after the episode that revealed Walt was in fact responsible for Brock's poisoning, "I read posts insisting that Walt was so discerning, so careful with the dosage, that Brock could never have died. The audience has been trained by cable television to react in this way: to hate the nagging wives, the dumb civilians, who might sour the fun of masculine adventure. *Breaking Bad* increases that cognitive dissonance, turning some viewers into not merely fans but enablers."

Nussbaum, Emily. "My *Breaking Bad* Bender." *The New Yorker*. 27 August 2012. nymag.com. Web. June 2014.

Nussbaum describes the special pleasures of binge-watching a TV series and discovers a Walter White who is "as much amoral artist as much as wannbe gangster.... The show felt like the crucial linking ring in a decade of cable meditations on masculine pathology."

Nussbaum, Emily. "That Mind-Bending Phone Call on Last Night's *Breaking Bad*." *The New Yorker*. 16 September 2013. nymag.com. Web. June 2014.

In what is sure to be a useful move to all of us who want to discuss the phenomenon, Nussbaum coins the term "Bad Fans" as a way of referring to a type of series viewer who so personally identifies with a particular character that they insist upon viewing every aspect of every episode only through that character's point of view. In the case of *Breaking Bad*, these viewers sometimes self-identify online as "Team Walt." Nussbaum asserts that these viewers are "watching wrong" and that they are often addressed by a series' writers through a new character who arrives late in the series and performs a parody of the show's Bad Fans. In *Breaking Bad*, this character would be Todd who "saw Walt purely as a kick-ass genius, worthy of worship." And was able to tell his gang members the story of the train heist without any mention of the fact that it involved the killing of an innocent child. She goes on to read Walt's phone call to Skyler in "Ozymandias" (514) as the writers giving Walt an excuse to parody the harsh Skyler-hating often found among Team Walt.

Poniewozik, James. "*Breaking Bad*'s Morality—And Our Own." *Time*. 24 September 2013. Web. September 2014.

    Citing Nussbaum and Seitz, the author examines what the relationship between Walter White and Heisenberg means, concluding: "But if you step back from the debate ... something pretty impressive is going on: a TV show is pushing crowds of fans to have an engaged discussion about the nature of morality."

Poniewozik, James. "*Breaking Bad* Watch: Say Hello to My Little Friend." *Time*. 30 September 2013. Web. July 2014.

    The author recaps the final episode of the series asserting that it is a western at heart and that Walter went out with his usual "DaVincian invention and Machiavellian manipulation." Noting that the finale could be read either as a victory or a defeat for Walt, the writer compares Walter's last moment to that of Gollum in *Lord of the Rings*.

Read, Jason. "'Look on My Works, Ye Mighty, and Despair!' *Breaking Bad* as Austerity Allegory." Unemployed Negativity. 29 September 2013. Web. July 2014.

    The writer (an associate professor of philosophy at the University of Southern Maine) reads the series as "taking the mundane anxieties of health care costs, unemployment, work and retirement and infusing them with enough of the danger and excitement of the illicit drug trade to make them (just barely) watchable and enjoyable. Now, with one episode left, it remains unclear how those anxieties will play out, but it seems clear that all the speculation on how it will end is also speculation of what will become of us." Interesting observation: "The three bosses of *Breaking Bad*, Tuco, Gus, and Lydia, follow a trajectory from feudal control of territory, Tuco; to Fordist standardization of production, Gus; and finally to Lydia's control over brand identity."

Rosenberg, Alyssa. "How Anna Gunn's Performance as Skyler White Changed Television." *The Washington Post*. 26 August 2014. Web. September 2014.

Writing immediately after *Breaking Bad* won several Emmy Awards, the author praises the decision to give Best Supporting Actress to Anna Gunn, concluding: "Gunn's drawn face in the last two seasons of *Breaking Bad* might not have brought about the end of the anti-hero era in television. But Gunn's performance marked the end of a time when the creators of such shows could get away with writing anti-heroes' wives as flat, cartoonish characters, or when audiences could get away with worshiping difficult men without encountering strong opposition."

Rosenberg, Alyssa. "Stop Hating the Wives: In Praise of *Breaking Bad*'s Skyler White." Slate. 16 July 2012. Web. September 2014.
   The writer argues that Skyler is a more complex character than Carmela Soprano.

Rosenberg, Alyssa. "Walter White, Abuser." Thinkprogress. 13 July 2012. Web. September 2014.
   The writer outlines Walter's systematic, abusive manipulation of Skyler and Jesse. Her analysis of Walter and Jesse's relationship is particularly insightful.

Ryan, Maureen. "*Breaking Bad*: Five Reasons It's One of TV's All-Time Greats." *The Huffington Post*. 11 July 2012 Web September 2014.
   Acknowledging that part of the series' unique appeal is its morality, the writer asserts: "Walt had the seeds of sin inside him before he ever got cancer or cooked meth, and the show isn't interested in making us see him as an anomalous bad guy. *Breaking Bad* wants us to wonder, what seeds lurk inside us?" She admits, however, that, "Early in the show's run, despite Anna Gunn's capable performance, I found Skyler to be the ultimate 'shrewish wife in anti-hero drama.'"

Segal, David. "The Dark Art of *Breaking Bad*." *New York Times Magazine*. 6 July 2011. Web. June 2014.
   Because at the writing of this bibliography, *Breaking Bad* is at the peak of its popularity, it is interesting to note that as recently as the summer of 2011 it could be said that *Breaking Bad* "has yet to achieve pop cultural breakthrough status." The writer argues that this is due to the show's demographic appeal in that it "doesn't play to the coasts" and therefore makes Vince Gilligan TV's "first true red-state auteur." The piece incorporates the writer's observations while he watched the filming of the episode "Rabid Dog" (512).

Silver, Stephen. "'Skyler White Is Such a Bitch!' And Other Unfair *Breaking Bad* Observations." Technologytell. 13 July 2012. Web. September 2014.
   The writer observes that during the series' fourth season, online articles about *Breaking Bad* started seeing a surge of Skyler-hating comments from readers and

goes on to compare this to other TV series with anti-hero protagonists, concluding with a suggestion to those who read web write-ups of TV (and post comments on them): "So when you watch the fifth season of *Breaking Bad* and you read the recaps every Sunday night, and you ask yourself why Walt would put up with someone as nagging and indecisive as Skyler, try to ask, at the same time, why Skyler would put up with a meth lord who blows up nursing homes and poisons children."

Stepinwall, Alan. "Looking Back at the End of Walter White." Hitflix.com. 4 October 2013. Web. June 2014.
    The writer argues that Emily Nussbaum's theory that everything in the finale after Walt enters the car he plans to steal was a dream and he is actually found dead in the frozen vehicle (a theory—or wish—that Norm MacDonald and Joyce Carol Oates had taken up on their Twitter feeds) cannot be supported by the text.

Stepinwall, Alan. "Review: *Breaking Bad*—'Granite State': No Escape." 23 September 2013. Hitflix.com. Web. June 2014.
    The writer references Emily Nussbaum's term "bad fans" and observes that Skyler and Walt are both using Skyler's maiden name "Lambert" in this episode.

Stepinwall, Alan. "Review: *Breaking Bad*—'To'hajiilee': Nazis. I Hate These Guys." Hitflix.com. 8 September 2013. Web. June 2014.
    The writer observes that Walter White combing the desert in the episode "To'hajiilee" is reminiscent of the "Ecstasy of Gold" scene from *The Good, the Bad, and the Ugly*.

Stepinwall, Alan. "Revisiting the Series' Greatest and Most Devastating Hour from a More Sober Point of View." Hitflix.com. 26 December 2013. Web. June 2014.
    The writer makes the observation that Walt's angry telephone harangue to Skyler echoed the voice of "Team Walt" "bad fans" and represented, to some degree, things Walt thought but would never say. Among the trivia given here is the fact that the show got special permission to roll this episode's credits 19 minutes into the program and Baby Holly's "ma-mama" was a line the child ad-libbed during filming.

Stepinwall, Alan. "Walt Returns to Albuquerque to Settle Family Business." Hitflix.com. 29 September 2013. Web. June 2014.
    The author finds the series finale too neat for someone as reckless as Walt unless "the God of *Breaking Bad*" had arranged the faultless conclusion referencing the prayer Walt says in the stolen car ("Just get me home and I'll do the rest" upon which, the keys drop from above) and Vince Gilligan's previous references to God. The writer makes the apt observation that those who had binge-watched the series and watched the finale as it aired on TV must have had their patience tried by the commercial interruptions.

Touré. "*Breaking Bad* and the Downfall of the White 'Anyman.'" *Time.* 20 July 2012. Web. June 2014.

   Asserting the science is Walter's "superpower," the writer casts *Breaking Bad* among shows about white suburbanites losing control of their advantage (alongside *The Wire, Mad Men, The Sopranos*) but considers Walter White an exception among these anti-heroes in that he "became a criminal for reasons we can understand— and at his core he remains the guy next door. He is anyman in Hell."

Wrathall, John. "The Secret Life of Walter White." *Sight & Sound* 23.9 (2013): 34–36. OmniFile Full Text Mega. Web 16 May 2014. Web. July 2014.

   The author is a UK TV critic who outlines the tortured path *Breaking Bad* followed to the air in Great Britain, contextualizing the series within the tradition of American suburban fatherhood stories (from *Father Knows Best* to *Malcom in the Middle*). Comparing Walter to Macbeth, the writer calls the show "a 186-act tragedy." He also considers Bryan Cranston's previous television roles (*Malcom in the Middle* and *Seinfeld*) as informing audiences in their reading of Walter White and argues for a more than passing connection between *Breaking Bad* and the Alexander Mackendrick film (*Sweet Smell of Success*) reference in the second and third episode titles "The Cat's in the Bag" "...And the Bag's in the River."

Farther Afield

(Though these are not analyses of the series per se, the editor feels compelled to include this evidence of Breaking Bad*'s resonance among science professionals. The reader is invited to take these as serious cultural artifacts or comic relief according to his/her frame of mind.)*

Fanta, George F. "Disapproval of *Breaking Bad.*" *Chemical & Engineering News* 86.18 (5 May 2008): 4.

   In what the writer claims is his first letter to an editor, the writer asserts that a two-page description of the TV series in the March 3, 2008, edition of *Chemical & Engineering News* was "disgusting, to say the least" because such a show is "a disservice to [his] honorable profession."

Michael, Jeffrey. "Good Review for *Breaking Bad.*" *Chemical & Engineering News* 86.24 (26 June 2008): 7.

   The writer defends the journal's article about the series saying, "The dark humor of this series may have been lost on more conservative readers, but I trust the majority found this series (whose main subject is, after all, synthetic organic chemistry) to be refreshingly substantive in contrast to the mindless pap we are served by the major TV networks."

Ritchie, Burke. "Disapproval of *Breaking Bad.*" *Chemical & Engineering News* 86.18 (5 May 2008): 4.

The writer's brief letter exclaims: "The ACS President should retract and apologize for the article '*Breaking Bad.*' Is this how you try to make chemistry look good: by writing about a TV show about a chemistry Ph.D. and high school teacher turned methamphetamine manufacturer and distributor?"

Sumulong, Solito A. "Other Opinions of *Breaking Bad.*" *Chemical & Engineering News* 86.21 (26 May 2008.): 51.
    The writer defends the journal's publication of the brief article on *Breaking Bad* by saying "to argue that such illegal activity is taboo for discussion and artistic expression because we work in such a noble profession is just simple."

Volp, Robert F. "Other Opinions of *Breaking Bad.*" *Chemical & Engineering News* 86.21 (208): 51. 26 May 2008.
    In response to the letters by Fanta and Ritchie, the writer expresses his "surprise" that colleagues would write to denounce the journal's mention of *Breaking Bad* because "a TV show about a chemical professional who synthesizes illicit drugs is clearly within the scope of the magazine and should be reported regardless of how distasteful it may be to some."

Episode List

Episodes are listed here in chronological order with the episode number
(first digit indicating the season, following digits indication its number in that season),
episode title, primary credited writer, the director, and the original air date.

101, "Pilot." Writ. & Dir. Vince Gilligan. 20 January 2008.

102, "The Cat's in the Bag." Writ. Vince Gilligan. Dir. Adam Bernstein. 27 January 2008.

103, "...And the Bag's in the River." Writ. Vince Gilligan. Dir. Adam Bernstein. 10 February 2008.

104, "Cancer Man." Rit. Vince Gilligan. Dir. Jim McKay. 17 February 2008.

105, "Gray Matter." Writ. Patty Lin. Dir. Tricia Brock. 24 February 2008.

106, "Crazy Handful of Nothin.'" Writ. Bronwen Hughs. Dir. George Mastras. 2 March 2008.

107, "A No-Rough-Stuff-Type Deal. Writ. Peter Gould. Dir. Tim Hunter. 9 March 2008.

201, "Seven Thirty-Seven." Writ. J. Roberts. Dir. Bryan Cranston. 8 March 2009.

202, "Grilled." Writ. George Mastras. Dir. Charles Haid. 15 March 2009.

203, "Bit by a Dead Bee." Writ, Peter Gould. Dir. Terry McDonough. 22 March 2009.

204, "Down." Writ. Sam Catlin. Dir. John Dahl. 29 March 2009.

205, "Breakage." Writ. Moira Walley-Beckett. Dir. Johan Renck. 5 April 2009.

206, "Peekaboo." Writ. J. Roberts and Vince Gilligan. Dir. Peter Medak. 12 April 2009.

207, "Negro y Azul." Writ. John Shiban. Dir. Félix Enríquez Alcalá. 19 April 2009.

208, "Better Call Saul." Writ. Peter Gould. Dir. Terry McDonough. 26 April 2009.

209, "Four Days Out." Writ. Sam Catlin. Dir. Michelle MacLaren. 3 May 2009.

210, "Over." Writ. Moira Walley-Beckett. Dir. Phil Abraham. 10 May 2009.

211, "Mandala." Writ. George Mastras. Dir. Adam Bernstein. 17 May 2009.

212, "Phoenix." Writ. John Shiban. Dir. Colin Bucksey. 24 May 2009.

213, "ABQ." Writ. Vince Gilligan. Dir. Adam Bernstein. 31 May 2009.

301, "No Más." Writ. Vince Gilligan. Dir. Bryan Cranston. 21 March 2010.

302, "Caballo Sin Nombre." Writ. Peter Gould. Dir. Adam Bernstein. 28 May 2010.

303, "I.F.T." Writ. George Mastras. Dir. Michelle MacLaren. 4 April 2010

304, "Green Light." Writ. Sam Catlin. Dir. Scott Winant. 11 April 2010.

305, "Más." Writ. Moira Walley-Beckett. Dir. Johan Renck. 18 April 2010.

306, "Sunset." Writ. & Dir. John Shiban. 25 April 2010.

307. "One Minute." Writ. Thomas Schnauz. Dir. Michelle MacLaren. 2 May 2010.

308, "I See You." Writ. Gennifer Hutchinson. Dir. Colin Bucksey. 9 May 2010.

309, "Kafkaesque." Writ. Peter Gould. Dir. Michael Slovis. 16 May 2010.

310, "Fly." Writ. Sam Catlin. Dir. Moira Walley-Beckett. 23 May 2010.

311, "Abiquiu." Writ. John Shiban and Thomas Schnauz. Dir. Michelle MacLaren. 30 May 2010.

312, "Half Measures." Writ. Sam Catlin. Dir. Adam Bernstein. 6 June 2010.

313, "Full Measure." Writ. & Dir. Vince Gilligan. 13 June 2010.

401, "Box Cutter." Writ. Vince Gilligan. Dir. Adam Bernstein. 17 July 2011.

402, "Thirty-Eight Snub." Writ. George Mastras. Dir. Michelle MacLaren. 24 July 2011.

403, "Open House." Writ. Sam Catlin. Dir. David Slade. 31 July 2011.

404, "Bullet Points." Writ. Moira Walley-Beckett. Dir. Colin Bucksey. 7 August 2011.

405, "Shotgun." Writ. Thomas Schnauz. Dir. Michelle MacLaren. 14 August 2011.

406, "Cornered." Writ. Gennifer Hutchinson. Dir. Michael Slovis. 21 August 2011.

407, "Problem Dog." Writ. & Dir. Peter Gould. 28 August 2011.

408, "Hermanos." Writ. Sam Catlin and George Mastras. Dir. Johan Renck. 4 September 2011.

409, "Bug." Writ. Moira Walley-Beckett and Thomas Schnauz. Dir. Terry McDonough. 11 September 2011.

410, "Salud." Writ. Peter Gould and Gennifer Hutchison. Dir. Michelle MacLaren. 18 September 2011.

411, "Crawl Space." Writ. George Mastras and Sam Catlin. Dir. Scott Winant. 25 September 2011.

412, "End Times." Writ. Thomas Schnauz and Moira Walley-Beckett. Dir. Vince Gilligan. 2 October 2011.

413, "Face Off." Writ. & Dir. Vince Gilligan. 9 October 2011.

501, "Live Free or Die." Writ. Vince Gilligan. Dir. Michael Slovis. 15 July 2012.

502, "Madrigal." Writ. Vince Gilligan. Dir. Michelle MacLaren. 22 July 2012.

503, "Hazard Pay." Writ. Peter Gould. Dir. Adam Bernstein. 29 July 2012.

504, "Fifty-One." Writ. Sam Catlin. Dir. Rian Johnson. 5 August 2012.

505, "Dead Freight." Writ. & Dir. George Mastras. 12 August 2012.

506, "Buyout." Writ. Gennifer Hutchison. Dir. Colin Bucksey. 19 August 2012.

507, "Say My Name." Writ. & Dir. Thomas Schnauz. 26 August 2012.

508, "Gliding Over All." Writ. Moira Walley-Beckett. Dir. Michelle MacLaren. 2 September 2012.

509, "Blood Money." Writ. Peter Gould. Dir. Bryan Cranston. 11 August 2013.

510, "Buried." Writ. Thomas Schnauz. Dir. Michelle MacLaren. 18 August 2013.

511, "Confessions." Writ. Gennifer Hutchison. Dir. Michael Slovis. 25 August 2013.

512, "Rabid Dog." Writ. & Dir. Sam Catlin. 1 September 2013.

513, "To'hajiilee." Writ. George Mastras. Dir. Michelle MacLaren. 8 September 2013.

514, "Ozymandias." Writ. Moira Walley-Beckett. Dir. Rian Johnson. 15 September 2013.

515, "Granite State." Writ. & Dir. Peter Gould. 22 September 2013.

516, "Felina." Writ. & Dir. Vince Gilligan. 29 September 2013.

About the
Contributors

Brian **Cowlishaw** is an associate professor of English at Northeastern State University in Oklahoma. His scholarly essays have appeared in *Americana* and *Studies in Popular Culture*. He is co-chair of the Southwest Popular/American Culture Association's Science Fiction & Fantasy area and writes about science fiction and fantasy and postmodern literature for *Sequart.org*.

Bridget Roussell **Cowlishaw** is an independent scholar. She holds a Ph.D. in rhetoric, composition, and literacy from the University of Oklahoma. Her work has been published in *Prospects: An Annual of American Cultural Studies*, the *Journal of Popular Culture*, and the *Journal of American and Comparative Cultures*.

Ian **Dawe** is an independent scholar writing for *Sequart.org*. He has been published in *Studies in Comics* and has written articles and essays on *Star Trek*, James Bond, and Alan Moore.

R. Nicholas **Gerlich** is the Hickman Professor of Marketing at West Texas A&M University. His work has appeared in several professional journals including the *Journal of the Academy of Marketing Science*, *Publications Review*, and the *Journal of Retail Analytics*, among others. He is working on books about Route 66 and vintage neon signage.

Stephanie Stringer **Gross** is an associate professor of English at Husson University in Bangor, Maine, where she has served in various administrative positions, and also teaches in the University of Maine's Honors program. She has published in *The Cather Review* and *Critical Insights: Willa Cather*.

Susan **Johnston** is an associate professor and graduate chair in the Department of English at the University of Regina in Canada. She has published popular culture criticism in *The Journal of Adaptation in Film and Performance*, *Mythlore*, and *Logos: A Journal of Catholic Thought and Culture*. She is working on a book about George R.R. Martin's *A Song of Ice and Fire* series.

Jeffrey Reid **Pettis** teaches secondary English and history. His poetry and short stories have been published in *From the Cerulean Sea*, *Ultraviolet Magazine*, *521: An Anthology*, *NoD Magazine*, and *OffSIDE Magazine*. He is editor-in-chief of *Ultraviolet Magazine* and his research interests include the literature of Vladimir Nabokov, Samuel Beckett and Edmond Jabès.

Robert G. **Weiner** is an associate humanities librarian at Texas Tech University. He is the author of *Marvel Graphic Novels and Related Publications* (2008) and the editor of *Captain America and the Struggle of the Superhero* (2009) and *Graphic Novels and Comics in Libraries and Archives* (2010), all from McFarland, among other works.

Lori Smith **Westermann** is a lecturing professor at West Texas A&M University. She has published in the *International Journal of Business,* the *Academy of Educational Leadership Journal,* the *Academy of Marketing Studies Journal,* the *International Journal of Accounting Information Science and Leadership,* and the *Journal of Business and Economics Research.* Her research interests concern the impact of social media on popular culture fandom.

Index